THE HISTORIC INDIAN TRIBES OF LOUISIANA

THE HISTORIC INDIAN

TRIBES OF LOUISIANA

From 1542 to the Present

Fred B. Kniffen
Hiram F. Gregory
George A. Stokes

LOUISIANA STATE UNIVERSITY PRESS
Baton Rouge and London

Designer: Christopher J. Wilcox
Typeface: Aster
Typesetter: G & S Typesetters, Inc.
Printer: Thomson-Shore, Inc.
Binder: John Dekker & Sons, Inc.

10 9 8 7 6 5 4 3 2 1

Library of Congress Cataloging-in-Publication Data

Kniffen, Fred Bowerman, 1900–
    The historic Indian tribes of Louisiana.

    Includes index.
    1. Indians of North America—Louisiana.   I. Gregory,
Hiram F.   II. Stokes, George A., 1920–   III. Title.
E78.L8K59   1987   976.3'00497   86-27601
ISBN 0-8071-1295-X

To the Indian people of Louisiana

CONTENTS

ILLUSTRATIONS

Maps

PREFACE

This book tells part of the story of the Indian people of Louisiana, with particular attention to their experiences in historic times. Although the span covered—from 1542 to the present—is only a moment of their time in Louisiana, it was marked by such catastrophic events as the disappearance of tribes, the extinction of languages and other ancient culture traits, large-scale migration, and traumatic changes in economic and political status and custom.

Perhaps this book will remind a generation or two of others who went before them. Perhaps it will recall to ethnocentric Europeans their obligation to the land they have named Louisiana; it had had generations of well-nigh perfect care before they arrogated to themselves most of that responsibility.

Deeply felt is the hope that this book will generate greater interest, among Indians and their contemporaries alike, in the Indians' contributions to their common heritage. If a single young person is persuaded to ask his grandparents about Indian culture, the effort has been worthwhile. It has been even more worthwhile if the reader tells others what the old Indian people have asked teachers to teach, that is: "We are still here. We are alive; we are Indian people. This is our home."

ACKNOWLEDGMENTS

Telling this story with a useful degree of accuracy and understanding has required much help. To all of those who have contributed the information so essential to this work, we say "Yakoke." Many Indian people have generously shared their personal and tribal experiences and lore. It is a pleasure to name them here. Any error of omission is unintentional and deeply regretted. The Indian people are listed as follows. CADDO: Mary Burnett, Charlene Hodge, Phil Newkumet, Hank Shemayme, Irvin Whitebead, Mr. and Mrs. Melford Williams, Thompson Williams; CATAHOULA LAKE—BLACK RIVER: Napoleon Book, Claribel Gregory Burford, Delson Chevalier, Clinton Enlow, Hildred Fuqua, Charles Hampton, Emma Phillips Hampton, W. W. Hampton, Adele Kinney, Calvin Kinney, Will Nichols, Dennis Oneal, Emerick Sanson, Gilbert Sanson, Luther Sanson, Steve Sanson, David Smith, Louis White, Charles "Joe" Wiley, Louis Wiley, Oliver Wiley, Virgin Wiley; CHITIMACHA: Larry Burgess, Leroy Burgess, Lydia Darden, Pete Mora, Benjamin Paul, Pauline Paul, Chief and Mrs. Emile Stouff, Mr. and Mrs. LeMay Wahl; CLIFTON CHOCTAW: Luther Clifton, Pearl Shackleford, Mr. and Mrs. Amos Tyler, Carroll Tyler, Mr. and Mrs. Norris Tyler, Paul Tyler; EAST BATON ROUGE CHOCTAW: David Broom, Ralph "Black Hawk" Murphy; JENA BAND OF CHOCTAW: Beverly Jones Allen, George Allen, Clyde Jackson, Mary Jones, Anderson Lewis, Jesse Lewis, Lily Lewis, Dorothy Nugent; EBARB CHOCTAW—APACHE: Beto Castie, Kenneth Ebarb, Mr. and Mrs. (Marie) Martin Ebarb, Mr. and Mrs. Raymond Ebarb, Mr. and Mrs. "Red" Ezernack, Maggie Manshack, Frank Martínez, Monsignor George Martínez, Mr. and Mrs. Lonnie Martínez, Mr. and Mrs. Wesley Martínez, Rheet Paddie, Mr. and Mrs. Tom Parie, Ed and Callie Procell, Ed and Sally Procell, Joe Remedies, Steve Remedies, Edna Sepulvado, Dr. Lester Sepulvado,

Thomas Sepulvado, Mr. and Mrs. Jim Toby; HOUMA: Antoine Billiot, Ernest Billiot, John Billiot, Marie Dean, Helen Gindrat, Roy Parfait; KOASATI: Bel Abbey, Martin Abbey, Mona Abbey, Nora Abbey, Margie Abbey Baptiste, Solomon Baptiste, Bertney Langley, Joe Langley, Lorena Langley, Rosaline Langley, Jamison Poncho, Joyce Poncho, Lovelin Poncho, Robert Poncho, Ruth Poncho, Ernest Sickey, Curtis Sylestine, Lowell Sylestine, Mona Sylestine, Marie Thompson, Sam Thompson, Myrna Abbey Wilson, Wilifred Wilson; TUNICA-BILOXI: Earl Barbry, Nathan Barbry, Mr. and Mrs. Sam Barbry, Sylvester Barbry, Arthur Bordelon, Clementine Broussard, Harry Broussard, Florence Jackson, Ana Mae Juneau, Norma Kwajo, Alice Picote, Horace Pierite, Joseph Pierite, Jr., Joseph Alcide Pierite, Sr., Merlan Pierite, Rosa Pierite, Mary Vercher, Rose Pierite White; PAN-INDIAN GROUPS: Lloyd Elm (Mohawk), Jerry Hill (Oneida), Arlinda Locklear (Lumbee), Sarah Peralta (Apache), W. J. Strickland (Lumbee).

We also turned to our colleagues and students for information and encouragement. The late Richard Joel Russell had much influence on our views of man's relationships to the land, as had the late Carl O. Sauer. William B. Knipmeyer read proof, critiqued, and helped in other ways, while Marietta M. LeBreton imparted her profound knowledge of Louisiana Indian and colonial policies. Their patience and help are gratefully acknowledged. The late William Willis shared with us his view of the New Anthropology, which was being "reinvented" in the 1970s. His help, along with that of Vine Deloria, Jr., led us to seek a new approach to the integration of the ancient and modern aspects of Louisiana Indian culture.

Coupled with the efforts of Deloria, those of Ernest C. Downs, consultant to the Institute for the Development of Indian Law, resulted in a grant from the Sachem Fund of the Mellon Foundation that made fieldwork possible and supported visits to tribal areas. Donald Juneau, attorney with the Native American Rights Fund, promoted tribal developments, and his *ad hoc* lectures on Indian law are reflected in the last chapter of this book.

A number of dedicated Mennonite Central Committee Volunteers shared their knowledge with us: Greg Bowman and Jan Roper-Curry (with the Houma), Mary Vanrheenan and Janet Shoemaker (with the Choctaw-Apache), and Sherry Miller and Miriam Rich

ACKNOWLEDGMENTS

(with the Clifton Choctaw). Their sojourns, though all too brief, made the tribal areas better places.

We are grateful to Donald G. Hunter of Alexandria for photographs and access to valuable field data on Koasati culture. We must also thank Michael Schene and James Eisenagle of the National Park Service team at Jean Lafitte National Park, who worked with us on documentation and ethnohistory. Paula Johnson of Abita Springs spent much time researching the Choctaw of southeastern Louisiana and kindly shared her findings and experiences with us.

A special measure of appreciation is due Clarence H. Webb of Shreveport, William G. Haag of Baton Rouge, the late Robert S. Neitzel of Marksville, and the late James A. Ford of the American Museum of Natural History in New York City. These eminent archaeologists have provided insights into change and culture that have guided much of the historicity in this book.

Recognition must also be accorded to the work of amateur ethnologists who have given us much help. Among those who have known and loved the traditional Indian cultures of Louisiana are Tom Colvin of Mandeville, his mother, Melba Colvin, and his late father, who made major contributions to Choctaw materials. Others sharing with us their knowledge of the Choctaw were "Jo" Evans of Ferriday and the late U. B. Evans.

The late Caroline Dormon knew the Indian people well. Her fascination with the Indians prevailed throughout her lifetime, and she actively sought to help them and to preserve their traditional way of life. Her contributions to this work are second only to those of the people she loved.

Claude Medford, Jr., a part-Choctaw from east Texas, helped us time and again in the course of our work. This book may fall short of the detailed description and analysis of southeastern Indian culture he would prefer, but we tried to learn from his good criticisms. Emanuel Drechsel kindly read much of the linguistic and ethnographic material presented here, and consulted with us on it. We hope he finds it stronger because of his critical approach.

Don R. Sepulvado, of Natchitoches, is responsible for the lion's share of the photography included in this work. We hope that the pictures, most of which are being published herein for the first time, will help the reader see the Indian people as we do. Personnel

ACKNOWLEDGMENTS

of the Louisiana State University Cartographic Section drafted the maps and the charts. The skillful work of Clifford Duplechin, Mary Lee Eggart, and James Kennedy is both admired and appreciated.

Of enormous value to us has been the editorial advice and assistance provided by members of the Louisiana State University Press. The highly professional work of Catherine Landry and the rest of the editorial staff, combined with their unfailing patience and good humor, has made our labor on this book both pleasant and productive. The support of key administrative personnel is well-nigh essential to the completion of a study such as this. We are grateful for the encouragement of President Robert Alost, Vice-President Dale Thorn, former president Joseph J. Orze, former vice-president Thomas P. Southerland, and Maxine F. Taylor of Northwestern State University.

Finally, we must thank our families, particularly Mary Jane, Jeanette, and Virginia. They, over the years, have coped with our absences, edited and criticized our work, and shared our troubles and frustrations as we struggled to learn and produce what appears herein.

THE HISTORIC INDIAN TRIBES OF LOUISIANA

INTRODUCTION

The American Indian is one of the most popular, familiar figures in the world. For generations he has been portrayed, often sympathetically, in the media at hand, and books on the Indians abound. This particular book seeks to introduce to Louisianians and others their Indian neighbors and to give the Indian community a synopsis of tribal history and tradition as assembled by tribal and other historians, linguists, ethnologists, and geographers.

Louisiana has the third largest native American population in the eastern United States. Only North Carolina and Florida have more than the 16,040 Louisiana Indians counted in the census of 1980. Yet most non-Indians in the state are unaware of Louisiana's Indian heritage, or they assume that the tribes are dead or have moved to Oklahoma.

The naturalist Caroline Dormon came to know the tribal groups in the 1930s and called them "the invisible people." Somehow, they still seem unreal to a people conditioned by Hollywood to envision Indians galloping on horseback, wearing feathered headdresses, living in tepees, and dancing to war drums. The Louisiana Indian in the real world today can be found driving a bulldozer, directing an oil-field crew, playing a fiddle in a New Orleans restaurant, or cutting pulpwood. He converses not in a series of primal sounds but rather in English, French, Choctaw, or Koasati. He well may belong to one of the nation's most expressive peoples, since numbers of Louisiana Indians, in addition to their native languages, speak French, Spanish, and English. In a way, the Indian is still invisible, traditional headdress having given way to straw hats and safety helmets, and breechclouts to blue jeans. Trailers, prefabricated houses, and tract homes stand in the former locales of thatched and wattle-and-daub native structures, and a journey into the forest is likely to be made in a pickup truck.

The Indian is an important contributor to the wealthy cultural heritage of Louisiana. He participates fully in the changes that affect everyone in the region every day. The future of the Louisiana Indians is unknown, and much of their past is yet a mystery. The most diligent research has thus far failed to reveal how and when they first went to Louisiana. Even discoveries of the magnitude of the Poverty Point site in northeast Louisiana answer few questions while raising many new ones.

The principal body of information on which this study is based is the record of Indian life that began to accumulate in the sixteenth century. Unfortunately, early accounts of Indian ways are incomplete, and their reliability must be carefully weighed. Untrained observers often interpreted what they saw in terms of Old World concepts, values, and practices. The white men naturally tended to concentrate on the aspects of Indian life they found interesting, leaving others alone. Even so, we must acknowledge our debt to those who produced the flawed but priceless documentary record.

The early records of Indian and European contacts often create doubt, confusion, and controversy. Especially difficult is the task of setting apart those things in contemporary Indian life that are purely aboriginal and those that were introduced by outsiders. European influences marked the tribes before they saw white men. Alien epidemic diseases decimated communities living far from any European. Domesticated plants, pigs, and fowl escaped from their European owners and traveled farther and faster into Indian territory than white men did.

Today, many Indian groups are culturally and racially mixed; entire languages will never be heard again. Students, of necessity, are concerned increasingly with the processes of acculturation, that is, the mixing of modes of living. Researchers must seek to identify the nature of change and adaptation among the Indians rather than try to retain or restore Indian culture traits they might consider worthy of a place in modern life.

It has been suggested that Amerigo Vespucci sailed along the entire coast of the Gulf of Mexico as early as 1497. If so, he was surely the first European to see any of present-day Louisiana, but no evidence has been found to corroborate his voyage. In 1519 Alonzo Alvarez de Pineda cruised the Gulf coast from east to west and back again, entering at one point the mouth of a large river. There he found a sizable Indian town, and he located forty more villages within a distance of six leagues upstream. The river may have been the Mississippi, but observations recorded at the time do not match that stream's natural setting. It seems more probable that Pineda sailed into Mobile Bay.

Panfilo de Narvaez, sailing westward along the Gulf coast in 1526, reached the mouth of the Mississippi River and then continued westward at some distance from shore. Disembarking to investigate smoke it had seen on the land to the north, his party found some survivors of a severe storm, who had been cast ashore near the site of modern Galveston. From one of the castaways, Cabeza de Vaca, has come the earliest description of Texas coastal Indians related to the Atakapa of southwest Louisiana.

The first descriptions of Louisiana Indians are contained in the accounts kept by members of Hernando de Soto's expedition that set out from Tampa Bay in May, 1539. Livestock with the party included horses, hogs, mules, and bloodhounds. Following a circuitous overland route, and plagued throughout the journey by bad relations with the Indians, de Soto reached the Mississippi River somewhere near the mouth of the Arkansas River in May, 1541. The explorers noted with interest the presence of many bison in the area, the first they had seen. The party wintered on the Ouachita River near present-day Camden, Arkansas. Judging from the complaints registered by the Spaniards, the winter of 1541–1542 was unusually severe.

In March, 1542, nearly three years after his departure from Tampa Bay, de Soto may have moved down the Ouachita River into what is now Louisiana. He possibly crossed the Ouachita at Ayays, perhaps near Columbia, and went southward to Anilco, a large and evidently prosperous agricultural settlement, possibly at present-day Jonesville. From there, it is speculated, the expedition turned eastward to Guachoya, on the Mississippi near Ferriday. Subsequently, it visited Catalte, which may have been at modern Fort Necessity, and two towns on the Mississippi, Aminoya and Teguanote, both farther upstream than Guachoya. The inhabitants of these towns may have been Tunica, Koroa, or ancestral Taensa, the last a Louisiana tribal group closely related to the Natchez.

At some point in this part of his journey, de Soto died and was

succeeded by Luis de Moscoso. The weary Spaniards set out overland under their new leader, hoping to reach Mexico. Not far along
the way, they found two places where the Indians made salt, which
might have been Drake's Well, or Drake's Lick, northwest of present-
day Winnfield, and the Bistineau saline in what is now southern
Webster Parish. Four days journey beyond the latter, the party
reached Amaye, east of Red River at about the latitude of Shreveport. There they experienced language difficulties. The inhabitants
spoke Cahinnio Caddo, a language quite different from those to
the east and evidently unfamiliar to the interpreters accompany-
ing the expedition. Moving westward, the Spaniards reached Red
River, making their crossing a few miles north of what is today
Shreveport. The party encountered more Caddoan tribes as it
marched southwestward across present-day Louisiana and into
the region that is now Texas.

Giving up its attempt to reach Mexico overland, the expedition
returned eastward to spend the winter of 1542–1543 at Aminoya
on the Mississippi River. In July, 1543, the surviving Spaniards em-
barked small boats they had built and set off downriver on the long
trip to Mexico. For several days they were pursued and attacked by
the people of Quigualtam, who surely were the Natchez Indians.
Nearing the mouth of the Mississippi, and following a few days' respite, the expedition was attacked by Indians of a different tribe,
tentatively identified as Chawasha, Quinapisa, or Washa, since
these assailants were armed with spears and ancient spear throw-
ers, or atlatls. Turning westward from the river's mouth, the Spaniards probably camped that night on the Timbalier Islands. In September, 1543, the tattered remnants of de Soto's grand expedition
finally reached rest and safety in Mexico.

Accounts provided by de Soto's expedition, despite many inade-
quacies, are most useful as the earliest written sources of information on the southeastern Indians. They are sufficiently exact regarding the terrain and the Indians encountered to permit some
debatable reconstruction of de Soto's irregular course, but they do
not provide accurate locations of recognizable Louisiana tribes of
the 1540s. That had to await the influx of Europeans around 1700,
and in the meantime there occurred a considerable shifting of
populations. The Caddo-speaking Ouachita, for example, had not

reached the Ouachita River in de Soto's time. The towns he visited on the west bank of the Mississippi were largely abandoned by 1700, their places taken by large towns on the higher eastern wall of the river valley in present-day Mississippi. The shift has been attributed to rather improbable periodic increases in flooding. It is much more likely that the people moved because of the onset of epidemic European diseases and their consequent desire to avoid the older living sites. Afterward, no permanent Indian settlement was established in what is today northeastern Louisiana, though the area was eminently habitable. There were only temporary camps of Chakchiuma, Koroa, and Tunica, people normally resident on the Yazoo River in what is now Mississippi.

De Soto had found large towns at places made permanently attractive by their fertile soils and situation on significant land and water routes—sites occupied since prehistoric times by mound builders. The highest density of native population seems to have been reached in late prehistoric time, possibly with the rise of a new level of agricultural production. However, there was still no great pressure on supplies of wild and cultivated foods, and hence no need to change basic food habits. The apparent beginning of population decline, even prior to de Soto's time, thus cannot be ascribed to a failure of the food supply.

The departure of de Soto's men from present-day Louisiana ushered in nearly a century and a half in which no European is known to have set foot in the area. Guido de Bazares approached closest in 1558, when he sailed along the Gulf coast from Mexico to Mobile Bay, where a Spanish colony was established in the following year.

Although Europeans were absent from Louisiana during this long period, the effects of their passage across the continent were substantial within the area. Epidemic diseases that may have been implanted by de Soto's party decimated the tribes of present-day northeastern Louisiana. Vacated areas attracted other tribes or remained abandoned. Precious bits of iron found their way to remote tribes and were used for tipping arrows. Once introduced, foreign influences continued to spread under their own impetus.

In the latter half of the seventeenth century, Europeans in numbers began to reach what was to be Louisiana. They were Frenchmen instead of Spaniards, with the notable exception of Alonzo de Leon, whose expedition of 1690 crossed overland from Mexico and reached the Caddoan Adai east of the Sabine River.

The chief avenue of approach for the Frenchmen was the Mississippi River. Louis Joliet and Father Jacques Marquette descended the river as far as the Quapaw towns near the mouth of the Arkansas in 1673, and five years later René Robert Cavelier de La Salle completed his epic trip down the Mississippi River to its mouth. In 1686, Henri de Tonti, La Salle's lieutenant, repeated the journey. He visited the Taensa villages on Lake St. Joseph in 1690 and then pushed overland to the Caddoan-speaking Natchitoches Indians on Red River. From Tonti and other participants in La Salle's ventures have come a number of valuable accounts of the Indians, among them Father Zenobius Membre's description of the Taensa and, notably, Henri Joutel's account of the Caddo.

Energized by La Salle's journey, a host of missionary priests descended on Louisiana, and from them have come invaluable observations on the Indians to whom they ministered. About the turn of the eighteenth century, Dumont de Montigny, Father Antoine Davion, and Father Jean François Buisson de St. Cosme worked with Louisiana Indians or with their neighbors in adjoining regions. The Jesuit Jacques Gravier recorded observations on the Indians he encountered as he descended the Mississippi River in 1699. In the same year, Pierre Le Moyne, Sieur d'Iberville, left his base at Old Biloxi and sailed up the river as far as the Houma town at present-day Angola. On a second ascent his party reached the Taensa villages, from which Jean Baptiste Le Moyne, Sieur de Bienville, retraced Tonti's overland march to the Natchitoches town on Red River. Present on both trips was M. Penicaut, a carpenter, whose account has been much used.

Benard de la Harpe, who went up Red River in 1716 to occupy his land grant, traveled widely and left a journal containing many valuable data on Louisiana Indians. Compiled at about the same time were notes on the Indians that were ultimately to appear as the anonymous *Luxembourg Narrative*. Antoine Simon Le Page du Pratz, a colonist, spent the years from 1718 to 1734 among the Natchez and later produced a history of Louisiana that is a prime source on the Indians. Father Pierre Charlevoix, who descended the Mississippi in 1723, left a history valued for its treatment of tribal annals. Additional information was recorded by Father le Petit, who was living among the Natchez at about the same time. Some of the above accounts and many others appear in the collections compiled by John Shea, B. F. French, Pierre Margry, and Reuben Thwaites.

Somewhat more recent, but still prized as Indian source materials, are Jean Bernard Bossu's travels, published in 1771, Thomas Hutchins' narrative of 1784, and the works of William Bartram, published in 1792. The source materials also include Baudry de Lozieres' account of the Avoyel and Bayougoula, and other accounts from the period 1794 to 1798. Near the end of the eighteenth century, Martin Duralde, who was commandant of the Atakapa and Opelousa posts, composed a manuscript on the Chitimacha and Opelousa that is now invaluable as virtually the only source on the latter. John Sibley, in a government report of 1806, included detailed information on the status of Louisiana tribes derived from data based on the knowledge of François Grappe, who was part-Caddo.

While the foregoing accounts are substantive and useful, the reports of travelers with only casual interest in the Indians are also of importance. Difficulties stem from the fact that the Indians had largely withdrawn from the principal routes of travel by the nineteenth century and so had to be deliberately sought out. Furthermore, they were living much as poor whites did, and were too easily dismissed, by unthinking observers, as being ignorant of their ancestral ways. Professional ethnologists finally penetrated the shell of negative outward appearances and revealed the rich underlying store of traditional Indian ways and knowledge still preserved. Since the latter part of the nineteenth century, trained observers, armed with a thorough knowledge of the older accounts, have worked with Louisiana Indians in an effort to fill gaps in knowledge about them.

Indian experts on the various tribal cultures include Ely Johnson, also known as Etienne Chiki, a Tunica who worked on the Tunica and Biloxi languages. Another who helped analyze and preserve the Tunica language was Sesosterie Yuchigant. One dedicated chief, Elijah Barbry, even traveled to Washington on behalf of his people. Volsin Chiki and Joseph Pierite, Sr., both Tunica chiefs, made great efforts to see that tribal history and culture were recorded and carried on by members of their tribe. Joseph Pierite, Sr., traveled and politicked to gain tribal recognition and aid.

Benjamin, Christine, and Pauline Paul, all Chitimacha, were very nearly the last speakers of their language. A chief, Benjamin Paul freely gave information on their tradition and worked on a lengthy, detailed analysis of the language. Pauline Paul, an expert basket maker, was responsible for much of the technology of her people, largely through her efforts to teach her craft to younger women and girls.

Emile Stouff, the last traditional chief of the Chitimacha, and his wife, Faye, spent many hours sharing their knowledge of traditional culture. Faye collected and published the unwritten stories of her people. She also encouraged young people to learn basketry. At this writing, she is preparing a more detailed collection of tribal materials under a grant from the Louisiana State Division of the Arts.

Less well known are the authorities on the Jena Choctaw: Louise Allen, Mary Jones, Anderson Lewis, and Lily Lewis. All have worked with linguists and ethnologists to preserve their traditional culture, and have spent much time teaching the old ways to young people. George Allen, Clyde Jackson, Jessie Lewis, Dorothy Nugent, and Cheryl Smith teach the traits of Indian culture to their own people and outsiders as well.

The Koasati tribe has produced its own remarkable experts. Arzalie Langley, Jackson Langley, and Mark Robinson were deeply involved in efforts to share Koasati culture with non-Indians and sought to reinforce knowledge among their own people. Jackson Langley and Robinson were active in the 1930s. Arzalie Langley, a medicine woman, was one of the last speakers of the Mobilian Jargon. Although aged and bedridden, she gave freely of her knowledge. Also of the Koasati, Bel Abbey and his family have worked with linguists, ethnohistorians, and cultural geographers seeking to record and preserve tribal culture. Bel has been recognized widely for his expertise in training younger anthropologists in Indian studies.

The Koasati tribal chairman Ernest Sickey has dealt actively with economic and health programs for his people and other Indians in Louisiana. He has also sought to collect and preserve as much as possible of Koasati and Choctaw tradition. Through his efforts, an excellent tribal history has been published, and with further aid from Eugene Burnham of the Summer Institute of Linguistics, the first readers for the Koasati language have been produced.

Vynola Newkumet, Sadie Bedoka Weller, and Melford Williams, all of whom now live in Oklahoma, have been recognized widely for their efforts to preserve Caddo culture. John Billiot, Sr., spent several years in the 1930s collecting the tribal history of the Houma. More recently, Antoine Billiot and Marie Dean, largely unassisted, have preserved and taught the wide spectrum of Houma crafts. Another Houma, Helen Gindrat, has continued to encourage and teach others at every opportunity.

Clementine Broussard and her son, Harry Broussard, of the Tunica, and Wesley Martínez, Rheet Paddie, Callie Procell, Ed Procell, Edna Sepulvado, and Jim Toby, all of the Ebarb community, have made great efforts to attract the interest of outsiders and to gain help for their communities so that ancient culture might be recorded and preserved. Two Choctaw from Bayou LaCombe, the late Sanville and Mathilda Johnson, not only carried on their traditional way of life but left a rich legacy in their students, particularly Tom Colvin and Hazel Cousins.

Claude Medford, Jr. has collaborated effectively with ethnohistorians, linguists, and artisans in the recording of music and crafts. He has published on the Tunica, Houma, Chitimacha, and Koasati crafts, and his efforts have helped the tribes maintain and revitalize them. The number of Indians actively interested in the preservation of their ancient way of life gives insight into the vitality of the cultural traditions themselves.

John R. Swanton is universally recognized as the premier authority on the ethnology of Louisiana Indians. Swanton's first work on the state, appearing in 1907, dealt with the mythology of the Louisiana tribes. This was followed by a long succession of valuable publications, culminating in 1952 in his *Indian Tribes of North America*. Of the twenty-four of Swanton's works bearing wholly or in part on Louisiana, three embrace much of what is known of the aboriginal cultures of the state's historic Indians: "Indian Tribes of the Lower Mississippi Valley," published in 1911; "Source Material on the History and Ethnology of the Caddo Indians," published in 1942; and "The Indians of the Southeastern United States," published in 1946.

More intimately concerned with at least some aspects of Louisiana Indian cultures have been Albert S. Gatschet, M. R. Harrington, and Cyrus Byington, who was a missionary and a fine student of the Choctaw language as spoken by a number of Louisiana tribes. Others include Andrew Albrecht, David I. Bushnell, Jr., Robert D. Calhoun, James Crawford, H. B. Cushman, Frances Densmore, George Dorsey, James D. Dorsey, Ann Fischer, John Fischer, Hiram F. Gregory, Mary Haas, Daniel Jacobson, Jeffrey Kimball, Claude Medford, William A. Read, Frank Speck, Morris Swadesh, Ruth Underhill, Le Baron Marc de Villiers, and Gene Weltfish.

A group of students has been concerned with Louisiana Indians in an areally broader consideration of Indian languages. Also concerned with physical anthropology and other topics, these students, some of whom have not actually visited Louisiana, include Daniel Brinton, Lucien Carr, George Catlin, Frederick Hodge, William H. Holmes, Alex Hrdlicka, James Mooney, J. W. Powell, Henry Schoolcraft, and Erminie Voegelin.

REFERENCES

Recourse to the narratives of the de Soto expedition, the earliest sources of information about the initial European contact with the Indians, has been inevitable. There are several narratives of varying quality. The best evaluation of them is that of the United States de Soto Commission, established by the United States Congress. In its turn, the work of the commission has been appraised as further reviews have been undertaken by individuals.

Fordyce, John R.
1929   Trailing de Soto. *National Research Council Bulletin* 74, Washington, D.C.

Swanton, John R.
1912   De Soto's Line of March from the Viewpoint of an Ethnologist. *Mississippi Valley Historical Association Proceedings* 5: 147–57.
1932   The Ethnological Value of the de Soto Narratives. *American Anthropologist* 34(4): 570–90.
1939   Final Report of the United States de Soto Commission. *House Documents*, 76th Cong., 1st Sess., 71, Washington, D.C.

Duke, John
1978   The U.S. de Soto Commission. M.A. thesis, Northwestern State University.

Also available are extensive discussions of Swanton's and the commission's interpretations, including:

Phillips, Philip, James A. Ford, and James B. Griffin
1951 Archaeological Survey in the Lower Mississippi Alluvial Valley, 1940–1947. *Papers of the Peabody Museum of Archaeology and Ethnology* 25: 347–90, Harvard University, Cambridge.

Swanton answered criticisms of his work and the commission's work in *American Antiquity*.

Swanton, John R.
1952 Hernando De Soto's Route Through Arkansas. *American Antiquity* 18: 156–62.

The Spanish accounts of Luis Hernandez de Bïedma, Garcilaso de la Vega, and Rodrigo Ranjel are available in a two-volume translation.

Bourne, Edward G., ed.
1904 *Narratives of the Career of Hernando de Soto.* Trailmakers Series, New York.

The most popular contemporary work on the de Soto expedition is probably that of Garcilaso de la Vega.

De la Vega, Garcilaso (Jeannette Varner, John Varner, eds.)
1980 *The Florida of the Inca.* Austin.

The Bossu narratives are now available in translation and have been carefully annotated.

Dickinson, Samuel Dorris, ed. and trans.
1982 *New Travels in North America by Jean-Bernard Bossu, 1770–1771.* Natchitoches.

Another valuable account is also available in translation, though the English version lacks much of the information found in the French editions.

Le Page du Pratz, Antoine Simon
1758 *Histoire de la Louisiane.* Paris, 3 vols. Reprint of original English translation published in 1975 in Baton Rouge.

The narrative accounts of Henri de Tonti are to be found in several translated sources, one of which is especially accurate and convenient.

Giraud, Marcel
1974 *A History of French Louisiana, Volume 1: The Reign of Louis XIV, 1698–1715.* Baton Rouge.

Virtually the only attempt to synthesize the wide range of historical materials on the Caddo was John Swanton's 1946 effort.

Swanton, John R.
1946   Source Material on the Ethnohistory of the Caddo. *Bureau of American Ethnology Bulletin* 43, Washington, D.C.

Accounts by Jacques Gravier, Zenobius Membre, and other clergy appear in the chronicles edited by Reuben Thwaites. Some Canadian priests, often called the "seminary priests," left the Quebec seminary and went to Louisiana. Their materials are less available but of equal interest. Father Antoine Davion, missionary to the Tunica, left a number of primary sources at the seminary archives. These include good materials on the tribes, but none have yet been translated from the French.

Thwaites, Reuben, ed.
1896–1901   *Jesuit Relations and Allied Documents: Travels and Explorations of Jesuit Missionaries in New France, 1610–1791.* Cleveland.

Mildred Wedel has reworked the la Harpe narrative and offers new insights into the data.

Wedel, Mildred Mott
1978   La Harpe's 1719 Post on Red River and Nearby Caddoan Settlements. *Bulletin 30, Texas Memorial Museum.* Austin, 1–20.

Perhaps the best handy source of information on the Louisiana tribes is provided by the United States government.

American State Papers
1882–1834   *Documents Legislative and Executive, Class II, Indian Affairs* 1–2, Gale and Seaton, Washington, D.C.
1832–1861   *Documents of the Congress of the United States in Relation to the Public Lands* 1–8, Gale and Seaton, Washington, D.C.

Further information on the West is available.

Berenger, Jean
n.d.   *Mémoire sur Louisiane.* MS at Newberry Library, Chicago.

One account of the Caddoan area of northwestern Louisiana is especially valuable for its detail.

Bolton, Herbert E.
1914   *Athanase de Mézières and the Louisiana-Texas Frontier, 1768–1780.* Cleveland. 1970 rpr., New York.

Most sources of information on the Choctaw will be cited elsewhere in this work, but a number of good generalized materials are at hand.

Bushnell, David I., Jr.
1909 The Choctaw of Bayou Lacombe, St. Tammany Parish, Louisiana. *Bureau of American Ethnology Bulletin* 48, Washington, D.C.
1910 Myths of the Louisiana Choctaw. *American Anthropologist*, n.s., 12: 526–35.
1919 Native Villages and Village Sites East of the Mississippi. *Bureau of American Ethnology Bulletin* 69, Washington, D.C.
1922 Some New Ethnological Data from Louisiana. *Journal of the Washington Academy of Sciences* 12: 303–307.
1927 Drawings of A. De Batz in Louisiana, 1713–1735. *Smithsonian Miscellaneous Collections* 35.
1934 Tribal Migration East of the Mississippi. *Smithsonian Miscellaneous Collections* 85.

Byington, Cyrus (H. S. Halbert and John R. Swanton, eds.)
1915 A Dictionary of the Choctaw Language. *Bureau of American Ethnology Bulletin* 46, Washington, D.C.

I

THE NATURAL SETTING

To every generation of its residents Louisiana has offered resources both rich and varied. The state's position at the edge of a continent facing a sea makes for diversity of landforms and climates. Location near the tropics gives rise to long growing seasons and abundant, varied plant and animal life. Contributing further to landscape variety, the Mississippi River, a major resource, traverses the state from north to south and links the sea to vast interior lands. An area so large, rich, and useful is bound to attract and hold people. So it has been with the Indians who were first to occupy this splendid country and whose descendants live there today.

The state of Louisiana covers 48,523 square miles, an area slightly larger than Pennsylvania and half the size of West Germany. From east to west, the state stretches about 290 miles, and nearly 280 miles from north to south. The distance from New Orleans to Shreveport is about 285 miles, equal to the journey from Boston to Philadelphia or from Bonn to Berlin. New Orleans, at thirty degrees north of the equator, lies in the same latitude as Cairo and Shanghai.

Relief in Louisiana is generally low; all of the state lies within the Atlantic–Gulf Coastal Plain. The elevation ranges from sea level to 535 feet at the state's highest point, Mount Driskill, in Bienville Parish.

Much of Louisiana consists of alluvial valleys and grassy prairies that stand less than one hundred feet above sea level. Broad, wet marshlands line the coast of the Gulf of Mexico. The remainder of the state is made up of low hills that stretch across the inland portions of the state and are largely the product of the erosion of a gently elevated sea bottom. In both hill country and lowland there are numerous streams and lakes, making an extensive, highly complex drainage system flowing toward the gulf. Particularly notable is the Red River, which rises in New Mexico and flows southeastward to and across Louisiana. Below the junction of the Red and the Mississippi, streams flow directly to the Gulf of Mexico. They are useful north-south traffic arteries and at the same time formidable barriers to movement east and west.

Louisiana's humid subtropical climate is subject to varying marine and continental influences. Spring is a season of winds and showers, produced as frequent but weakening cool fronts move across the state. Summers are hot and steamy both day and night, with thundershowers of convectional origin most frequent near the coast. Tornadoes occur, as do the giant tropical storms and hurricanes that at times sweep inland over the coastal marshes, bringing dangerous winds and flooding. Often, however, they produce welcome general rains.

Fall tends to be dry. Days are still warm but more comfortable because of lower humidity, and nights are cool. Winters are short, and rains accompany the passage of cold fronts. Precipitation sometimes takes the form of light snow or freezing rain.

Temperature ranges may be considerable. Daytime highs in summer may reach one hundred degrees Fahrenheit, and on winter nights temperatures of fifteen or twenty degrees may be recorded. For January and July, average temperatures of about fifty and eighty degrees, respectively, may be expected. Slight differentials in ecology are sometimes important. Cold air drainage into lower swamps, for example, may occur, leaving some areas almost free of frost.

Growing seasons are long, ranging from an average of 230 days in the northern parishes to 300 or even more along the coast. No truly dry season occurs, though precipitation amounts in some years may be well below average. Near the coast, average annual rainfall totals about sixty inches, and fifty-two inches or so fall each year in the north.

While Louisiana is noted for its diversity of ethnic groups and cultures, it displays an equally impressive range of natural environments. Each of the major topographic regions is distinctive in soils, flora, and fauna. The principal regions are the hills of central and northern Louisiana, the blufflands along the Mississippi River in the eastern part of the state, the prairie country of southwestern

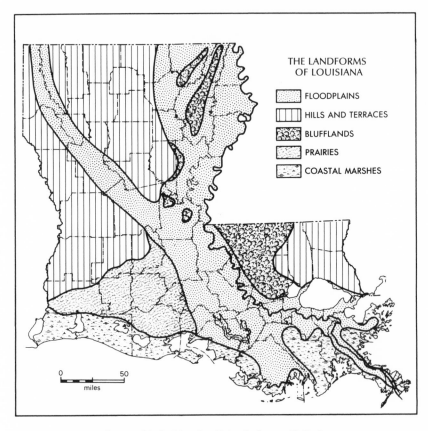

Courtesy of the Louisiana State University Cartographic Section

Louisiana, the coastal marshes, and the great alluvial floodplains of the Atchafalaya, Mississippi, and Red rivers and lesser streams.

The hills of Louisiana, produced by the erosion of gently uplifted areas, are not prominent by some standards. Great sedimentary layers once almost horizontal have been subjected to isostatic pressures. Seaward, the layers are warped downward, culminating in the great geosyncline under the Gulf of Mexico. Northward, at about the latitudes of Alexandria and Winnfield, the change in attitude of the beds has been upward, revealing the edges of resistant layers and forming cuestas trending from southwest to northeast. These ridges, sculptured by erosion, are sources of chert, quartzite,

DRAINAGE
IN LOUISIANA

Courtesy of the Louisiana State University Cartographic Section

and sandstone. Although the hills are not high, they stand in marked contrast to the rest of this low-lying state, where a difference in elevation of as little as five feet may be significant.

Other uplands in Louisiana originated as alluvial deposits formed during the worldwide oscillations of sea level associated with the glacial and interglacial stages of the Pleistocene epoch. Each time ice accumulated on the continents and sea level fell everywhere, the Mississippi River cut a broad trench along its lower course. With each succeeding interval of glacial decay, sea level rose and the Mississippi partially filled the extensive valley, thus gradually creating wide deposits of riverborne sediments.

The same forces that had raised the older ridges continued to lift the alluvial valley fillings to higher levels over much of the state. Subsequent erosion has had little effect on some of these surfaces, called terraces, but others have been considerably modified. Much terrace land is good farming country. Coarse gravels occurring in their basal sections have been reworked and deposited on the point bars of major streams. Useful rock types include cherts, jasper, quartzites, and petrified wood.

With their rocky and acidic clay soils, the hills were a unique ecological area. Pure stands of pine, usually longleaf, grew on high ground, while lower elevations supported extensive oak and hickory forests. Deer and bear were plentiful, and great numbers of smaller animals, particularly squirrels and birds, lived in the oak- and beech-covered bottoms.

The first Louisiana settlers found the uplands attractive. Clovis, Scottsbluff, and San Patrice projectile points are scattered across the hills and prairies of the area. Relics such as these are clear signs of prehistoric hunting Indians, marking their arrival in the area at about ten or twelve thousand years before the birth of Christ. Upland sites are virtually everywhere—near springs, around fossil lakes, and at the margins of hills and bottoms. Such locales provided deer and abundant small game, fresh water, vast quantities of beech, hickory, oak, and chinquapin mast, stone for tools, and hardwood for implements and fuel. Of special value were the local areas of salt concentration near present-day Winnfield and Shreveport. Springs had developed around large salt domes, and the Indians were quick to exploit them, first as hunting locales and later in support of their farming operations. They produced salt by boiling or dehydrating the spring waters, as white men were to do later.

As the Indians turned to agriculture, numbers of them were drawn to richer alluvial lowlands, but many still preferred life in the great forests of the hill country. The Caddoan-speaking tribes were strong in the northwest, settling along the wide creek bottoms or beside the ephemeral "raft" lakes at the margins of the Red River floodplain.

The migrant Choctaw, too, were attracted to the pine woods, an environment reflecting their ancient homes east of the Mississippi River. An additional, political impetus toward settlement in the hills was supplied by the Spanish. Fearing Anglo-American pressures, they encouraged the location there of Alabama, Apalachee, Biloxi, Choctaw, Koasati, and Taensa.

Along the eastern margins of the Mississippi River floodplain in Louisiana and Mississippi there extends a north-south belt of buff-colored material called *loess*. The thick deposits of this fine-grained sediment form the conspicuous bluffs so well displayed in the Natchez, Mississippi, area. Almost vertical cliffs standing along the left bank of the Mississippi from Vicksburg to just north of Baton Rouge comprise a major part of the blufflands environment in which substantial numbers of Indians once lived.

Smaller deposits of loess are located on the Catahoula Hills and Sicily Island to the west of the Mississippi alluvial valley, and others are present on older surfaces of Maçon Ridge in northeast Louisiana. Although much like the blufflands to the east, these in the west were not developed extensively until after white contact with the Indians had been established.

The fertile loess supported a wide variety of hardwoods, including oak, hickory, and black walnut. Cane flourished in wet areas, and cedar grew extensively in badly eroded sections. These higher lands were free of floods, the bluffs rising as much as 100 to 150 feet above flood level. They were not troubled by the pyrophytic palmetto and saw briers that quickly invaded clearings in the floodplain, and so were coveted by the many tribes that cleared land by burning. The Houma, Koroa, Natchez, Tunica, and their allies clung to these fine lands. The first Europeans found in them some of the greatest concentrations of Indians they encountered.

A most distinctive region is the prairie country of southwestern Louisiana. The land is comparatively dry and very flat, the grassy surface broken only by islands of trees, woods lining the bayous, and coulees that cut across it. The prairie is extensive, covering all or portions of eleven parishes and having a total area about twice that of Delaware. Much of it is underlain by a clay hardpan which contributes to the current agricultural value of the region but may have thwarted development of the soil in aboriginal times.

The grasslands have been of little importance as producers of wild game. The bison that the Atakapa Indians hunted there seasonally for the most part disappeared early. Europeans later found a few deer and buffalo on the prairie, and other game was limited to waterfowl in ponds and streams.

The aborigines, viewing other parts of Louisiana more favorably, were never drawn to the grasslands in significant numbers. The Chitimacha and Opelousa had occupied portions of it but preferred lands along the natural levees of Bayou Lafourche, and the former eventually moved into the vast depths of the Atchafalaya swamp. The Opelousa, not well known, apparently shifted about on the Prairie Terrace west of what is today Lafayette. Of the lesser prairies in Louisiana, some were occupied at least for a time. One such region was the Avoyelles Prairie, home of the Indian people of a similar name.

The great coastal marshes of Louisiana extend for three hundred miles along the margins of the Gulf of Mexico, from Texas to Mississippi. Beginning as salt marsh near the active shoreline, this region stretches inland an average distance of about thirty miles, grading into brackish and finally freshwater marsh.

In some respects the coastal marshes are hostile to man. The low land is wet much of the time, the tall grasses are coarse and sharp, the swarms of deerflies and mosquitoes are nearly unbearable, and from time to time the area is beaten savagely by the great tropical storms. But life-forms in the marsh offered man vast food supplies. Enormous molluscan resources were at hand on beach strands or could be reached by short boat trips: freshwater mussels (*unio*), brackish water clams (*rangia*), and saltwater species including oysters (*ostrea*). For thousands of years the Indians of the coastal marshes fed upon these excellent foods. Available to them also were crabs, crayfish, and other crustaceans. Fish of many edible kinds abounded. Ducks, geese, heron, and other waterfowl from all over North America wintered here. Brackish and freshwater grasses supported great numbers of mink and otter that, in turn, helped maintain a large alligator population. Even deer were present in a few places, such as the island remnants of natural levee crests and relict shorelines. Thousands of acres were covered with marsh elder and cattail, and coco grass roots were plentiful.

In outward appearance the Louisiana marsh country is unattractive, but it was occupied throughout Indian times. In this stoneless alluvial environment, shellfish provided not only food but the raw materials for implements and containers. Further enticements to settlement were pearls, feathers, asphalt (bitumen), and salt. Perhaps the treasure most anxiously sought by the marsh dwellers

was safety. Harassed tribes such as the Houma found refuge literally at land's end, occupying the attenuated natural levees that extended toward the Gulf of Mexico. Places of concentration included
Barataria, Bayou du Lac, Grand Caillou, and Isle Jean Charles. The
settlements in these places were the antecedents of the line villages
of later French populations.

Some Indians settled under the great oak trees covering fossil
beaches in southwest Louisiana. Called *cheniers* by the French, the
beaches, which appear as low sand ridges, offered wet heels and
haunches a respite from that watery world. At early dates, other
Indians colonized the "Five Islands" of southernmost Louisiana—
Jefferson, Avery Island, Weeks, Cote Blanche, and Belle Isle. Standing atop great salt domes, these oak-clad hills were virtual islands
of elevated lands, even offering, like their north Louisiana counterparts, the desirable deposits of salt underlying them.

Unusually extensive in Louisiana are the floodplains of the numerous rivers flowing southward to the Gulf of Mexico. These low-
lying areas once were subjected to periodic overflows from the
Mississippi, Red, and Atchafalaya rivers and other sizable streams.
The floods deposited horizontally sorted sediments, bringing into
existence the battures (sandy borders of the rivers), natural levees,
and backswamps so typical of this land. The streams themselves,
seeking shorter routes to the Gulf of Mexico, meandered constantly
across and down the broad Mississippi alluvial valley. The floodplain was littered with their relics as old river bends, cut off or
abandoned, partially filled with silt to become oxbow lakes, elon-
gated swamps, and brakes.

In former times, the better-drained silty loam soils of the natural
levees were dominated by rich stands of live oak, sweet gum, hickory, and pecan. Some portions supported immense brakes of wild
cane, and on the long, gentle slopes of the wetter silts leading to the
backswamps grew thickets of palmetto. Water stood in the backswamps much of the time, and from the wet clays rose forests of
giant cypress and tupelo gum. The battures sustained dense, curving ribbons of willows and cottonwoods.

Deer and bear inhabited all parts of the floodplains, and particularly numerous were the small creatures—the rabbits, birds, am-
phibians, and reptiles that sought shelter along the battures. Great
clouds of migratory waterfowl moved across the area, some win-

tering in the coastal marshes and others resting before moving on to Central America or South America. In the spring, the flow was northward as the birds returned to their nesting grounds. Even today, the Catahoula Lake area on the western margin of the Mississippi floodplain is visited each winter by more than forty thousand ducks.

The streams and other waters were homes for turtles, alligators, and catfish, and yielded great numbers of alligator gar, buffalofish, and freshwater mussels. If these resources were exploited to their full potential, they and such wild foods as pecans and freshwater lotus seeds could have sustained relatively large human populations without agriculture of any sort.

Like the white farmers who eventually succeeded them almost everywhere, Indian agriculturalists were drawn to the natural levees. Although the rich lands were covered with cane and hardwoods, this vegetation was easily cleared by fire and slashing. There was little or no deep sod to break.

Actual settlement on the floodplain was based on a restricted choice of environments. Great, fertile natural levees closely paralleled the large oxbow lakes such as Larto Lake, Lake St. Joseph, and Lake Concordia. For a long time the levees were at least partially occupied by Indian farmers, but, eventually, agricultural efforts were abandoned and the ancient fields given over to hunting and gathering. Their maximum utilization came only with the advent of European agriculture and modern mechanized farming.

Today, the decline in Louisiana's Indian population is matched by the deterioration and outright destruction of the state's once magnificent natural environments. Many tribes have disappeared; the rest are decimated. The likelihood of their eventual demise is strengthened by environmental ruin. The problem is one for all Louisianans. Irreparable ecological damage can be tolerated no longer, and the Indian, like his neighbors, has begun to demand protection.

Chitimacha basket makers lament the destruction of the cane brakes. The Choctaw and Koasati echo that lament. Houma fishermen and trappers mourn the loss of thousands of acres of marsh environments, chopped apart by hundreds of miles of industrial canals and their polluted waters.

The great natural levees and their flanking backswamps have

been turned into giant fields of milo and soybeans, crops to be exported to other parts of the earth. Logging operations have violated the hill country, and the "endless" pure stands of longleaf pine have given way to new, faster growing trees. The Koasati basket makers must travel farther each year to collect their straw.

Described individually, these changes may seem insignificant. Collectively, they are overwhelming, particularly to elderly Louisianians. Future generations may never see the present landscape. Industrialization, expanding populations, and their waste products demand new strategies for survival from everyone.

REFERENCES

Louisiana may well be the most misunderstood state in the Union. In some ways, the land and people seem remote, their images screened by both real and imagined swamps, marshes, and pine woods, and blurred by generations of racial and cultural mixing and migration. The casual observer almost always has a perception of Louisiana that is far from reality. Even Louisianians are constantly surprised by the nature and variety of their surroundings.

Much of the "real" Louisiana has been well described. The research findings cited here represent a body of knowledge about the state that is remarkable for its clarity and its persistence as a firm point of departure for further inquiry. Much of this work was done half a century ago but continues to show its value. The foundation laid by such investigators as Clair Brown, Harold Fisk, James Ford, Fred Kniffen, and Richard Russell still supports the research efforts of their successors.

For general coverage of Louisiana's physical and cultural attributes, see:

Kniffen, Fred B.

1968 *Louisiana, Its Land and People.* Baton Rouge.

Newton, Milton B., Jr.

1972 *Atlas of Louisiana.* Miscellaneous Publication 72–1, School of Geoscience, Louisiana State University.

The following are significant discussions of the physiography and geomorphology of Louisiana's major regions.

Chawner, W. D.

1936 Geology of Catahoula and Concordia Parishes, Louisiana. *Louisiana Geological Survey Bulletin* 9: 5–49, Louisiana Department of Conservation, Baton Rouge.

Cline, Isaac Monroe
1926   *Tropical Cyclones.* New York.
1927   *Floods of the Lower Mississippi Valley.* Board of Trade, New Orleans.

Coleman, James M., and William G. Smith
1964   Late Recent Rise of Sea Level. *Geological Society of America Bulletin* 75: 833–40.

De Bow, J. D. B.
1858   The Levees and the Overflows of the Mississippi. *De Bow's Review* 25 (Oct.): 436–42.

Fenneman, Nevin M.
1938   *Physiography of the Eastern United States.* New York.

Fisk, Harold N.
1938   Geology of Grant and La Salle Parishes. *Louisiana Geological Survey Bulletin* 10: 5–66, Louisiana Department of Conservation, New Orleans.
1944   *Geological Investigation of the Alluvial Valley of the Lower Mississippi River.* No. 52, Mississippi River Commission, Vicksburg.

Foster, J. H.
1912   Forest Conditions in Louisiana. *Forest Service Bulletin* 11, United States Department of Agriculture, Washington, D.C.

Hilgard, E. W.
1872   On the Geology of Lower Louisiana and the Salt Deposit on Petite Anse Island. *Smithsonian Contributions to Knowledge* 23(3), Washington, D.C.

Russell, Richard J.
1933   Larto Lake, An Old Mississippi River Channel. *Louisiana Conservation Review* 3: 18–22, 46.
1936   Lower Mississippi River Delta: Reports on the Geology of Plaquemines and St. Bernard Parishes. *Louisiana Geological Survey Bulletin* 8: 3–193, Louisiana Department of Conservation, New Orleans.
1940   Quaternary History of Louisiana. *Geological Society of America Bulletin* 51: 1199–1234.
1944   Lower Mississippi Valley Loess. *Geological Society of America Bulletin* 55(1): 1–40.

Russell, Richard J., and H. V. Howe
1935   Cheniers of Southwestern Louisiana. *Geographic Review* 24: 449–61.

Saucier, Roger T.
1964   Recent Geomorphic History of the Pontchartrain Basin. *Louisiana State University Coastal Studies Series* 9, Baton Rouge.

The native vegetation of Louisiana, a world in itself, has received its share of attention. Clair Brown's work was seminal.

Brown, Clair A.
1936   The Vegetation of the Indian Mounds, Middens and Marshes in Plaquemines and St. Bernard Parishes. *Louisiana Geological Survey Bulletin* 8: 407–22, Louisiana Department of Conservation, New Orleans.
1945   *Louisiana Trees and Shrubs.* Louisiana Forestry Commission, New Orleans.
1972   *Wildflowers of Louisiana and Adjoining States.* Baton Rouge.

Dormon, Caroline
1934   *Wild Flowers of Louisiana.* New York.

Penfound, W. T.
n.d.   Plant Distribution in Relation to the Geology of Louisiana. *Proceedings of the Louisiana Academy of Sciences* 8: 25–34.

Penfound, W. T., and E. S. Hathaway
1938   Plant Communities in the Marshlands of Southeastern Louisiana. *Ecological Monographs* 8: 1–36.

Small, John E.
1933   *Manual of the Southeastern Flora.* New York.

In-depth surveys of birds and mammals allow one to gauge the amount and kind of resources the Indians must have known and utilized. Surveys also show how resources have changed since the advent of the Europeans.

Arthur, Stanley C.
1931   *Fur Animals of Louisiana.* Louisiana Department of Conservation, New Orleans.

Beyer, George
1900   The Avifauna of Louisiana, with an Annotated List of Birds of Louisiana. In *Proceedings of the Louisiana State Society of Naturalists,* 75–120.

Lowery, George H., Jr.
1955   *Louisiana Birds.* Baton Rouge.
1974   *The Mammals of Louisiana and Its Adjacent Waters.* Baton Rouge.

St. Amant, Lyle
1959   *Louisiana Wildlife Inventory and Management Plan.* Louisiana Wildlife and Fisheries Commission, New Orleans.

Indian occupations have been related, through time, to landforms, flora, and fauna. Most such studies reflect the theoretical directions established by Fred B. Kniffen and Richard J. Russell at Louisiana State University.

Gagliano, Sherwood M.
1963 A Survey of Preceramic Occupations in Portions of South Loui-
      siana and South Mississippi. *Florida Anthropologist* 16(4):
      105–32.
1964 *An Archaeological Survey of Avery Island.* Baton Rouge.
1964 Post-Pleistocene Occupations of Southeastern Louisiana Terrace
      Lands. *Proceedings of the 19th Southeastern Archaeological Con-
      ference, SEAC Bulletin* 1: 18–26.
1967 Point Bar Agriculture. *Proceedings of the 22nd Southeastern Ar-
      chaeological Conference, SEAC Bulletin* 5: 13–14.
1967 Late Archaic-Early Formative Relationships in South Louisiana.
      *Proceedings of the 23rd Southeastern Archaeological Conference,
      SEAC Bulletin* 6: 9–22.

Gregory, Hiram F.
1968 Maximum Forest Efficiency: Swamp and Upland Potentials. *Pro-
      ceedings of the 21st Southeastern Archaeological Conference,
      SEAC Bulletin* 3: 52–59.

Huner, John
1967 Ecology of the Lower Mississippi Valley. *Proceedings of the 22nd
      Southeastern Archaeological Conference, SEAC Bulletin* 5: 11–12.

Kniffen, Fred B.
1936 Preliminary Report on the Indian Mounds and Middens of Pla-
      quemines and St. Bernard Parishes. H. V. Howe, ed., *Louisiana
      Geological Survey Bulletin* 8: 407–22, Louisiana Department of
      Conservation, New Orleans.

McIntire, William G.
1958 Prehistoric Indian Settlements of the Changing Mississippi River
      Delta. *Louisiana State University Coastal Studies Series* 1, Baton
      Rouge.

Williams, Stephen
1967 Ecology of the Upper Lower Valley. *Proceedings of the 22nd South-
      eastern Archaeological Conference, SEAC Bulletin* 5: 15–16.

Significant regional studies have been published, as have others generally
broad in scope.

Bushnell, David I.
1908 Primitive Salt-Making in the Mississippi Valley. *Man* 35.

Caldwell, Joseph R.
1958 Trend and Tradition in the Prehistory of the Eastern United States.
      American Anthropological Association Memoir 88.
1965 Primary Forest Efficiency. *Proceedings of the 21st Southeastern Ar-
      chaeological Conference, SEAC Bulletin* 3: 66–69.

Fairbanks, Charles H.
1965 Gulf Complex Subsistence Economy. *Proceedings of the 21st Southeastern Archaeological Conference, SEAC Bulletin* 3: 57–62.

Ford, James A.
1936 An Analysis of Indian Village Site Collections from Louisiana and Mississippi. *Anthropological Study* 2, Louisiana Geological Survey, Department of Conservation, New Orleans.

Griffin, James B.
1961 Some Correlations of Climatic and Cultural Change in Eastern North American Prehistory. *Annals of the New York Academy of Sciences* 95: 710–14.

A number of early accounts, including that of Le Page du Pratz, contain firsthand information on plants and animals in aboriginal times.

Le Page du Pratz, Antoine Simon
1758 *Histoire de la Louisiane.* Paris, 3 vols. Reprint of original English translation published in 1975 in Baton Rouge.

Lauren Post, a geographer, has synthesized a number of sources on domestic plants and animals introduced into French Louisiana. The animals and their uses spread rapidly to the Indians, and the animals had significant impact on wildlife as competitors and predators.

Post, Lauren C.
1933 The Domestic Animals and Plants of French Louisiana as Mentioned in the Literature with Reference to Sources, Varieties, and Uses. *Louisiana Historical Quarterly* 16(4).

John James Audubon, the nineteenth-century painter and naturalist, left, in addition to the magnificent paintings for which he is famed, classic descriptions of Louisiana's flora and fauna.

Audubon, John James
1848 *Quadrupeds of America.* The Cabildo, New Orleans.

Also of value are the accounts left by the botanist William Bartram.

Van Doren, Mark, ed.
1928 *The Travels of William Bartram.* New York.

Ethnographic accounts of relatively recent Indian manipulations of land and resources are scarce in comparison with archaeological studies of relationships between man and the land. One study must be considered a model for what might be done.

Speck, Frank G., and Ralph W. Dexter
1946 Molluscan Food Items of the Houma Indians. *Nautilus* 60(1): 34–40.

II

PREHISTORY: A SYNOPSIS

The first Indians seem to have reached Louisiana by late Pleistocene or early Holocene time. These hunters left a vague but,
fortunately, distinctive trail in the form of lost and spent projectile
points. These ancient leaf-shaped stone relics exhibit bifacial flutes,
where long flakes were removed from the points' flat sides to facilitate hafting. From the Great Lakes to Ecuador, they are known to
date the earliest Indian hunters' presence.

The hunters of ten to twelve thousand years ago saw a different,
almost unimaginable America. Sea level was lower, broad grasslands extended toward the Gulf of Mexico and to Lake Pontchartrain, and mammoths, ground sloths, and other mammals now
extinct were abundant in Louisiana. In other states, the fluted missiles known as Clovis Points have been found imbedded in the
skeletons of such animals.

By 6000 to 8000 B.C., a welter of early hunting complexes appears
to have developed, identifiable in some instances by unique point
types: Scottsbluff, Eden, Clovis, Plainview, and the delicate San
Patrice. Much remains unknown about the people who made and
used these ancient weapons; only the San Patrice sites have been
adequately isolated and tested archaeologically. Thumbnail-shaped
end scrapers, denticulated scrapers, and various other small scraping and cutting tools now seem as typical of these hunters as their
projectile points. Taken as a whole, the earliest sites are surely evidence of the widespread migration of Ice Age hunters into North
America.

As the Ice Age ended, climates began to assume their contemporary ranges, and Louisiana, like the rest of the Southeast, became
humid and heavily wooded. Once-broad grasslands shrank to relict

prairies or were flooded by the rise of sea level, and many land surfaces were buried under sediments washed toward the gulf by the Mississippi River. Gradually, the landscape came to resemble that which one sees today. The climax forests of pine, mixed hardwoods, and swamp hardwoods that evolved, like the biomass they once supported, baffle the imagination. These were the environments to which remnant populations of the early hunters, sometimes called the Paleo-Indians, entrusted themselves.

The combination of Indian hunting pressures and changes in the natural habitat seems to have been fatal for the giant mammals. Consequently, the specialized way of life of the hunters gave way to a broader accommodation. By 5000 B.C., many had begun adapting themselves to the woodlands. Archaeologists have termed this period of intense forest utilization and a widespread marsh and delta adaptation the Archaic. Life became more sedentary, and populations gradually increased.

New technology developed during the Archaic. Ground and polished stone tools appeared: axes; adzes; ungrooved axes, or celts; milling stones, or mortars; pitted nutting stones; net weights; bola weights; and elaborate weights for the atlatl. Late in the Archaic, complex lapidary forms made their appearance, reflecting a growing preoccupation with certain animals, including locusts, owls, frogs, and cats. A variety of stone objects, including beads and atlatl weights, was given these configurations. A widespread trade network grew, covering most of the southeastern part of the country. Hematite and galena from present-day Missouri, banded slate from present-day Illinois, soapstone (steatite) from the Appalachians, and quartz crystals from what is today Arkansas were exchanged for Louisiana resources. White sandstone, shells, and bitumen may have been the Louisiana Indians' stock-in-trade.

Hunting continued to be a basic pursuit, but emphasis shifted to the white-tailed deer and the bear. Smaller animals became important food items. Along the Gulf coast, great mounds of shells, refuse from innumerable meals, began to accumulate.

Projectile points changed, too. The large, lanceolate, fluted tips were replaced by shorter, wide, notched and stemmed varieties. Cutting edges were multiplied by serration, and notches gradually evolved into large barbs. These are the familiar points that fill bags and boxes in countless private collections all over Louisiana. Few of the collectors know that their treasured "arrowheads" actually antedate the bow.

The archaeologist Joseph Caldwell views these Archaic developments as having climaxed in what he has termed "maximum forest efficiency." Never before had the Indian had such effective, intimate knowledge of his environment.

Hickory nuts, even more nutritious than domesticated maize, were plentiful and became a major food source. Archaic sites often clustered along large swampy lakes, near oak and hickory climax forests. Catahoula Lake, in central Louisiana, and the lakes along the Red River valley have extremely high densities of these sites, in accord with researchers' expectations. Waterfowl in the fall and winter, and fish, alligators, and turtles in the summer, assured a year-round food supply. Venison, along with acorns and hickory nuts, seasonal fruits, and other foods, probably made agriculture unnecessary and, according to some anthropologists, kept the Indian populations strong and healthy.

Although the Paleo-Indians lived in most parts of Louisiana, few traces are left of their simple way of life, particularly of those culture traits of a nonmaterial nature, such as religion. Deliberate burials have occasionally been found at Archaic sites in Louisiana, but they reveal little of how the Paleo-Indians thought and felt. In Bienville Parish, a burial was found in which the skeletons were extended on their backs and interred with the body of a dog. Low earth mounds near Saline Bayou in Natchitoches Parish yielded burials with cremated remains in shallow pits, together with tubular stone beads and a few notched projectile points. The beads seem to have been in the cremations.

Archaeologists presently disagree on the origins of the new ideas that emerged as the Archaic period moved toward its close. Some suggest that, by 1000 B.C., influences were being felt from the Olmec theocracy of Mexico. Others believe that new cultures developed locally as logical outcomes of a trajectory of changes beginning with the Archaic shifts to "Maximum Forest Efficiency."

Changes were certainly afoot in the region by the time of the rise of the Poverty Point culture, about 1000 B.C. At the Poverty Point site, conical mounds were erected to cover scattered ashes from cremations, and a town was laid out on concentric ridges ordered to conform with relationships between the sun and the earth. A giant effigy mound, representing a bird with outstretched wings and tail, dominated the entire community. Towering seventy-five feet above the flat alluvial plain, the huge structure is probably the second largest mound ever built in the eastern woodlands of America. The construction of such monumental public works at so early a date has led archaeologists to marvel at the superior levels of sociopolitical organization that must have existed. Some speculate that this must have been one of the earliest chiefdoms in the whole country. By plotting the distribution of more than ninety thousand artifacts collected at the site, archaeologists have isolated possible workshops and higher status areas, and have postulated matriarchal residences arranged in an orderly fashion across the site.

Slowly but surely, a picture of a widespread cultural development stretching from the present-day Missouri lowlands to what is today Florida, with its center at Poverty Point, is being disclosed. The development included regional adaptations to environmental conditions and, on some occasions, anticipation of later trends toward horticultural practices. It is certain that the axe and hoe, the primary implements of eastern Indian agriculture, were known and used by these people.

The axe and adze, developed by the beginning of the Archaic, seem to have made possible the construction of dugout canoes and thus to have facilitated the expansion of the trade networks of the late Archaic. At Poverty Point, hematite, magnetite, banded flint from present-day Tennessee, massive white and gray flint from what is today Illinois, schistose stones and steatite from present-day Georgia, and copper from the region of the Great Lakes were added to the inventory of trade goods. Novaculites and tan cherts from local sources were made into regional varieties of stemmed projectile points, while delicate barbed and notched points were manufactured from the gray flints of the Illinois area. Point-bar gravels were sifted for nodules of fine-grained chert that could be used as cores for the thin flakes, twice as long as they were wide, that archaeologists call blades. These were used as knives, scrapers, and drills, or perforators. Some of this work is very small; indeed, microlithic tools were most common. Thousands upon thousands have been found at Poverty Point. The blade and other microlith industries, rare pottery, and millions of fired-clay objects used in earth-oven cookery distinguish the Poverty Point sites from those of the Archaic, with their flake tools, fire-cracked cooking stones, and absence of ceramics.

Certain of the Poverty Point items were also used in the periods archaeologists have termed Burial Mounds I and II. Conical burial mounds exhibiting multiple construction stages, blades, and ceramics were retained. Work in copper was intensified. Copper bracelets, earspools, and strips appeared. Some major sites, such as the one at present-day Marksville, were enclosed in giant walls or levees. An elaborately decorated, grog-tempered ceramic—thought by some to have been specialized funerary pottery—was made. The design of a "double-headed" bird (actually, an attempt to render both sides of the creature on a flat surface) representing various birds, among them vultures, shoveler ducks, and roseate spoonbills, appeared. Negative designs on a dentate or smooth rouletted background were common.

Maize has been reported at one of the sites (Marksville proper), but it seems probable that these people were more often dependent upon a "pre-corn" plant combination comprising *Chenopodium* and amaranth, both now considered weeds. These plants were widely cultivated in the Mississippi drainages and may have been grown on point bars and in the fertile soils of natural levees in Louisiana.

The widespread burial-mound tradition that characterized the Tchefuncte and Marksville (Southern Hopewell) cultural periods gave way to a new orientation in Indian life. This change has been attributed by some to Mexican influences, but a resolute cadre of archaeologists holds that it was the by-product of the concentration of settlements at the end of the Marksville and Troyville periods, at about A.D. 800 to 1000. These left mounds of midden refuse upon which houses were built. The pro-Mexican argument points out the appearance of truncated earth mounds that served as temple bases and the foundations of the houses of chiefs.

Pottery became superabundant in the Burial Mound I and II periods, including, as well as cookware, special burial wares and pipes. Most was made of clay mixed with crushed sherds (grog) or grit for temper, the material added to prevent shrinking and cracking. By Temple Mound II, crushed shell was commonly used for tempering. In the Temple Mound II stage, ceramics and iconography appear to echo the vessel forms and iconography found in Mexico. Beautifully made, delicate arrow points, called "bird" points by collectors, first appeared then.

Maize, beans, and squash, along with sunflowers, melons, tobacco, and gourds, had become the dominant cultigens by Temple Mound II (sometimes termed the Mississippian Period). Trade grew in salt, always a precious commodity. Sources in Louisiana including present-day Avery Island and Drake's Lick were widely

Fig. 1
JONESVILLE TEMPLE MOUND, CATAHOULA PARISH
Courtesy of Representative Bill Atkins and the Williamson Museum, Northwestern State University, Natchitoches

used by the Indians. Burials were most often in cemeteries, but in both the Mississippi Valley and the Caddoan area of upper Red River, the paramount elite were often interred, together with family members or retainers sacrificed for burial with them, in truncated rectangular mounds. At Mounds Plantation, about A.D. 1000, a truncate mound was raised over a central log tomb, a custom that appeared in Burial Mound II! The Caddoan area exhibited a number of such conservative elements but, on the whole, moved quickly toward the Mississippian tradition. The separate stages

Caddo I–V mirror this continuity into historic times in north-western Louisiana.

The practice of sacrificing retainers, and iconography such as the hand and eye, barred ovals, lightning, flying serpents, skulls with long bones, cloud symbols, arrow symbols, rattlesnakes, and magnificent birds like the eagle, hawk, and cormorant, seem to have increased in popularity. Embossed copper plates and "long-nosed god" masks, also made of copper, were found at the Gahagan site in Red River Parish in burials in truncate mounds. Animal and other representations were engraved on ceramics, bone, stone, and shell artifacts. Carinated bowls, plates, and varied bottle forms appeared. New traits left their novel memorials, like the beautifully made stones rolled along alleys in the chunkey game. The atlatl and spear were almost entirely replaced by the bow and arrow.

Louisiana seems to have felt these influences from several directions: from the west via Red River, from the middle Mississippi Valley, and from the Gulf coast. It is probable that the great cult center at Cahokia, near what is today East St. Louis, Illinois, exerted a powerful influence all across the South. Louisiana could not have escaped that potent pressure.

Archaeology, which remains the most revealing source of information about the prehistoric cultures of Louisiana, has roughly drawn this much of the picture. The model is detailed enough to show that the powerful temple mound–building cultures were probably on the decline when the first whites reached the native tribes. Certainly, by then, temple mounds were less common, surviving in only a few places.

Upon this ebb and flow of people and cultures the Europeans encroached. Much has been learned about what happened thereafter, but we are left with two great questions: How much continuity was there in Indian life after the advent of the Europeans, and what would have happened had the Louisiana Indian cultures not been ravaged by war and disease, and otherwise affected by the European cultural presence?

REFERENCES

A number of excellent syntheses of Louisiana archaeology are available. The best overview is probably that of Robert W. Neuman.

Neuman, Robert W.
1984 *An Introduction to Louisiana Archaeology.* Baton Rouge.

A good compendium of early source material has also been published. With these two works, one can quickly acquire the sources needed for the pursuit of Louisiana archaeology.

Neuman, Robert W., and Lanier Simmons
1969 A Bibliography Relative to the Indians of the State of Louisiana. *Anthropological Study* 4, Louisiana Geological Survey, Department of Conservation, Baton Rouge.

The earliest occupations of Indians in the state have attracted attention only in recent years. Some archaeologists seem to have assumed that the thick mantle of Recent alluvium in south and central Louisiana precluded work on the early sites, but others, particularly Clarence H. Webb of Shreveport, pointed out the presence of early artifacts in northern Louisiana where older geological surfaces were exposed.

Webb, Clarence H.
1948 Evidences of Pre-Pottery Cultures in Louisiana. *American Antiquity* 13(3): 227–32.

Although a decade passed before those seeds took root, Webb's paper opened a Pandora's box of Pleistocene and early Holocene occupations in the state. The Indians had been in Louisiana longer than anyone had believed. Webb, William G. Haag, and their students examined the Lithic, Archaic, and Formative stages of Louisiana prehistory.

Haag, William G.
1961 The Archaic of the Lower Mississippi Valley. *American Antiquity* 26(3): 227–32.

Gagliano, Sherwood M., and Hiram F. Gregory
1965 A Preliminary Survey of Paleo-Indian Points from Louisiana. *Louisiana Studies* 4(1): 62–67.

Haag's interest in Archaic occupations in Louisiana had developed early, as he addressed his attention to the entire Southeast.

Haag, William G.
1942 Early Horizons in the Southeast. *American Antiquity* 7(3): 209–22.

Haag's work was followed by that of his students and colleagues. By the 1970s these studies of Archaic and earlier sites had spread to north and central Louisiana, and a more complete picture of the Archaic had begun to emerge.

Gagliano, Sherwood M.
1963 A Survey of Preceramic Occupations in Portions of South Louisi-
      ana and South Mississippi. *Florida Anthropologist* 16(4): 105–32.
1964 *An Archaeological Survey of Avery Island*. Baton Rouge.

Gibson, Jon L.
1966 A Preliminary Survey of Indian Occupations in LaSalle Parish,
      Louisiana. *Louisiana Studies* 5(3): 193–237.
1968 Cad Mound: A Stone Bead Locus in East Central Louisiana. *Bul-
      letin of the Texas Archaeological Society* 38: 1–17.
1977 Archaeological Survey of Portions of Little River, Boeuf River and
      Big Creek, East Central and Northeastern Louisiana. *University
      of Southwestern Louisiana Center for Archaeological Studies, Re-
      port 3*, Lafayette.

Webb, Clarence H., Joel Shiner, and E. Wayne Roberts
1971 The John Pearce Site (16CD56): A San Patrice Site in Caddo
      Parish, Louisiana. *Bulletin of the Texas Archaeological Society*
      42: 1–50.

Smith, Brent
1975 Prehistoric Settlement Patterns of the Young's Bayou Drain-
      age, Natchitoches Parish, Louisiana. *Louisiana Archaeology* 2:
      163–200.

Gregory, Hiram F., and Hugh K. Curry
1978 *Prehistory: Natchitoches Parish Cultural and Historical Resources*.
      Natchitoches Parish Planning Commission, Natchitoches.

Largely at the instigation of Sherwood M. Gagliano, the nonceramic occupations of southern Louisiana, eventually confirmed as Archaic, have
been explored in some depth.

Gagliano, Sherwood M.
1967 Late Archaic-Early Formative Relationships in South Louisiana.
      *Proceedings of the 23rd Southeastern Archaeological Conference,
      SEAC Bulletin* 6: 9–22.

Poverty Point has been of compelling interest to both archaeologists and
laymen since it was first visited in 1913 by Clarence B. Moore. Years of patient investigation have not solved this magnificent riddle. A large settlement in 1000 B.C., the site still offers many research possibilities. The
extensive literature on Poverty Point, its significance to the American Formative, and its relationships to other sites in Louisiana and across the
Southeast has been brought together in two major works.

Broyles, Betty, and Clarence H. Webb, eds.
1970 The Poverty Point Culture. *Southeastern Archaeological Confer-
      ence Bulletin* No. 12, Morgantown.

Webb, Clarence H.
1982   The Poverty Point Culture, 2nd ed., revised. Vol. 17 of *Geoscience and Man*, Baton Rouge.

Now a state commemorative area, Poverty Point is protected, and work there is continuing. Pollen studies and geomorphological and stratigraphic investigations have recently provided new insights into the development of the major site. Models of Poverty Point grew from the work of Robert Bell, James Ford, Sherwood Gagliano, Jon Gibson, Glenn Greene, Hiram Gregory, William Haag, Donald Hunter, Carl Kuttruff, John Lenzer, Robert Neitzel, J. S. Perry, Philip Phillips, Roger Saucier, William Spencer, and Cynthia Weber.

Ted Brasher offered new conceptions of Poverty Point as the center of a widespread cultural development. Jon Gibson described it as evidence of a formal chiefdom.

Gibson, Jon L.
1974   Poverty Point: The First North American Chiefdom. *Archaeology* 27(2): 96–105.

Hiram Gregory suggested a horticultural component. Don Hunter noted small, specialized camps. Roger Saucier and Sherwood Gagliano demonstrated that the culture extended to and across the Gulf coast. Clarence Webb monitored and oversaw all the research.

Gibson, Jon L., ed.
1980   Caddoan and Poverty Point Archaeology: Essays in Honor of Clarence Hungerford Webb. *Louisiana Archaeology* 6.

Some amateurs have made contributions of great importance to Louisiana archaeology. After 1960, the Catahoula Basin and Poverty Point were the focal points of amateur fieldwork. Carl Alexander amassed the great general collections, Les Davis worked diligently in the Tensas Basin, and William Baker discovered the burials at Cowpen Slough. Brian Duhe worked the Lake Pontchartrain area.

Archaeology in Louisiana was sporadic from 1916 through the 1930s. From 1920 to 1940, work was dominated by three archaeologists from the Smithsonian Institution: Gerard Fowke, Frank Setzler, and Winslow Walker. Fowke and Setzler, both trained in the classical Hopewell culture of the Ohio Valley (Burial Mound II or Marksville Period in Louisiana), were attracted to Louisiana. Fowke discovered the Hopewellian connections of the Marksville mounds (now Marksville Prehistoric Park) and worked on the site with Setzler. With their activities, Louisiana archaeology took on a new dimension and, for the first time since the days of Squier and Davis, received national attention.

Fowke, Gerard
1927 Archaeological Work in Louisiana. *Smithsonian Miscellaneous Collections* 78(7): 254–59.
1928 Archaeological Investigations—II: Explorations in the Red River Valley in Louisiana. In *Forty-fourth Annual Report of the Bureau of American Ethnology, 1926–1927*, Washington, D.C., 339–436.

Frank Setzler's work grew directly from that of Fowke and gave Louisiana archaeology a truly scientific culture-history orientation.

Setzler, Frank M.
1933 Hopewell Type Pottery from Louisiana. *Journal of the Washington Academy of Sciences* 23(3): 149–53.
1933 Pottery of the Hopewell Type from Louisiana. *Proceedings of the United States National Museum* 82(22): 1–21.

Caroline Dormon, a naturalist and artist, asked John R. Swanton to send an archaeologist to Louisiana to help with the work of the de Soto commission. Swanton sent Winslow Walker. The tireless Walker reconnoitered mounds, outlined for the first time the prehistoric cultures of Louisiana, wrote the first formal description of Caddoan ceramics, and conducted perhaps the earliest salvage archaeology in the eastern United States, all between 1932 and 1936.

Walker, Winslow M.
1932 A Reconnaissance of Northern Louisiana Mounds. In *Explorations and Fieldwork of the Smithsonian Institution in 1931*. Washington, D.C., 169–74.
1932 Prehistoric Cultures of Louisiana. In *Conference on Southern Prehistory, Division of Anthropology and Psychology, National Research Council*. Washington, D.C., 42–48.
1933 Trailing the Mound Builders of the Mississippi Valley. In *Explorations and Fieldwork of the Smithsonian Institution in 1932*. Washington, D.C., 77–80.
1934 A Variety of Caddoan Pottery from Louisiana. *Journal of the Washington Academy of Sciences* 24(2): 99–104.
1935 A Caddo Burial Site at Natchitoches, Louisiana. *Smithsonian Miscellaneous Collections* 94(14): 1–13.
1936 The Troyville Mounds, Catahoula Parish, Louisiana. *Bureau of American Ethnology Bulletin* 113, Washington, D.C.

Walker was among the first to recognize the significance of Caddoan archaeology. His work at the Natchitoches Fish Hatchery and at Jonesville resulted from Dormon's intervention and well demonstrates the worth of cooperation betwen amateurs and professionals. Dormon was one of a cadre of highly effective amateur archaeologists that was developing in

Louisiana at that time. Others were Mr. and Mrs. U. B. Evans in the Catahoula Basin, and Edward F. Neild and Clarence H. Webb of Shreveport. In
south Louisiana, Randolph Bazet of Houma and the McIlhenny family at
Avery Island collected artifacts and encouraged additional archaeological
research, including the work of professionals.

Traditional archaeology began in Louisiana in the 1930s. As elsewhere,
pottery was the essential tool for establishing the chronological sequence
of cultural development for the region. Applying the direct historical
method, James Ford began to extend his work into Mississippi and to seri-
ate ceramics (potsherds) so as to identify the chronology of cultural development in the Southeast. The basis for that development was what Ford
called the Red River Mouth sequence. He defined historic Caddo, Choctaw,
Natchez, and Tunica ceramic complexes, which he could extend back to
prehistoric roots. These efforts had great influence on the development of
southeastern archaeology, and the lower Mississippi Valley sequence that
grew from this initial work remains a fine example of the merits of these
techniques.

Ford, James A.
1936   An Analysis of Indian Village Site Collections from Louisiana and
        Mississippi. *Anthropological Study* 2, Louisiana Geological Sur-
        vey, Department of Conservation, New Orleans.
1951   Greenhouse: A Troyville-Coles Creek Period Site in Avoyelles Par-
        ish, Louisiana. *Anthropological Papers of the American Museum
        of Natural History* 44(1), New York.
1953   Measurements of Some Prehistoric Design Developments in the
        Southeastern United States. *Anthropological Papers of the Ameri-
        can Museum of Natural History* 44(2), New York.

The series of excavations conducted in Louisiana during the intensive
archaeological fieldwork supported by the Works Progress Administration led to a more detailed knowledge of these cultural sequences. Under
James A. Ford's direction at Louisiana State University, the excavations
were designed to test and expand the sequence as known for the lower Mississippi Valley. The cultural sequences have been expanded, largely since
the 1960s, which tells us something about the difficulty of funding archaeological research. A neat synthesis is:

Phillips, Philip, James A. Ford, and James B. Griffin
1951   Archaeological Survey in the Lower Mississippi Alluvial Valley,
        1940–1947. *Papers of the Peabody Museum of Archaeology and
        Ethnology* 25: 347–90, Harvard University, Cambridge.

Efforts to refine these earlier sequences began in the 1950s. Primarily the
work of the Harvard "school"—Philip Phillips, Stephen Williams, David
Halley, John Belmont, Ian Brown, and Jeffrey Brain—these efforts have

continued to concentrate on ceramic analysis and the refining of "culture history."

Phillips, Philip
1970 Archaeological Survey in the Lower Yazoo Basin, Mississippi, 1949–1955. *Papers of the Peabody Museum of Archaeology and Ethnology* 60, Harvard University, Cambridge.

One interested in the "personality" of archaeology and the *esprit de temps* should turn to two personal tributes to seminal figures in archaeology.

Williams, Stephen
1970 *Philip Phillips, Lower Mississippi Survey, 1940–1970*. Peabody Museum, Harvard, Cambridge.

Brain, Jeffrey P., and Ian W. Brown
1982 Robert S. Neitzel: The Great Sun. *Lower Mississippi Survey Bulletin* 9, Peabody Museum, Harvard, Cambridge.

Despite the difficult times of the Great Depression and World War II, a group of local amateurs led by the Shreveport pediatrician Clarence H. Webb began laying the foundation for yet another ceramic sequence in northwestern Louisiana. In the late 1930s, only Walker's single report on the Natchitoches Fish Hatchery site and Ford's 1936 attempt to define Caddoan ceramics existed. Webb, though closely associated with the Louisiana State University teams of Ford, Phillips, Griffin, and Neitzel, broadened his contacts with archaeologists to include Alex Krieger in Texas and Robert Bell in Oklahoma. The "Caddo-ologists" were subsequently to develop their archaeology with new orientations, terms, and labels. Not until the 1960s did the four-state area (Arkansas, Louisiana, Oklahoma, and Texas) begin to seek correlations with the lower Mississippi Valley sequence.

Webb, Clarence H.
1939 Further Excavations of the Gahagan Mound: Connections with a Florida Culture. *Bulletin of the Texas Archaeological and Paleontological Society* 11: 92–126.

1945 A Second Historic Caddo Site at Natchitoches, Louisiana. *Bulletin of the Texas Archaeological and Paleontological Society* 16: 52–83.

1948 Caddoan Prehistory: The Bossier Focus. *Bulletin of the Texas Archaeological and Paleontological Society* 19: 100–43.

1959 The Belcher Mound. *Memoirs of the Society for American Archaeology* No. 6, Salt Lake City.

1961 Relationships Between the Caddoan and Central Louisiana Culture Sequences. *Bulletin of the Texas Archaeological Society* 31: 11–12.

1983 The Bossier Focus Revisited: Montgomery I, Werner and Other Unicomponent Sites. In *Southeastern Natives and Their Pasts: Papers Honoring Dr. Robert E. Bell* (Don Wychoff and Jack L. Hoffman, eds.), Studies in Oklahoma's Past No. 11, Norman, 183–238.

Webb, Clarence H., and Ralph R. McKinney
1975 Mounds Plantation (16-CD-12), Caddo Parish, Louisiana. *Louisiana Archaeology* 2: 39–127.

Webb, Clarence H., and David R. Jeane
1977 The Springhill Airport Sites: J. C. Montgomery I and II. *Newsletter of the Louisiana Archaeological Society* 4(3): 3–6.

Working with Hiram Gregory, Webb has synthesized much of Caddoan archaeology.

Webb, Clarence H., and Hiram F. Gregory
1978 The Caddo Indians of Louisiana. *Anthropological Study* 2, Louisiana Antiquities Commission, Department of Culture, Recreation, and Tourism, Baton Rouge.

Beginning in the 1960s, the influence of the Department of Geography and Anthropology at Louisiana State University in Baton Rouge began to be felt in Louisiana archaeology. The early work of Fred B. Kniffen, James A. Ford, Harold N. Fisk, William G. Haag, and Richard Joel Russell on mounds, villages, and the meandering Mississippi and its deltas began to open new approaches to teams of geomorphologists, geologists, and archaeologists. A wedding of cultural and physical science took place, resulting in what Kniffen in 1958—with a premonition of what was to happen nationwide in the 1970s—called the birth of cultural ecology. The impetus of the group at Louisiana State University and the lonely voice of Joseph Caldwell at the University of Georgia launched this approach in the Southeast.

Kniffen, Fred. B.
1936 Preliminary Report on the Indian Mounds and Middens of Plaquemines and St. Bernard Parishes. H. V. Howe, ed., *Louisiana Geological Survey Bulletin* 8: 407–22, Louisiana Department of Conservation, New Orleans.

McIntire, William G.
1958 Prehistoric Indian Settlements of the Changing Mississippi River Delta. *Louisiana State University Coastal Studies Series* 1, Baton Rouge.

Caldwell, Joseph R.
1958 Trend and Tradition in the Prehistory of the Eastern United States. *American Anthropological Association Memoir* 88.

Gregory, Hiram F.
1968   Maximum Forest Efficiency: Swamp and Upland Potentials. *Proceedings of the 21st Southeastern Archaeological Conference, SEAC Bulletin* 3: 52–59.

Gagliano, Sherwood M.
1967   Point Bar Agriculture. *Proceedings of the 22nd Southeastern Archaeological Conference, SEAC Bulletin* 5: 13–14.

Gibson, Jon L.
1970   Archaeological Checklist of Edible Flora in the Lower Mississippi Valley, the Poverty Point Culture. *Southeastern Archaeological Conference Bulletin* 12: 90–98.

Byrd, Kathleen
1976   The Tchefuncte Subsistence: Information Obtained from the Excavation of the Morton Shell Mound, Iberia Parish, Louisiana. *Southeastern Archaeological Conference Bulletin* 19: 70–75.
1976   The Brackish Water Clam (*Rangia cuneata*): A Prehistoric "Staff of Life" or a Minor Food Resource? *Louisiana Archaeology* 3: 23–31.

By the latter 1960s, settlement-pattern studies, ecologically adaptive models, and faunal analysis had become part of the archaeology of Louisiana. These studies extended into the 1980s.

Gregory, Hiram F.
1969   Plaquemine Period Sites in the Catahoula Basin: A Cultural Microcosm in the Catahoula Basin. *Louisiana Studies* 8(2): 112–35.
1980   A Continuity Model for Caddoan Adaptation on the Red River in Louisiana. In *The Hanna Site, an Alto Village in Red River Parish, Louisiana* (Thomas, Campbell, and Ahler, eds.), *Louisiana Archaeology* 5: 347–60.

Since 1970, studies assessing the cultural resources of the state and the concomitant management of those rapidly vanishing resources have increased. Nonrenewable, this heritage is indeed fragile. Efforts have integrated state, federal, and private support systems for archaeology in Louisiana. Surveys and assessments have been made in all parts of the state via these interests, and salvage and mitigation projects have been instituted over the area.

New techniques, including sophisticated coring, air photo interpretations, and computer analysis and the use of data banks, are transforming Louisiana archaeology into a strong scientific discipline with its theoretical basis firmly rooted in both physical and social science. The journal

Louisiana Archaeology and the Louisiana Archaeological Society involve both lay and professional archaeologists in the field and in data analysis. The Office of Archaeology in the Louisiana Division of Culture, Recreation, and Tourism, Baton Rouge, offers a wide range of statewide information and field services. Louisiana archaeology is growing in scope and quality.

III

THE TRIBES IN 1700

The identities and locations of Louisiana's Indian tribes cannot be determined for any period prior to about 1700. De Soto's brief visit in 1542 was like a flash of lightning—spectacular, but providing little illumination. With the advent of the French some 150 years later, the area and its occupants came under the observation of literate men who had come to stay and who recorded much of what they saw and did.

The French documents, though far from complete, provide the best view of pre-Columbian Indian life and of the general scene in Louisiana in 1700. Even with their help, the work of sorting pre-European and postcontact culture traits remains difficult, particularly in the case of the lesser tribes that lived along the Mississippi River and elsewhere in what is today southeast Louisiana, and who were early and profoundly affected by the aliens.

Literature on Louisiana's tribes varies extensively in coverage. The greater tribes generally were accorded closer attention than, for example, the Atakapa, whose chief distinction lay in the very meagerness of their material culture.

Like many Indians, the Atakapa called themselves *Ishak*, "the people." The name *Atakapa* is of Choctaw, or Mobilian, origin and means "eater of human flesh." Cannibalism was indeed practiced among these people but was limited to the eating of portions of slain enemies.

Atakapa lands included all of what is today southwestern Louisiana, extending from upper Bayou Teche to the Sabine River and from the Gulf of Mexico northward almost to present-day Alexandria. Theirs was a dispersed occupation, and sizable areas were left vacant. Atakapa territorial boundaries, like those of other tribes, thus were ill-defined zones rather than neat lines.

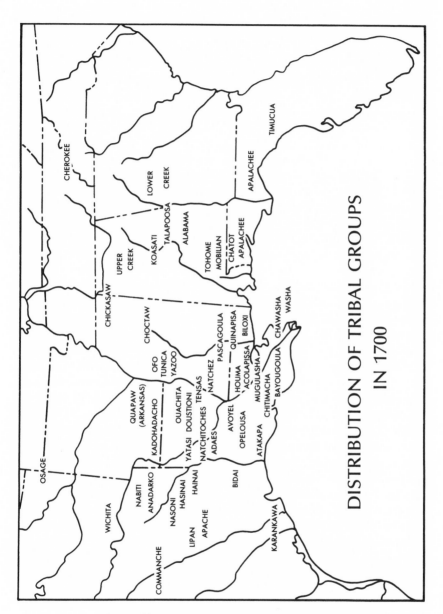

DISTRIBUTION OF TRIBAL GROUPS IN 1700

CHEROKEE
LOWER CREEK
TIMUCUA
APALACHEE
UPPER CREEK
TALAPOOSA
KOASATI
ALABAMA
TOHOME
MOBILIAN
CHATOT
APALACHEE
CHICKASAW
CHOCTAW
OFO
TUNICA
YAZOO
PASCAGOULA
QUINAPISA
BILOXI
WASHA
CHAWASHA
NATCHEZ
HOUMA
ACOLAPISSA
MUGULASHA
BAYOUGOULA
QUAPAW (ARKANSAS)
KADOHADACHO
OUACHITA
DOUSTIONI
TENSAS
NATCHITOCHES
YATASI
ADAES
AVOYEL
OPELOUSA
CHITIMACHA
ATAKAPA
OSAGE
NABITI
ANADARKO
HASINAI
HAINAI
BIDAI
NASONI
LIPAN
APACHE
WICHITA
KARANKAWA
COMMANCHE

Courtesy of the Louisiana State University Cartographic Section

The Atakapa comprised four sovereign bands, each of which had one or more villages. Dialectic differences distinguished the two eastern bands, the sunrise people, from the *Hikike Ishak*, the sunset bands. A fifth band, the Opelousa, were related only linguistically.

At one time or another, the eastern Atakapa bands occupied locations on upper Bayou Teche, on lower Vermilion River, near Plaquemine Brule, near Lake Arthur on the Mermentau River, on the western Grand Lake, on lower Bayou Nezpique (Nezpique Prairie), on Bayou Queue de Tortue, and on Lacassine Island. The two western bands situated themselves along the Calcasieu River and the lakes around Lake Charles. Occupied in the twentieth century, the last Atakapa village was on Indian Lake, now Lake Prien. The principal nineteenth-century Opelousa village was some fifteen miles west of the Opelousas church, at the edge of the great swamp that is the Atchafalaya River floodplain. Other sites have been reported to the north and west of this village and on Bayou Plaquemine Brule.

To early explorers, the Louisiana Atakapa were an almost invisible people, seen rarely in their boats along the coast in summer. They sometimes betrayed their presence by distant smokes and marsh fires. According to tradition, the Louisiana Atakapa came from the West, where their cultural kinsmen survived well into historic times. The easterners probably were much like their neighbors in present-day Texas, whose Spanish visitors noted their low order of cultural development and a general scarcity of natural resources.

The Louisiana Atakapa, however, enjoyed singular advantages. The coastal marshes of Louisiana are given variety by the long, low, inshore sand ridges that parallel the coast. These *cheniers* combine with the numerous local waterways to create a changing maze of lagoons, lakes, and active streams. These waters are of varying degrees of salinity and, in marked contrast to their Texas counterparts, are rich in fish, shellfish, bird and animal life, and useful vegetation.

The *cheniers* present a mystery of their own. Atakapa settlements extended seaward only as far as the edge of the high ground bordering the marsh some twenty miles inland from the beaches, so that, apparently, the marshes were left without permanent residents. Abundant evidence, however, demonstrates that the *cheniers* were once the home of people much superior in culture to the later Atakapa. Excellent pottery has been found on the ridges, as have trade artifacts of copper, galena, and stone. In addition to these relics, dozens of large mounds and middens have been located, and a great shell mound, in the shape of an alligator six hundred feet long, could be seen on a ridge in Vermilion Parish Grand Lake until a few years ago. This ancient culture has no Texas counterpart.

The Caddo tribes in Louisiana in 1700 included the Adai, Doustioni, Natchitoches, Ouachita, and Yatasi. The shifting stream channels, driftwood accumulations, and ephemeral lakes so typical along the Red River for more than one hundred miles upstream from Natchitoches have obscured the village sites of these notable people. Frequent flooding forced settlements to move, at times considerable distances. In the 1790s, the Kadohadacho, the Caddo proper, moved to Caddo Lake from present-day Arkansas.

The Doustioni and Natchitoches, the original Natchitoches confederacy, remained near their traditional homes in the vicinity of Natchitoches. The Yatasi, from south of the Shreveport area, and the Adai, from near present-day Robeline, shifted about freely and originally may not have been Caddoan speakers. The Ouachita moved from the Red River to the Ouachita after de Soto's arrival, and their frontier town there, according to reports, was destroyed on two occasions.

The Louisiana Caddo were fundamentally a southeastern people. Their languages were unlike those to the east but may have been distantly related to other non-Muskogean languages in the Southeast. It is not strange to find cultural differences in a marginal people such as the Caddo. Even so, they were bound to the tribes east of them by social organization and religious beliefs and rituals. Their cultural attainments approached those of the Natchez.

The Caddo lived well in a fertile country. Their economy was bolstered by active trade, hunting, and fishing, in addition to agriculture. Even the bison was at hand and was hunted along the northwest Louisiana buffalo trails as late as 1700.

The principal towns of the linguistically related Tunica, Koroa, and Yazoo, in 1700, were situated on high ground along the Yazoo River, not far above present-day Vicksburg. Westward, beyond the Mississippi, stretched what is today northeast Louisiana, empty of people as far as the Ouachita River save for transients plying the salt trade and occasional Tunica hunting and gathering parties. At that time, the area was cloaked in mystery, and much of its story is still unknown.

De Soto found at least thirty sizable towns between the mouths of the Arkansas and Red rivers, lying along the west side of the Mississippi. By the time of the advent of the French, according to estimates, the thriving population the Spaniard saw had shrunk some 80 percent. Despite reports of villages in 1700, none have actually been found; only about a thousand Taensa and Avoyel remained in Louisiana. Losses have been attributed to increasingly severe, frequent flooding and, more probably, the lethal character of European diseases.

The Tunica were an active people, outstripping even the Natchitoches and Koroa as traders in salt and busy with farming, hunting, and fishing. Some have characterized Tunican culture as comparatively plain, but it is possible that this characterization stems from a lack of more detailed knowledge of the people.

The Natchez speakers, in 1700, were of three tribes: the Taensa and Avoyel in Louisiana, and the Natchez of the Mississippi River's left bank. Cultural similarities among them were strong, as attested by their identical speech, though some customs were less widely accepted. About 1700, the Taensa and Natchez were at odds, even though the latter had rekindled their sacred flame at the perpetual fire in the Taensa temple. Antipathy of this sort was often observed among tribes separated by the lower Mississippi River, perhaps because the shared resource of the river heightened the sense of rivalry.

In the late seventeenth century, the Taensa occupied seven or eight villages on the western end of Lake St. Joseph and another, Little Taensa, on the Tensas River near present-day Clayton, in northern Concordia Parish. There may have been other settlements in what are today Madison and East Carroll parishes. The Mississippi's west bank in this area is low ground, and Taensa village site selection of necessity emphasized freedom from flooding as well as the proximity of agricultural lands, game, and wild food supplies.

The numerous people seen by de Soto at Guachoya and Aminoya may have been Taensa. By 1700 their large population had been reduced to no more than eight hundred, in spite of their agricultural skills based on methods and ceremonies similar to those among the Natchez.

Little is known of the Avoyel. Never numerous, they faded early from history's view. When first contacted by Europeans, the Avoyel had only recently parted from the Natchez and still closely resembled them. Villages are known to have existed for a time at present-day Marksville and Alexandria, the former site supporting a stockaded town. The Avoyel controlled Red River from Alexandria to its junction with the Mississippi, the lower Black River, and the upper Atchafalaya, with easy access to upper Bayou Teche.

In the tribe's own language, the word *Avoyel* means "people of the rocks," or "flint people." The name was appropriate, since they were producers and traders of stone projectile points and blanks. The trading role of the Avoyel was reinforced by their location, and they were widely known as middlemen. It was Avoyel territory, in later years, that constituted the land bridge, a constriction of the drainage system, across the swamps west of the Mississippi River, over which were driven the cattle and horses stolen in Spanish Texas.

Occupying the margins of the Florida parishes—that portion of the "toe" of the Louisiana "boot" north of the Isle of Orleans—and, intermittently, the Mississippi River's banks from the Red River southward, were seven sovereign tribes, none of which was large. Culturally, the seven tribes, known as the Muskogeans, conformed to the regional pattern. They spoke Choctaw dialects but were not members of the Choctaw confederacy. They had no significant settlements in the interior of the Florida parishes, a region of infertile soils that nevertheless held a major resource in the form of abundant cherty gravels. The evidence of numerous workshops where gravel is available suggests that periodic visits were made to secure stones for weapons and other implements.

The primary Houma village in 1700 stood on blufflands flanking the portage between the big meanders of the Mississippi River where a westward loop received Red River, now the site of Angola. Iberville spoke of 140 cabins, arranged in a circle, and estimated the population to include some 350 potential warriors and many children.

The Houma may have been an offshoot of the Chakchiuma, a Yazoo River tribe with whom the Houma shared their tribal symbol, the red crayfish. *Houma* is Choctaw or Mobilian Jargon for "red," possibly derived from the last two syllables of the parent tribe's name, *Chakchiuma.*

The Houma move from the Yazoo to the Louisiana village could not have been made long before 1700, perhaps occurring between de Soto's passage and the coming of the French. Some believe that the rectangular floor plan of Houma houses, so different from the round plans of the Yazoo Chakchiuma and other Choctaw speakers, indicates that the Houma may have sojourned among the Natchez longer than among the Muskogean speakers.

Bayougoula is Choctaw or Mobilian Jargon for "bayou people." What may have been the tribe's name for itself, *Pischenoa*, Choctaw or Mobilian Jargon for "ours," appears once in an early account. The tribe's totem animal was the alligator.

The four to five hundred Bayougoula in 1700 were clustered about a single village on the site of modern Bayou Goula. Iberville found the settlement a quarter of a mile from the right bank of the Mississippi River, on a little stream that provided the domestic water supply.

Comparatively little is known about the other Muskogean-speaking tribes of Louisiana—the Acolapissa, Mugulasha, Okelousa, Quinapisa, and Tangipahoa. Even their identities remain uncertain. Those in more remote places were not exposed to the influx of French observers. All were on the move in historic times, fleeing more powerful oppressors and seeking refuge in settlement on the lower Mississippi River close to French towns. They rapidly lost numbers, merged with other relict tribes, and finally disappeared from the record.

From the name *Acolapissa*, Choctaw or Mobilian Jargon for "those who see and hear," it might be inferred that the members of this border tribe served as outposts against possible enemy incursions from the west. The name also suggests recognition of the Acolapissa as a Choctaw tribe. The combined numbers of Acolapissa and Tangipahoa, as of 1650, have been reckoned to be 1,500, possibly an overestimate.

In 1699 the Acolapissa were living in six towns lying along Pearl River, the town farthest downstream being some four leagues above the mouth of the river. Recent archival research places the other five villages on streams flowing into Lake Pontchartrain from the north. Precise sites of the six towns have not been determined, and one early account suggests that settlement was more or less continuous along the river in the diffused manner distinctive of that time in the Southeast. There are "old fields" in the area that may have been Acolapissa in origin; conditions there favored agriculture and other subsistence activities.

Shortly after 1700, the Acolapissa moved close to Lake Pontchartrain on Bayou Castine to escape English and Chickasaw slave hunters. Fleeing a deadly epidemic in 1718, they established a village on the Mississippi River above New Orleans. Afterward, they declined greatly in numbers and were eventually absorbed by the mixed tribal group that came to be identified as Houma.

The Quinapisa may have been an offshoot of the Acolapissa, both being derived, perhaps, from the Choctaw-speaking Napochi of the Moundville, Alabama, area. In 1682 they occupied a village on the right bank of the Mississippi River, near Hahnville. Once the tribe had been much more numerous, living in several villages down toward the mouth of the Mississippi. By 1700 they had joined with another diminishing tribe, the Mugulasha, and were established with the Bayougoula at their village. In the same year, the Bayougoula fell on the Quinapisa-Mugulasha and slaughtered numbers of them. The survivors were absorbed by other tribes, and their names passed from the record.

The Quinapisa attacked La Salle's party as it passed their village and then sent messengers to their allies, the Natchez and Koroa, suggesting that they do the same. The Quinapisa-Mugulasha were also allies of the Houma and Acolapissa. Their friendship with the Houma doubtless contributed to the Bayougoula attack on them, in view of the animosity between the Houma and the Bayougoula.

Almost nothing is known of the Quinapisa's distinctive traits, though they may have been the Indians who used atlatls to attack the remnants of de Soto's party a half-league above the mouth of the Mississippi. The name Quinapisa is Choctaw for "those who see," also suggesting an outpost function. However, their villages on the Mississippi could hardly have been outposts.

The tribal name *Mugulasha* is a corruption of *Imongolasha*, Choctaw for "people of the other side," referring to a social division. The language of these Indians probably was a Choctaw dialect, judging by their association with Bayougoula and Quinapisa. Although confused with the Quinapisa because the two were joined at an early date, the Mugulasha once occupied villages below the Bayougoula and had their own temple and perpetual fire.

As early as 1699, a party of Mugulasha and Bayougoula hunters greeted Iberville at Biloxi, an incident revealing how far hunters actually ranged. On his ascent of the Mississippi in the same year, Iberville encountered Mugulasha and Bayougoula at the latter's village.

Accounts relate that the Mugulasha and Quinapisa maintained their separate identities and organizations in the Bayougoula settlement and that they danced separately in observing the calumet ceremony with Iberville's party. They maintained friendly relations with the Houma, despite the enmity between the Houma and the Bayougoula. They may have retained sovereignty over their former lands downstream from the Bayougoula, since the chiefs had precisely bounded hunting grounds whose invasion was an occasion for war. The Mugulasha, like the Quinapisa, disappeared from the area after their massacre by the Bayougoula in 1700.

Tangipahoa is Choctaw for "corn gatherers" or "corncob people." The people with this name were said to have been a seventh town of the Acolapissa on Pearl River. Yet, before 1682, at least some of them had moved to the Mississippi River to establish a village on the left bank two leagues below the Quinapisa town. By 1682 the town had been destroyed by the combined Houma and Okelousa, the survivors fleeing back to the Acolapissa on Pearl River.

Sometime between 1702 and 1705, when the Acolapissa were driven from Pearl River by slave hunters and had taken refuge on Bayou Castine, the Tangipahoa moved to the river that bears their name. Their subsequent history is unknown. They may have joined other tribal remnants that gathered on the Mississippi near New Orleans.

Okelousa is Choctaw for "black water," a name said to have been given to this small tribe because it occupied lands around two small lakes in which the water was darkened by its high organic content. The lakes are presumed to have been to the west of and above Pointe Coupee. The group is further characterized as "wandering people west of the Mississippi" and elsewhere, with the Washa and Chawasha, as "wandering people of the seacoasts."

In 1682 the Okelousa were allied with the Houma in the destruction of the Tangipahoa village on the Mississippi River. The combined Chawasha, Okelousa, and Washa of 1699 were said to have numbered seven hundred, of whom two hundred were warriors. Iberville and Bienville considered the three tribes to be speakers of Choctaw dialects, but doubt persists on this point. The elusive Okelousa faded soon from the record, perhaps absorbed by a larger tribe.

The name *Chitimacha* may be the people's own term for "those living on Grand River," or it may be Choctaw for "those who have pots." The latter allusion is difficult to understand, since all tribes of the lower Mississippi made and used pottery. More recently, the Chitimacha have called themselves, in their own language, "men altogether red." Another name, *Yaknechito*, meaning "big country," was early coupled with a separate group of people called the Chitimacha. Its significance can only be guessed at. Might it refer to the Atakapa, because of their connection with the marsh and prairie, or to a geographical division of the Chitimacha themselves?

The Chitimacha were a numerous people. An estimated population of four thousand in 1650 has been proposed for the three tribes, a figure none too high in view of the number of villages recorded. Up to the twentieth century, thirteen to fifteen names of villages could be recalled and the sites identified, and earlier there were many more. Most of the remembered villages were on Bayou Teche, while others were on the main shore or inlets of Grand Lake, on Butte la Rose, on Grand River, and at the mouth of Bayou Plaquemine.

It has been suggested that there were two divisions of the Chitimacha, one occupying villages on upper Bayou Lafourche and the Mississippi, and the other oriented to lower Bayou Teche, Grand Lake, and the Atchafalaya River. Evidence at hand does not support such a division for any time prior to the appearance of the French on the lower Mississippi River. Bayou Lafourche belonged to the Washa and Chawasha, while Chitimacha settlements on the Mississippi and Bayou Plaquemine were established well into the eighteenth century.

Chitimacha tradition locates a former home in the Natchez area, and the Natchez claimed kinship ties. Perhaps the western movement of Muskogean tribes split the preexisting Tunican stock, forcing them both northward and southward. Areally rare social structures embracing ranks of nobles and commoners distinguish both

Fig. 2
CHITIMACHA INDIANS DANCING THE CALUMET, 1718
from a drawing by Le Page du Pratz
National Anthropological Archives, Smithsonian Institution

Natchez and Chitimacha, though not necessarily relating them. The Chitimacha are among the lower Mississippi River tribes that display the highest attainments within the southeastern culture area.

The term *Washa* is possibly Choctaw for "hunting place," an appropriate name in view of the abundance of game in the lowlands the Washa occupied. Lake Washa, more commonly called Lake Salvador, in St. Charles Parish, and another, smaller Lake Washa, in lower Terrebonne Parish, still bear the name.

The extent to which Washa material and social culture traits paralleled those of their presumed linguistic kin, the Chitimacha, is unknown. In 1699 they lived around a central village on upper Bayou Lafourche near what is today Labadieville, so agriculture may have been an economic mainstay. At the same time, the Washa ranged widely to the coast and the lower Mississippi, thus sharing in the special resources of those areas. They may have been the bison hunters seen by La Salle in a meadow below New Orleans, and they might even have been among those attacking the retreating de Soto party on the lower river.

After the arrival of the French, the Washa were frequently on the move. John Sibley reported that they had originally lived in the Barataria area. If his report is true, this was only one of many sites they occupied. In 1718 they moved to the banks of the Mississippi River, and in 1739 their village was near the Côte des Allemands post. Their name was known into the nineteenth century. Then it was lost, perhaps in the fusion of tribes called Houma. Never a numerous people, the Washa were reckoned, in 1699, together with the Chawasha and Okelousa, to comprise no more than two hundred warriors.

The people known as the *Chawasha*, a Choctaw name for "raccoon place," resembled the Washa in many respects. The tribes were said by the French "to have the same character," so it seems strange that they maintained their separate identities well into the eighteenth century. Like the Washa's, the Chawasha's earliest known village was on Bayou Lafourche. It was located below the principal Washa town. These people frequented the lower course of the Mississippi River to its mouth.

The Chawasha contributed forty warriors to the French punitive expedition against the Chitimacha in 1707, but this display of loyalty to the white men gained them little. In 1713, while still on

Bayou Lafourche, they were visited by a party of Natchez, Yazoo, and Chickasaw on pretense of smoking the calumet. At an unguarded moment, the visitors attacked the Chawasha, killing the great chief and several of his family, and carrying away eleven others as slaves, including the chief's wife. The raid may have been instigated by an English trader to provide slaves for the seaboard colonists.

Following the establishment of New Orleans, the shaken Chawasha moved to the banks of the Mississippi River, locating in a village downstream from the French. Another blow fell in 1730, when Governor Perrier directed an attack of black slaves on the Chawasha settlement, said by one observer to number only thirty people. Despite reports that they were all slain, the Chawasha remained identifiable for another fifty years. Like the members of other small tribes, they frequently shifted their village location while constantly decreasing in number, and finally vanished.

The people of the Louisiana tribes in 1700 had reached a level of living that, by almost any reasonable standard, compared favorably with that of the European newcomers. The aborigines had raised their tribal skills to good ranges of performance. They were competent agriculturalists, their tools were serviceable, and their farm lore was based on long, successful experience. Housing was good, and weapons were excellent and used with great skill. Some items, such as pottery and basketry, had outstripped utilitarian needs and become media of artistic achievement and expression.

Some deficiencies must be acknowledged. There were no animals that could serve as beasts of burden, and the lack of a domesticated root crop forestalled diversification of the food supply. Clothing was rudimentary at best and offered only limited protection against insects and the elements.

The Indians' lot, however, must have been no worse than that of people in other lands. Indian doctors were capable, except as surgeons, and there was no self-abuse through excessive use of tobacco, alcohol, or other stimulants. There was no environmental pollution and no depletion of natural resources. Although the Great Sun of the Natchez held powers of life and death over his subjects, an ambitious person nevertheless could climb the political and social ladders through display of superior talent and application. Opportunities for personal advancement were even greater among the democratic Choctaw. The spirit world of the Indians proclaimed its priests and promises, and its taboos and terrors, but the individual was no more encumbered by fears and obligations than was his European contemporary.

The Indians engaged in active, joyous recreational pursuits, among them feasting and games. No modern sports event excites more interest than did chunkey and the ball game, or affords greater opportunities for gambling. Then, as now, aesthetic tastes and feelings were expressed in the dance, in music, through the decorative arts, and through the composition and telling of tales.

Europeans in 1700 enjoyed advantages in writing, technology, and the domestication of animals. In immunity from want and fear, and in individual freedom, the Louisiana Indians of that time were surely their equals.

REFERENCES

The definitive sources on the tribes of Louisiana in 1700 are probably those compiled by the ethnohistorian John Swanton.

Swanton, John R.
1911   Indian Tribes of the Lower Mississippi Valley and Adjacent Coast of the Gulf of Mexico. *Bureau of American Ethnology Bulletin* 43: 318–26, Washington, D.C.
1917   Unclassified Languages of the Southeast. *International Journal of American Linguistics* 1(1): 42–49.
1919   A Structural and Lexical Comparison of the Tunica, Chitimacha and Attakapa Languages. *Bureau of American Ethnology Bulletin* 68, Washington, D.C.
1922   Early History of the Creek Indians and Their Neighbors. *Bureau of American Ethnology Bulletin* 73, Washington, D.C.
1923   New Light on the Early History of Siouan Peoples. *Journal of the Washington Academy of Sciences* 13: 33–43.
1928   Aboriginal Culture of the Southeast. *42nd Annual Report of the Bureau of American Ethnology*, Washington, D.C.
1929   Myths and Tales of the Southeastern Indians. *Bureau of American Ethnology Bulletin* 88, Washington, D.C.
1931   The Caddo Social Organization and Its Possible Historical Significance. *Journal of the Washington Academy of Sciences* 21(9): 203–206.

1942   Source Material on the History and Ethnology of the Caddo Indians. *Bureau of American Ethnology Bulletin* 132, Washington, D.C.

1946   (rpr. 1979). The Indians of the Southeastern United States. *Bureau of American Ethnology Bulletin* 137, Washington, D.C.

Frederick Hodge edited short synopses on all the tribes north of Mexico, including those of Louisiana.

Hodge, Frederick Webb
1910   Handbook of American Indians North of Mexico. 2 vols. *Bureau of American Ethnology Bulletin* 30, Washington, D.C.

Herbert Eugene Bolton in 1914 corrected some of the entries, especially on the Adais, but these tribal sources are as nearly complete as can be found to date.

Other notable sources include an early work on the Chitimacha.

Gatschet, Albert S.
1883   The Shetimasha Indians of St. Mary's Parish, Southern Louisiana. *Transactions of the Anthropological Society of Washington* 2: 148–58.

Some of Gatschet's material, edited by Swanton, provides an excellent discussion of the Atakapa.

Gatschet, Albert S. (John R. Swanton, ed.)
1932   A Dictionary of the Attakapa Language, Accompanied by Text Material. *Bureau of American Ethnology Bulletin* 108, Washington, D.C.

David I. Bushnell, Jr., also left early materials on the former tribes of the state. It is likely that his most important contribution was publication of the detailed drawings left by A. De Batz. These furnish much detail essential to the ethnography on the original tribes.

Bushnell, David I., Jr., ed.
1927   Drawings of A. De Batz in Louisiana, 1713–1735. *Smithsonian Miscellaneous Collections* (35).

In western Louisiana, where the Caddoan speakers resided, the classic synthesis of eighteenth-century documents by Herbert Eugene Bolton left an indelible picture not only of the Caddoan people but of their French and Spanish neighbors as well. Bolton's most useful source pertinent to Louisiana is:

Bolton, Herbert Eugene
1914   *Athanase de Mézières and the Louisiana-Texas Frontier, 1768–1780.* Cleveland. 1970 rpr., New York.

A synthesis of early material on Spanish and French interaction with the Caddo, which includes much primary source material on the Caddo and Atakapa, is available.

John, Elizabeth A. H.
1975   *Storms Brewed in Other Men's Worlds.* 1, 3, College Station.

Other researchers have added an overview of Louisiana Caddo culture from prehistoric times into the 1930s.

Webb, Clarence, and H. F. Gregory
1985   *The Louisiana Caddo.* 2nd ed. Archaeological Study 2, Department of Culture, Recreation, and Tourism, Baton Rouge.

Many of the numerous primary sources have been translated from French and Spanish into English. Among the major, better-known ones is:

Le Page du Pratz, Antoine Simon
1758   *Histoire de la Louisiane.* Paris, 3 vols.

The more detailed French version is preferred to the reprint of the English edition now generally available.

Le Page du Pratz, Antoine Simon
1975   *History of Louisiana.* Baton Rouge.

Important documents in the original French were collected by Pierre Margry.

Margry, Pierre, ed.
1880–1883   *Découvertes et Etablissements des Français dans l'Ouest et dans le Sud de l'Amérique septentrionale (1614–1754).* Paris, 6 vols.

Margry first published the remarkable account of Penicaut, the French carpenter who traveled from Biloxi up the Red River and across the Southwest with Louis Juchereau de Saint Denis. This work has been published in English.

McWilliams, Richebourg Gaillard, ed.
1953   *Fleur de Lys and Calumet.* Baton Rouge.

Jean Bernard Bossu left other accounts of the tribes, and an excellent, carefully annotated version of his original work was recently published.

Dickinson, Samuel Dorris, ed. and trans.
1982   *New Travels in North America by Jean-Bernard Bossu, 1770–1771.* Natchitoches.

An excellent history of French Louisiana, based on essentially primary source materials, contains much detailed information on the Indian and French culture of the period 1698 to 1715.

60
THE HISTORIC INDIAN TRIBES OF LOUISIANA

Giraud, Marcel
1953   *Histoire de la Louisiane Française, tome 1: Le règne de Louis XIV
(1698–1715).* 1, 2, Paris.
A well-edited English version is available.
1974   *A History of French Louisiana, Volume 1: The Reign of Louis XIV,
1698–1715.* Baton Rouge.

This is probably the best, most concise historical source on the Natchez
and the smaller tribes along the lower Mississippi River.
A popular synthesis of Natchez history, published originally in 1899, remains of interest. The version edited by Angie Deboe is recommended.

Cushman, H. B. (Angie Deboe, ed.)
1962   *History of the Choctaw, Chickasaw and Natchez Indians.* New
York.

A rare discussion of the Taensa has been provided by a Louisiana historian.

Calhoun, Robert Dabney
1934   The Taensa Indians, I. *Louisiana Historical Quarterly* 17: 411–35.

Another outstanding, but increasingly difficult-to-find, source in English is
the early account of trade in Louisiana during the period of French rule,
1699–1763. It deals in large part with Indian regulations, trade activities,
resources, and trade routes. No other source provides comparable details.

Surrey, N. M. Miller
1914   The Commerce of Louisiana During the French Regime, 1699–
1763. *Studies in History, Economics, and Public Law* 71 (1), Columbia University, New York.

The diligent historical research of Andrew Albrecht has never been accorded the recognition it deserves. His manuscripts are on file at the Department of Geography and Anthropology, Louisiana State University,
Baton Rouge. His most important work was:

Albrecht, Andrew C.
1946   Indian-French Relations at Natchez. *American Anthropologist*
48(3): 321–54.

A brief synthesis by Fred B. Kniffen in 1975 was the prototype of the discussion in this chapter, which seeks to project a model of the tribes at first
contact. Kniffen's synthesis is still a concise, neat statement.

Kniffen, Fred B.
1975   Louisiana's Historic Indians. *Louisiana Archaeology* 2: 1–22.

Patricia Galloway has annotated Dunbar Rowland and A. G. Sander's classic source on the early eighteenth-century tribes. Using the same French

primary sources from the Mississippi State Archives in Jackson, she has added further material and new insights to Rowland and Sander's study. Her work probably contains the best available English data for the early contact period.

Rowland, Dunbar, and A. G. Sanders (Patricia Galloway, ed.)
1984 *Mississippi Provincial Archives: French Dominion*. Baton Rouge.

Although English sources dealing with early Louisiana are often neglected, especially those about the first half of the eighteenth century, some locational material has been particularly useful.

Bartram, William
1792 *Travels Through North and South Carolina, Georgia, East and West Florida*. London.

A less adequate edition is more readily available but should be consulted with care.

Van Doren, Mark, ed.
1928 *The Travels of William Bartram*. New York.

Another useful English account is that of Thomas Hutchins, a geographer who visited Louisiana in the 1750s. A carefully reproduced facsimile edition exists.

Hutchins, Thomas (Joseph G. Tregle, Jr., ed.)
1968 *A Historical Narrative and Topographic Description of Louisiana and West Florida*. Facsimile ed., Gainesville.

The English correspondence of John Thomas, British agent to the Louisiana tribes in the eighteenth century, is present in full at the Library of Congress and offers remarkable insights into the tribes.

Another necessary source is Verner W. Crane's study of the early English colonial frontier and its impact on the tribes of the Southeast. Crane, in 1928, wrote what remains the definitive history of English, French, and Spanish conflicts between 1670 and 1732. This work offers a new overview, that of the English, of the Louisiana Indians and their Indian neighbors. It has finally been reissued.

Crane, Verner W. (Preface by Peter H. Wood)
1981 *The Southern Frontier, 1670–1732*. New York and London.

IV

THE EUROPEANS

Beginning about 1700, the Louisiana Indian tribes perforce lived side by side with Europeans. There ensued the series of cultural contradictions, confusions, and errors that still haunt both Indians and non-Indians. The advent of the white men had both accidental and intentional consequences that were negative in effect. Although the introduction of highly lethal diseases from Europe may be considered unintentional, it probably was the cause of more suffering than the white man's deliberate resort to Indian slavery and wars of extermination.

At first the tribes welcomed the Europeans. Even after the villages had been ravaged by the heavy-handed de Soto expeditionary force, and Indians had been killed and landscapes wasted by the newcomers, the tribes remained surprisingly generous. In 1682, when La Salle claimed the country for France, he did so without their opposition.

Indian forbearance was ill rewarded. Measles, smallpox, common colds and influenza, cholera, and other infectious diseases took a disastrous toll on Indian populations. By the third decade of the eighteenth century, the Chitimacha had been decimated and driven from their villages near Bayou Lafourche. The bulk of the survivors were sold into slavery, while the rest hid in the Atchafalaya swamp. The Chawasha had been deliberately killed by black slaves acting on the orders of Governor Perrier. The Natchez, after attempting to save their sacred Grand Village from French expropriation, had mounted an all-out war. Predictably, they were driven from their territory and sold as slaves in the West Indies or forced into refuge among the Creek and Cherokee. The Chickasaw found themselves under attack by the French, ostensibly because they had Natchez refugees among them. In their turn, the smaller tribes were harassed by others moving away from or toward the Europeans. The Houma began absorbing smaller groups, like the Acolapissa. The Natchitoches, who had been resettled among the Acolapissa by the French, were attacked when the French decided to move them back to the banks of the Red River, and lost many of their people.

Frenchmen and *métis*, men of mixed blood, cohabited with Indian women in the villages, traded liquor—especially tafia, the cheap rum made from sugarcane juice—to the tribes, and corrupted the Indians. Traders, often with the help of tafia, abused the trade, and Indians became dependent on European goods. Everything from guns to glass beads was available in trade for deerskins and furs. By about 1720, the Spanish, seeking to block French expansion westward, had built a presidio in northwestern Louisiana. They practiced Indian slavery, moved the tribes closer to their mission at San Miguel de los Adaes, and otherwise disturbed the centuries-old culture of the Caddoan Adai and Natchitoches.

In Indian Louisiana, the eighteenth century was an amazing time. The Europeans had unleashed forces that even they failed to understand. The members of Indian communities, staggered by the impact of these forces and seeking to recover their equilibrium, finally abandoned their agricultural cropping and subsistence hunting, and became hide hunters, mercenaries, and other pawns of imperialism. These activities led to an increasing-dependency relationship. By about 1750, some symbiosis of whites and Indians seems to have begun to develop, but it was short lived. Within a few years the Spanish had acquired all the western bank of the Mississippi River, present-day Florida, and everything in the Isle of Orleans south of Bayou Manchac. The relationship between the French and Indians suddenly intensified as the French and Indian War sent the Cherokee, Creek, Chickasaw, and other allies of the English on the warpath. The small tribes near New Orleans, Fort Toulouse, and Mobile, threatened by the English auxiliaries, began shifting west, with great impact.

Christianity, in challenging the native religions, did its part to change Indian life. The Franciscans, Dominicans, Jesuits, and especially the seminary priests from Quebec all undertook missions to Louisiana. In some cases, the tribes welcomed them, but even in the friendliest villages, converts to Christianity were few. Among the Caddoan tribes, the Spanish Franciscans contended with magic and native religion, and acknowledged that they were able to baptize most members of their flocks only *in extremis*. The Spanish mission system, which "ordered" Indians by moving them into mission settlements where they were to be taught "civilized" customs, failed completely. The Caddoan speakers protested that they could not live as the Spanish wanted. In spite of these and other apparent defeats, however, the priests and lay brothers left their mark. Not even the sacred precincts of temple and cemetery were spared the influences of European culture.

The tribes attempted, as best they could, to adjust to the newcomers. The Choctaw created a special fictive lineage and named a full-time diplomatic chief, the *Fani mingo*, or Squirrel Chief, to deal with the French. As Patricia Galloway has pointed out, the French suggested that the Choctaw treat them as fathers, unaware that the Indians had more respect for their maternal uncles than for their biological fathers. This was but one of the weaknesses in the European approach to the tribes.

The Tunica, toward the middle of the eighteenth century, found themselves occupying a location between English and Spanish jurisdictions, the Spanish run by former French allies. Their chiefs responded by playing the administrative leaders of the European powers against each other. With much skill they extracted more goods and services from each until, just after the American Revolution, English and American pressures intensified and the tribe was forced westward.

All through that century, the chiefs asserted their sovereignty. They did not consider themselves a conquered or subservient people. The chiefs of the Tunica, Houma, and others are on record as having clearly notified the Europeans that they were free to do as tribal tradition dictated, no matter what the attitudes of the European powers might have been.

Sometimes the clashing interests of whites and Indians led to open warfare. The Chitimacha fought a long war with the French. The Natchez coup led to a short war of annihilation and enslavement that, in turn, helped bring on the Chickasaw War. The Tunica and Ofo attacked and defeated the British Twenty-Third Battalion as it marched to deliver Indian slaves to the Illinois post.

The Europeans lived in almost constant fear of tribal rebellion.

Northern Indian leaders, among them Pontiac and Tecumseh, jour-
neyed south to seek pantribal unification, but they ultimately
failed. Still, the Louisiana tribes were beginning to realize and acknowledge a commonality of interests. As disease spread and intertribal raiding intensified, small tribes increasingly wedded themselves to more powerful groups and formed pantribal alliances and
villages. The Tunica, Ofo, and Avoyel united in a set of villages on
the Mississippi River and the Avoyelles Prairie. The Acolapissa,
Houma, and, quite likely, the Washa fused into one group, seeking
refuge from the encroachment of the Europeans.

No institution was more feared and detested by the Louisiana Indians than slavery. The Tunica so abhorred slavery that one woman
of the tribe was said to have hanged herself to avoid it. Other tribes
were equally repulsed by the institution, but Europeans, who knew
of the Indians' aversion to it, nevertheless held numbers of Indian
slaves from a lengthy list of tribes. Most were Chitimacha, Natchez,
and Connechi (Lipan Apache), all of whom were traditional enemies
of the Europeans. Indians from the larger, more militant tribes, such
as the Caddo, Chickasaw, and Choctaw, were usually not enslaved.
Talapoosa slavers menaced the smaller tribes throughout the eighteenth century, and some Indians remained in bondage long after
the Spanish had abolished slavery in Louisiana near the end of
that century.

Slave and, later, former slave populations in Louisiana soon
were speaking the *Yuka anumpa,* or slave language, which Europeans found easier to learn than many of the native tongues. In
northwestern Louisiana, the Apache learned the local Spanish or
French dialect, or the Nahuatl used as a lingua franca by the Spanish to the west. This may have led to the wider use of the pantribal
jargon, Mobilian, toward the end of the century.

Contact with the Europeans cost the tribes dearly. The meeting
was a frontal attack that impacted every aspect of tribal life. Its
effects have persisted well into the twentieth century. One seeks the
positive effects of European contact with the Indians in the eighteenth century almost in vain. The tradition of gift giving the tribes
imposed upon their "fathers," both French and Spanish, gained the
Indians much in the way of European material culture. Guns, flints,
powder and shot, steel knives, iron axes, and even glass beads and

silver ornaments became more readily available throughout the century. Their wider adoption, however, led increasingly to the abandonment of Indian art and technology. This loss eventually led to the erosion of tribal independence and a quickly growing dependency relationship between the Indians and the European governments and traders.

The positions of white and Indian communities underwent a reversal. Small tribes attached themselves to European settlements that once had clung to Indian villages. Tribes that in earlier times had taught, fed, and protected the white people now were forced to rely upon their support. This ironic situation still prevails and colors Indian–non-Indian relations all over North America, including Louisiana.

European interference in the internal affairs of Indian communities was extreme in the 1700s. Medal chiefs, legal chiefs who dealt with political and military affairs, were favored in every way when friendly to the whites, and the displacement of those less willing to collaborate with the newcomers was deliberately undertaken by both French and Spanish, constituting a major threat to tribal sovereignty. Still, in spite of all adverse pressures, Indian culture held together in tribe after tribe. It is probable that they will never be subjected to more destructive forces.

REFERENCES

The impacts of European culture on Louisiana Indian life, though profound and lasting, have received only limited attention. Historians have considered them primarily from the European point of view. Some revisionist writings offer an alternative perception, that of the Indian. A major catalyst for such writings, all over North America, was the work of the Standing River Sioux, Vine Deloria, Jr.

Deloria, Vine, Jr.
1969 *Custer Died for Your Sins: An Indian Manifesto.* New York.
1971 *In Utmost Good Faith.* San Francisco.

The latter deals with the changing impacts of federal and state law that resulted from colonial conflicts and relations of the nation with Indian tribes. Two of Deloria's associates have taken the same tack in their treatment of North American Indian land rights.

Kickingbird, Kirke, and Karen Ducheneaux
1973 *One Hundred Million Acres*. New York.

Land loss to various European cultural groups and enterprises needs to be understood according to the perception of the Indian. Specific references to relations between Indians and whites in Louisiana are included in the above work; Choctaw, Chitimacha, Houma, and Tunica are all discussed.

It also seems reasonable to point to the normative histories of Louisiana. B. F. French has presented a wide range of historical approaches to Louisiana and the Indians.

French, B. F.
1869 *Historical Collections of Louisiana*. New York.

E. A. Taschereau's work on the Quebec seminarians gives an important view of colonial ecclesiastical life and the role of the Catholic church in lower Louisiana. Another good source is Jean Delanglez.

Taschereau, E. A.
1685 *Histoire du séminaire de Québec*, M.E. 322-F.S.A. 3, *Mémoire sur les missions du Canada*, Versailles.

Delanglez, Jean
1935 *The French Jesuits in Lower Louisiana, 1700–1763*. Catholic University of America Studies in American Church History, 21.

Roger Baudier's hard-to-find synthesis of Catholic church history in Louisiana remains the outstanding work in that area.

Baudier, Roger
1939 *The Catholic Church in Louisiana*. New Orleans.

Other early works cover the first European contacts.

Shea, John G.
1861 *Early Voyages Up and Down the Mississippi*. Albany.

Dickinson, Samuel Dorris, ed. and trans.
1982 *New Travels in North America by Jean-Bernard Bossu, 1770–1771*. Natchitoches.

Le Page du Pratz, Antoine Simon
1758 *Histoire de la Louisiane*. Paris, 3 vols.

Margry, Pierre, ed.
1880–1883 *Découvertes et Etablissements des Français dans l'Ouest et dans le Sud de l'Amérique septentrionale (1614–1754)*. Paris, 6 vols.

McWilliams, Richebourg Gaillard, ed.
1953 *Fleur de Lys and Calumet*. Baton Rouge.

Delanglez, Jean
1944 The Voyages of Tonti in North America, 1678–1704. *Mid-America*
      26: 255–300.
1945 Cadillac's Early Years in America. *Mid-America* 26: 3–39.

The best treatment of French Louisiana from 1698 to 1715 was prepared
by a French historian and is now available in both French and English.

Giraud, Marcel
1974 *A History of French Louisiana, Volume 1: The Reign of Louis XIV,
      1698–1715.* Baton Rouge.

Giraud's work gives details on primary source materials in France and includes a long-needed inventory of sources and libraries. Another excellent
account of early Louisiana history was written by a Creole historian. It
offers more traditional viewpoints, and the general synthesis is sound.

Martin, François-Xavier
1882 *The History of Louisiana from the Earliest Period.* New Orleans.

The best source on eighteenth-century French economics in Louisiana remains obscure.

Surrey, N. M. Miller
1914 The Commerce of Louisiana During the French Regime,
      1699–1763. *Studies in History, Economics, and Public Law*
      71(1), Columbia University, New York.

Two semipopular accounts of Natchitoches and its founding by the French
Canadian Louis Juchereau de Saint Denis give some details on French and
Indian relations on the frontier.

Portre-Bobinski, Germaine
1941 French Civilization and Culture in Natchitoches. *Natchitoches* 5:
      1–120.

Phares, Ross
1952 *Cavalier in the Wilderness: The Story of the Explorer and Trader,
      Louis Juchereau de Saint Denis.* Baton Rouge.

Herbert Bolton has left impressive chronicles of the Spanish borderlands
and the Texas missions, frontier conditions, and life in the 1700s.

Bolton, Herbert Eugene
1914 *Athanase de Meziérès and the Louisiana-Texas Frontier, 1768–1780.*
      Cleveland. 1970 rpr., New York.
1970 (rpr.) *Texas in the Middle Eighteenth Century: Studies in Spanish
      Colonial History and Administration.* Austin.

The latter work ushers in the advent of Spanish rule and its impact on
both the French and Indian populations of Louisiana. In general, Spanish

influences on the tribes were particularly strong because of the Spaniards' tribal relocation policies. Unfortunately, most discussions of the interactions between the Spanish, the French, and the Indians remain unpublished. A series of dissertations and theses based on primary materials from Louisiana, France, and Spain were written, under Bolton's oversight, at the University of California—Berkeley. Several of these are particularly informative.

King, Isabel Mae
1927   The Indian Policy of Carondelet in Louisiana. M.A. thesis, University of California.

Yerxa, Dorothy Ida
1926   The Administration of Carondelet in Louisiana. M.A. thesis, University of California.

Bjork, David Knuth
1923   The Establishment of Spanish Rule in the Province of Louisiana, 1762–1770. Ph.D. dissertation, University of California.

McGlashen, Marian Lee
1928   Manuel Gayoso de La Mar, Governor of Louisiana, 1779–1799. M.A. thesis, University of California.

Charles Gayarre's general work contains much on the Spanish.

Gayarre, Charles
1885   *The History of Louisiana.* New Orleans.

Several other basic studies are available that present general overviews of Spanish Louisiana.

Kinnaird, Lawrence, ed.
1946   Spain in the Mississippi Valley, 1765–1794: Translations of Materials from the Spanish Archives in the Bancroft Library. *Annual Report of the American Historical Association for the Year of 1945.* Washington, D.C., 3 vols.

Carter, Clarence E.
1915   *The Critical Period, 1763–1765.* State Historical Library, Springfield.

Caughey, John W.
1972   *Bernardo de Galvez in Louisiana.* Gretna, La.

Numerous primary Spanish sources remain in Louisiana, but most of them are uncataloged and not indexed. The *Papeles Procedentes de Cuba*, available at Loyola University, New Orleans, and at the University of Southwestern Louisiana, Lafayette, offer vast amounts of untranslated primary material.

When most of Louisiana went under Spanish rule, the Florida parishes and Mississippi became British territory. A literature has developed on these English dominions, but much research remains to be done.

Haynes, Robert V.
1976   *The Natchez District and the American Revolution*. Jackson.

Hutchins, Thomas (Joseph G. Tregle, Jr., ed.)
1968   *A Historical Narrative and Topographic Description of Louisiana and West Florida*. Facsimile ed., Gainesville.

Romans, Bernard
1962   (rpr.) *A Concise Natural History of East and West Florida*. Gainesville.

Rowland, Dunbar
1911   *Mississippi Provincial Archives, 1763–1766, English Dominion*. Mississippi State Archives, Jackson.

Starr, Joseph Barton
1971   Tories, Dons and Rebels: Three American Revolutions in British West Florida. Ph.D. dissertation, Florida State University.

Dalrymple, Margaret Fisher, ed.
1978   *The Merchant of Manchac: The Letterbooks of John Fitzpatrick, 1768–1790*. Baton Rouge.

Between 1690 and 1790 contacts with Europeans altered the population and material culture of the tribes. Once the east bank of the Mississippi became English country, the Spanish in Louisiana began to assert themselves. Intertribal conflict increased. Related British settlements began to replace the bulk of the isolated plantations. Tribes migrating westward passed through the region.

V

THE NATIVE LOUISIANA TRIBES
AFTER 1700

The Indian tribes living in what is now Louisiana at the time the Europeans went there to stay had already experienced European influences of varying kind and degree, and subtle changes in their way of life had begun. From about 1700 onward, they were to learn what it meant to live side by side with the white man himself.

In earlier times, the Indians had borrowed culture traits from the Europeans, but now that transfer became two-directional. The Indians' baskets, for example, and even their pottery, were useful to the newcomers. Palmetto houses of Indian design were widely built and occupied by white Louisianians until about 1950. European cuisine quickly incorporated Indian ingredients such as bear oil and filé (pounded sassafras leaves), and foods such as maize, beans, squash, pumpkins, wild rice (*Folle avoine*) that grew on the *prairies tremblantes* and in shallow lakes, and wild nuts and fruits. The white man was a greater borrower than the Indian and sometimes relied almost entirely upon the skill and knowledge of the Indians as hunters and farmers.

The Indians and Europeans of earlier colonial times were more interdependent and much closer in material ways than their successors. The gap between the two peoples widened after 1700 as the Europeans introduced Old World foods, crops, domestic animals, tools, modes of building construction, and other culture traits. Only in modern times have Indians come to live in ways somewhat similar to those of whites of comparable economic status.

Over the years, the importance of agriculture in Indian economic life declined as Indians found places in the white man's world. As they paid less attention to farming, they were dislodged from or gave up their good farmlands, and numbers of them eventually became mercenary warriors, traders, hunters, prostitutes, trappers, and even slaves, securing food by purchase or barter.

Although quick to adopt non-Indian material culture traits, the Indians found nonmaterial, or socioreligious, usages of the Europeans less attractive. Some Indians were converted to new religions, and were as tenacious of their new faith as they had been of the old. The Louisiana Choctaw, Koasati, and Tunica turned to Christianity only in the twentieth century. The Jena Choctaw and some Tunica-Biloxi maintained their old religion into the 1940s.

Intertribal relationships among the Indians, like their religions, were deep-seated and, for the most part, unchanging. Traditional enmities existed even between those sharing languages and other traits, as between Taensa and Natchez, and Houma and Bayougoula. Armed conflict among the lesser tribes often took forms viewed by some Europeans as contemptible and treacherous. The Tunica, for example, fled from their homes on the Yazoo River and took refuge in the village of the Houma. Soon afterward, the Tunica reportedly fell on their hosts, killing some and driving the others away. The Quinapisa-Mugulasha who had shared their settlement with the Bayougoula met much the same fate. The Taensa destroyed the Ouachita town on the Ouachita River, moved south to live with the Bayougoula, and then drove them out. The Chitimacha and Yakne Chitto, accepting a Taensa invitation to eat the Bayougoula corn, were imprisoned by the combative Taensa and sold into slavery. The Tangipahoa town on the Mississippi River was ravaged by a party of Houma and Okelousa who sent the survivors flying back to the Pearl River. When the Natchitoches who had been living for some years with the Acolapissa on Bayou Castine were about to return to their Red River village, the Acolapissa set upon them, killing some and enslaving others. A combined party of Chickasaw, Natchez, and Yazoo raided the Washa town on Bayou Lafourche and took slaves there. The frequency of incidents of this sort indicates clearly the lack of unity among the many small tribes. It shows, too, that the Indians did not share the concepts of conduct professed, if not practiced, by Europeans.

Louisiana Indians rarely engaged in prolonged war with Europeans, and it is remarkable that most battles between Indians and whites actually occurred outside of what is today Louisiana. In

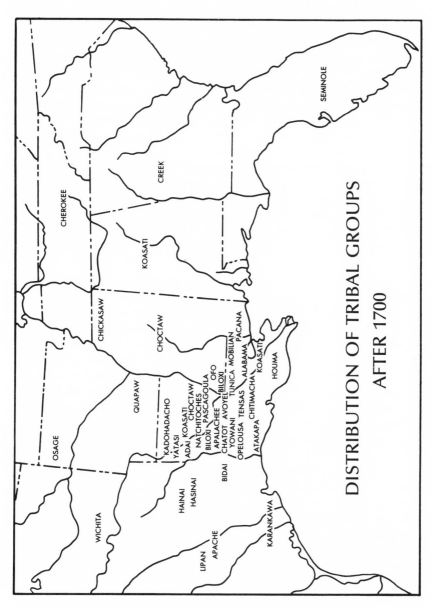

DISTRIBUTION OF TRIBAL GROUPS
AFTER 1700

SEMINOLE

CREEK

CHEROKEE

KOASATI

CHICKASAW

CHOCTAW

QUAPAW

OSAGE

KADOHADACHO
YATASI
ADAI KOASATI
CHOCTAW
NATCHITOCHES
BILOXI PASCAGOULA
OFO
APALACHEE BILOXI
CHATOT AVOYEL
TUNICA MOBILIAN
YOWANI PACANA
OPELOUSA TENSAS ALABAMA
CHITIMACHA KOASATI
ATAKAPA
HOUMA

HAINAI
HASINAI

BIDAI

WICHITA

LIPAN
APACHE

KARANKAWA

Courtesy of the Louisiana State University Cartographic Section

1799 it was reported that no Indian in present-day southwestern Louisiana had committed a hostile act against Europeans since Spain had assumed control in 1763. The nineteenth-century Caddo boasted that they had never shed the white man's blood.

Although the Indian people of Louisiana certainly possessed a martial spirit, they lacked the unity and numbers required to oppose the better-equipped Europeans and to match the power and confidence of the massed confederacies that the Creek and Choctaw east of the Mississippi commanded. From early times, the Indians generally maintained friendly relations with the French, the bonds being strongest between the French and the Tunica, the western Choctaw, and the small tribes clustered around Natchitoches and New Orleans.

The advent of the Europeans released forces that drove the ancient Louisiana tribes and others from their homes. The movements in Louisiana began early and continued even into the twentieth century, when some Choctaw took up free government land in Indian Territory, the region that was to become Oklahoma, in 1907. Soon after the beginning of French settlement in Louisiana, the smaller tribes of the lower Mississippi River country and the Florida parishes were subjected to raids, some British-inspired, by stronger tribes seeking slaves. Evidence of their decline as early as 1700 is found in the informal amalgamation of lesser tribes such as the remnants of the Quinapisa and the Mugulasha who shared the Bayougoula village. After the founding of New Orleans in 1718, many little groups sought protection by establishing themselves near the French settlement. The Florida parishes were virtually abandoned by their earlier Indian residents and were occupied by Choctaw from the north and east by the middle of the eighteenth century.

Even the most stalwart tribes were shaken by the heavy pressures of white encroachment. By 1700 only the Chitimacha retained their ancient holdings, and these strong people had given up productive lands along Bayou Teche. Nearly all their villages on Bayou Lafourche, Bayou Plaquemine, and the Mississippi had vanished. Although the Chitimacha had absorbed Taensa tribal remnants at the head of Grand Lake and some of the neighboring Houma as well, only fifty of them remained in 1909, confined to a small tract near Charenton. Individual Chitimacha joined the Atakapa, and others joined the mixed group known as Houma.

The Atakapa, in 1700, occupied villages scattered from Bayou Teche westward into what is today coastal Texas. Shielded by their isolation, they were long undisturbed by whites. Nothing that was known of Atakapa lands sufficed to draw whites across the difficult Atchafalaya Basin. The Atakapa sold some land between Bayou Teche and the Vermilion River to French settlers and furnished warriors for the Spanish governor Bernardo de Galvez' expedition against British forces along the Mississippi River during the American Revolution. They held their village on the Vermilion until the early nineteenth century.

In later times, the Atakapa worked as cowboys for white ranchers and sold moss and baskets. Still, their numbers declined. There were 175 Atakapa in Louisiana in 1805, but by the early twentieth century there remained only nine speakers of Atakapa, some living in Lake Charles. By 1934 only a few words were retained by a single person near there. A few other speakers from Louisiana survived a little longer at Vidor, Texas. Rosalie De Rosie, who lived near Vidor in 1935, was the last fluent Atakapa, according to the field notes of Caroline Dormon.

The Opelousa, presumably the linguistic kin of the Atakapa, were reported near Opelousas in 1725, evidently remaining there as long as their tribal identity was retained. In 1805 their tribal village was located some fifteen miles west of present-day Opelousas. There were twenty Opelousa in 1814; by the 1930s there were none. The remnant may have been absorbed by the Atakapa or Bayou Chicot Choctaw. According to Claude Medford, in the 1920s they played stickball with the Tunica. They camped at Ringrose Plantation and sold palmetto-stem and cane-splint baskets to the Fontenots, owners of Ringrose.

The scattered Louisiana Caddo in 1700 included the Doustioni, Natchitoches, and Ouachita near present-day Natchitoches. Upstream on the Red River, the Yatasi, also Caddoan, occupied several villages between what are today Coushatta and Logansport, forming a single band with a group called the Choya. Southwest, near present-day Robeline, were the Adai. Location changes, some forced, were so frequent and rapid that in many cases they are both uncertain and unimportant.

When the French built the fort at Natchitoches in 1714, the Yatasi were dispersed by the Chickasaw, some finding refuge to the north with the Kadohadacho and others reaching shelter at the Natchitoches post. Eventually, the Yatasi reoccupied their old territory, settling on the Sabine River near Logansport, and most of them were involved in the Caddo land cession to the United States after 1835.

As early as 1690, a number of the Ouachita had returned to Red River to settle near the Natchitoches Indians. Most of those remaining on the Ouachita River apparently were destroyed by the Taensa after they advanced to the southeast. Those who survived also joined their kinsmen, the Natchitoches, on the Red River. Another report, prior to 1734, relates that the Ouachita on the Ouachita River were scattered by the Chickasaw and that those who fled the disaster found places among the Kadohadacho. In either case, a map showing tribal distributions, presumably as of 1835, locates a Ouachita village on Red River south of Shreveport.

The upper Red, then, belonged to the Caddo. Their tribes seem to have held the stream from some distance south of Natchitoches upstream to the great bend in Arkansas and Texas, where the Kadohadacho lived. Since each tribe was sovereign, territorial claims were highly variable in extent when the Caddo sold their lands to the United States in 1835. One estimate places the total area at 500,000 acres. This is a conservative figure, since the Caddo ranged from the Sabine River in the west to the Ouachita River in the east. The Cahinnio Caddo lived in southern Arkansas, while the Ais, Hainai, Hasinai, Nacogdoches, and Nadarko Caddo made homes in eastern Texas.

The Caddo, in 1835, agreed to vacate their ancestral lands in all these areas within the year. Theirs was to be the only land cession treaty with the United States government to be signed in Louisiana. Nearly five years elapsed before they, in company with some other displaced tribes, took up new homes in what is now east Texas, with a few moving as far as Mexico. Ultimately, the Texans expelled virtually all Indians from the state, and in 1859 the Caddo moved to present-day Oklahoma. Today, their descendants, about one thousand strong, are concentrated about the towns of Binger, Fort Cobb, Gracemont, and Lokeba, near Anadarko, Oklahoma.

The Taensa on Lake St. Joseph in 1700 comprised the largest

Natchezan tribe in present-day Louisiana at that time, though diseases probably imported by de Soto had greatly reduced their numbers. Fearful of the Yazoo and the Chakchiuma, they abandoned their villages in 1706 and were admitted by the Bayougoula to that tribe's villages and lands. This generous gesture was a costly one. Soon after their new homes were established, the Taensa killed numbers of their hosts and drove out the others. They remained at the Bayougoula site until about 1715, when a number of them moved to Bayou Manchac, possibly because of the good bison hunting reported there but more likely in order to acquire control of the trade route. At the same time, other Taensa seem to have occupied a village on the right bank of the Mississippi River about thirty miles above New Orleans.

The ferocity of the Taensa seems to have been matched by their mobility. After 1730, they moved to sites in present-day Alabama north of Mobile Bay, giving their name to the Tensas River. After the English acquired control of that area, the Taensa moved to Red River and established themselves near the Apalachee, another Mobile Bay tribe, in the vicinity of modern Boyce. The French regime had granted the Taensa land on the Mississippi River at the head of Bayou Lafourche, but, apparently, they did not occupy it. In 1803 both Taensa and Apalachee sold their lands, and some of the former moved southward to Bayou Boeuf. Still another move came in 1812 when the Taensa shifted to Bayou Tensas, one of the many streams flowing into the northern end of Grand Lake. From this locality the Taensa were gradually assimilated by others, principally the Chitimacha. The Tensas language persisted among the Chitimacha at least until the latter part of the nineteenth century. Taensa tribal identity still existed in the 1930s.

The Avoyel, also speakers of a language related to the Natchez, apparently were a more stable people and seem never to have left the area they traditionally held. Their lands extended from the Red River rapids at present-day Alexandria to that stream's junction with the Mississippi. There were known villages near modern Marksville and at the rapids. The Avoyel became middlemen trading in horses and cattle stolen from the Spanish to the west, and in 1764 they joined the Choctaw, Ofo, and Tunica in attacking a British party ascending the Mississippi River. The decline in Avoyel numbers was rapid, so that by 1805 only a handful remained. A few people of Avoyel descent are still counted on the rolls of the Tunica-Biloxi tribe near Marksville.

La Salle came upon the Houma village near modern Angola in 1682. After their eviction by the Tunica in 1706, the surviving Houma settled on Bayou St. Jean near present-day New Orleans. From there they moved to Little Houmas, on the Mississippi some five miles south of what is today Donaldsonville, and to Great Houmas, which lay a mile or so inland on the left bank. Although characterized as indolent drunkards, the Houma were well treated by the French since they served as an outpost on the river. Although their lands were sold in 1776, English maps show them hunting on the Amite River as late as 1836.

Soon after the appearance of the French in Louisiana, the Muskogean-speaking Acolapissa, Bayougoula, Quinapisa, Mugulasha, and Tangipahoa lost their separate identities. Having deserted or been driven from their traditional homes, they gathered in settlements on the Mississippi River or along major distributary streams within New Orleans' sphere of influence. The thread of continuity with their tribal past seems to have been the separate chieftainships that were maintained after tribal lines were no longer distinct. In the minds of whites, these Indians fused into a single tribe called "Colapissas," and they eventually incorporated under the name *Houma*.

Some Washa and Chawasha, the Yakne Chitto, and refugees from Gulf coast tribes such as the Biloxi had also joined the Houma. The removal of the Houma and these tribes was a slow process. Some joined the Atakapa, but most found their way to the coastal bayous from Lafourche westward to Terrebonne. The common fate of small tribes was a steady decline in numbers and, finally, extinction, though some were absorbed by alien races. The pantribal Houma agglomerate managed to escape this end by making its way to an environment that forced a virtual abandonment of agriculture in favor of a hunting, fishing, and trapping economy—a transition also made by other tribes. Near the end of the eighteenth century, pressed by white settlers, all but three Houma families, or bands, moved back to the north and into oblivion. Although only about sixty Indians remained on the marshland bayous in 1803, their number today is estimated to be three thousand, in one of the rare instances of a population explosion among American Indians. The influence of Roman Catholicism and their French neighbors' insistence on large families seem the most likely causes. Today, most Houma possess French relatives, and among them French culture is strong. The use of the marshes as a refuge by so many people may be another contributing factor. The Houma occupied this territory almost in isolation until the development of petroleum resources there by outside interests in the 1940s. This tribal amalgam may be the only native Louisiana tribal group to join the western movement from west Florida in the Spanish period. As such, the Houma may be considered one of the immigrant tribes.

The identity, location, and fate of the Okelousa remain in doubt. Their place of residence at about 1700 has been located somewhere east of Pointe Coupee, yet they are also described as a wandering coastal people and are said to have once lived on Bayou Lafourche. They have disappeared, presumably having been absorbed by a larger tribe, probably the Houma.

The experience of the Washa and Chawasha was unique, since they were not Muskogean speakers and did not mix readily with more homogeneous tribes. They early deserted their villages on Bayou Lafourche and moved to the banks of the Mississippi River. The Washa occupied at least one village on the river below New Orleans in 1730, and nine years later the Washa and Chawasha were on the left bank of the Mississippi above New Orleans, near the Côte des Allemands post. In 1758 they were lodged in a village three or four leagues from New Orleans, and by the close of the eighteenth century the two tribes scarcely existed. The French at New Orleans ordered their black slaves to attack the Chawasha, almost annihilating them. Some probably escaped to join the Houma and Chitimacha, and thus were lost to the record. This aggressive employment of black slaves was but one of many techniques used by the French to alienate Indians and blacks from each other. Europeans generally were careful to keep these two groups at odds with each other.

So far, no account has been prepared that fully reveals the movements and relocations experienced by the original Indian tribes of Louisiana. The pressures that bore upon them so terribly not only drove them from their ancient lands but set them against each other as well. Many lesser tribes did not survive these experiences. That some of the original Louisiana tribes still exist reveals both the strength of the people and the durability of the institutions they had brought into being and relied upon for two centuries or more of wandering. The tribal stories may never be fully known, but efforts to unravel the tangled odysseys of the Indians and learn the sources of their strength are well justified.

REFERENCES

Virtually every historical source on eighteenth-century Louisiana contains material relevant to the European influences on the Indians after 1700. The Natchez, Chitimacha, and Chickasaw wars, actual wars between sovereign powers, are well described in the European tradition of history. Other European impacts, among them disease, famine, and enslavement, are far less systematically chronicled. The loss of land is even less favored in the literature. All these topics merit serious research, and entire books await those intrepid spirits who haunt archives. The sources listed here help one gain perspective and some general insight into the situation of the Indians after 1700. The best synthesis of the period is that of Marcel Giraud.

Giraud, Marcel
1974   *A History of French Louisiana, Volume 1: The Reign of Louis XIV, 1698–1715.* Baton Rouge.

Pierre François Xavier Charlevoix' work is excellent.

Charlevoix, Pierre François Xavier
1761   *A Journal of a Voyage to North America.* London, 2 vols.

In 1753 the memoirs of Dumont de Montigny, an excellent early source, became available.

De Montigny, Dumont
1753   *Mémoires historiques sur la Louisiane.* Paris, 2 vols.

The writings of Le Baron Marc de Villiers present a number of superb, well-edited primary sources.

De Villiers, Le Baron Marc
1922   Documents concernant l'histoire des Indiens de la région orientale de la Louisiane. *Journal de la Société Americanistes de Paris,* n.s., 14: 127–40.
1923   Notes sur les Chactas d'après les journaux de voyage de Regis du Roullet. *Journal de la Société Americanistes de Paris,* n.s., 15: 223–50.

1925 Extrait d'un journal de voyage en Louisiane de Père Paul du Ru (1700). *Journal de la Société Americanistes de Paris*, n.s., 17: 119–53.

The classic work on the Natchez, along with Dumont de Montigny's, remains that of the settler Le Page du Pratz.

Le Page du Pratz, Antoine Simon
1758 *Histoire de la Louisiane*. Paris, 3 vols.

Serious researchers will find this French version to be more useful than the readily available English translations, since it contains more detailed information.

The Jesuit chronicles cannot be disregarded in any attempt to obtain an overview of the entire lower Mississippi.

Thwaites, Reuben, ed.
1896–1901 *Jesuit Relations and Allied Documents: Travels and Explorations of Jesuit Missionaries in New France, 1610–1791.* Cleveland.

David Knuth Bjork was first to give Indian politics serious interpretation.

Bjork, David Knuth
1926 Documents Regarding Indian Affairs in the Lower Mississippi Valley, 1771–1772. *Mississippi Valley Historical Review* 13: 340–98.

Recently, a new, skillfully edited version of Dunbar Rowland and A. G. Sander's early work on the French archives in Mississippi has become available and should take precedence over earlier editions.

Rowland, Dunbar, and A. G. Sanders (Patricia Galloway, ed.)
1984 *Mississippi Provincial Archives: French Dominion*. Baton Rouge.

The "Survey of Federal Archives in Louisiana" remains unpublished, but the typescripts of it are a wonderful source on the tribes and are available at the Louisiana State University library in Baton Rouge.

Complete sets of important Spanish archival materials, the *Papeles Procedentes de Cuba*, are available at Loyola University in New Orleans and at the University of Southwestern Louisiana. Various parts of the French archives and the French Archive of the Marine are available in Louisiana and at the Library of Congress.

Although much is contained in B. F. French's *Historical Collections of Louisiana* and in Pierre Margry's *Découvertes et Etablissements des Français dans l'Ouest et dans le Sud de l'Amérique septentrionale*, it is probable that the best sources are the works of Herbert Eugene Bolton.

Bolton, Herbert Eugene
1914   *Athanase de Mézières and the Louisiana-Texas Frontier, 1768–1780.* Cleveland. 1970 rpr. New York.
1970   (rpr.) *Texas in the Middle Eighteenth Century: Studies in Spanish Colonial History and Administration.* Austin.

The Bexar Archives in San Antonio contain much information on upper Louisiana in the eighteenth century, as do the Blake Papers in the Nacogdoches County, Texas, archives. The latter are also available at Stephen F. Austin University at Nacogdoches, Texas, and at the Texas State Archives in San Antonio. Additional archival materials can be found at the Library of Congress, Washington, D.C., the Louisiana State Archives and the State Land Office in Baton Rouge, and the Eugene P. Watson Library and the Natchitoches Parish courthouse in Natchitoches, Louisiana.

VI

THE IMMIGRANT TRIBES
FROM 1764 TO 1900

At the end of the French and Indian War, the Indian tribes of what was to become the southeastern United States found themselves at odds with one another. Some large tribes, such as the Choctaw, had parted over whether to support England or France. Earlier in the eighteenth century, many smaller tribes had moved to the vicinity of French settlements near Mobile and New Orleans under the pressure of slave raids carried out by the Chickasaw, Talapoosa, and other more powerful groups. Slaves taken from them were sold to English colonists in the Carolinas, Georgia, and Virginia, so these small tribes, already alienated, fought fiercely for France and their own survival. With the end of the war, they began seeking lands to the west, distant from the Chickasaw and the Creek who had supported England.

The old alignments with the French no longer seemed secure. A number of minor tribes loyal to their French Catholic neighbors had been driven into a cul-de-sac at Mobile. Among them were the Apalachee, Taensa, Chatot, Mobile, and Pacana. Two other small groups, the Biloxi and Pascagoula, lived between Mobile and New Orleans, near present-day Bay St. Louis. The Okla Hannali, Yowani, or Six Towns Choctaw, a pro-French faction of the Choctaw, lived north of Lake Pontchartrain in what is today southern Mississippi. Between them and the lake some small Muskogean-speaking tribes, including the Acolapissa, Mugulasha, Quinapisa, and Tangipahoa, lived for a time, eventually shifting west and joining the Houma. The Tunica and Ofo, lesser tribes who had fled under Chickasaw pressure in the early eighteenth century, moved to the banks of the Mississippi River north of Baton Rouge, a strategic action that left the powerful Natchez tribe between themselves and their northern enemies.

The Mobile Bay tribes had crossed the Mississippi into Spanish territory by 1764, the Chatot settling near the rapids at Alexandria, the Biloxi near the Ofo and Tunica on the banks of the Mississippi River, and the Pascagoula not far from the others. The Taensa, having fled present-day Louisiana at the end of the French war with the Natchez in 1730 and having become closely affiliated with the Apalachee at Mobile Bay, settled with the Apalachee on the west side of Red River.

The Mobile proper, and the Alabama, Koasati, and Pacana, were shifted to the English east bank of the Mississippi north and south of the settlement at Manchac—a location some ten miles south of Baton Rouge and above the Houma living nearer New Orleans. The Spanish recorded that they had settled the tribes there in one village.

All of the foregoing tribes except the Apalachee, Chatot, and Taensa tried living along the new international boundary, the Mississippi River, where they sought to play the English against the Spanish. The effort failed; English land policy became more demanding, and tribe after tribe was driven across the river. Even the Houma peoples, an amalgam of Houma, Acolapissa, and other Muskogean groups living within the Isle of Orleans and not actually in British territory, felt compelled to move west.

The Indian allies of England were a pressing, constant threat to nonaligned Indians. When the English demanded that the tribes obey their governmental regulations, the chiefs resisted, affirming their autonomy. The Spanish governors de Galvez, Unzaga, and Carondelet were quick to court the tribal leaders, expecting that the tribes would help prevent Anglo-American ventures into vacant lands near the Ouachita and Red rivers, and into other parts of what is today central north Louisiana. The Spanish especially wooed the Choctaw, hoping to split the tribe further so that it would not become a powerful outpost of English influence on the frontier. The governors invited Choctaw into present-day north and central Louisiana, an act the Spanish soon regretted but could never correct. Hundreds of Choctaw moved into what is now upper Louisiana, first to hunt and then to settle or trade. There these powerful people were soon confronted by the Caddoan tribes who, for the first time since contact with whites, threatened open war. At the insistence of the Caddoan groups, the Choctaw were contained on Bayou Rapides and the Ouachita River.

The small migrant tribes isolated on Red River and in the woodlands of present-day northern Louisiana also complained of the Choctaw and Chickasaw incursions. Unable, or perhaps afraid, to control the Choctaw, the Spanish made plans to relocate the small tribes on Bayou Boeuf in a single intertribal area where they might be helped. Some Tunica, Ofo, and Biloxi, and a few Alabama and Yowani Choctaw, banded together near the Avoyelles Prairie, where Governor de Galvez established a garrison to protect them. The Choctaw remained on the banks of the Ouachita River and near Natchitoches, where they had attacked the peaceful Caddoanspeaking Adai. Choctaw communities were to remain the dominant Indian groups of the general region until the nineteenth and twentieth centuries.

The Apalachee, Biloxi, Pascagoula, and Taensa, steadfastly resisting Spanish efforts to move them near Bayou Boeuf or Catahoula Lake, remained on Red River until the Americans went there, between 1805 and 1830. By 1801 or 1802, some Anglophobes had fled to Spanish Texas, as determined to avoid the Americans as they had been to escape the British.

The Spanish authorities in present-day Louisiana sought to manipulate the tribes but soon found themselves in constant conflict with the chiefs or, in the case of the Choctaw, with roving bands far from the influence of their traditional leaders. The Houma, whether moving or not, were a source of consternation to the Spanish, who finally abandoned all thought of forming a fixed Indian policy for this mixed group.

The Taensa, Pascagoula, and Houma experienced conflicts among themselves, often over Pascagoula threats to steal or rape Houma women, and what is today southern Louisiana seethed with tribal threats and counterthreats. The Tunica and others growled of war. The Talapoosa raided for slaves, then apparently fled back to Pensacola, and as late as the nineteenth century, Talapoosa words were still heard in local Indian languages. European officials protested against the taking of open-range cattle and hogs. Dugout canoes were frequently stolen. Slaves, especially Indian ones, were set free to find refuge in forests and swamps.

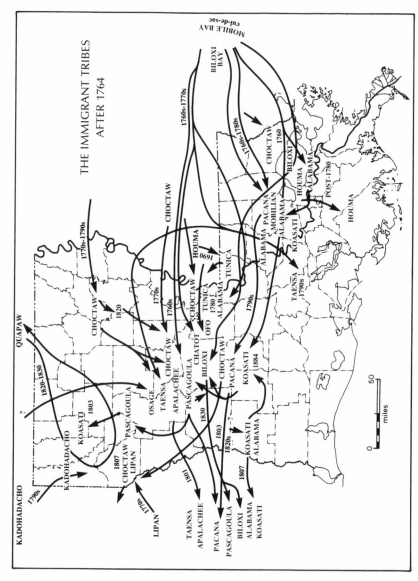

Courtesy of the Louisiana State University Cartographic Section

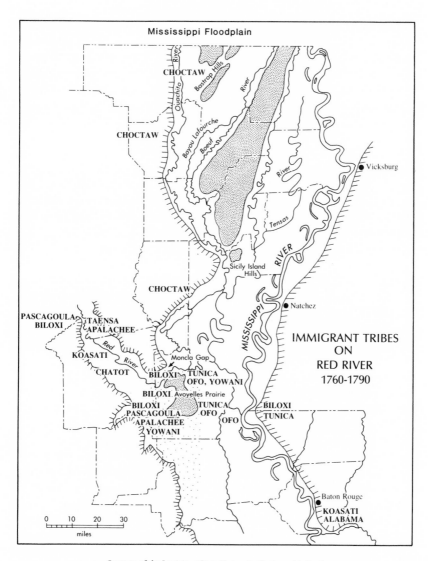

Mississippi Floodplain

CHOCTAW

CHOCTAW

● Vicksburg

CHOCTAW

Sicily Island Hills

● Natchez

PASCAGOULA
BILOXI
TAENSA
APALACHEE

KOASATI

CHATOT

Moncla Gap

BILOXI TUNICA
OFO, YOWANI

BILOXI Avoyelles Prairie

BILOXI
PASCAGOULA
APALACHEE
YOWANI

TUNICA
OFO

OFO

BILOXI
TUNICA

IMMIGRANT TRIBES
ON
RED RIVER
1760-1790

● Baton Rouge
KOASATI
ALABAMA

0 10 20 30
miles

Courtesy of the Louisiana State University Cartographic Section

The Tunica chief Lattanache told both the Spanish and the English that his was a sovereign tribe with the right to move, hunt, and do as it pleased. When the Spanish attempted to curb the practice of infanticide among the Houma, Chief Calabe warned them that Houma ways were not the ways of Europeans. The Caddo chiefs, in turn, threatened to kill all the Choctaw if the Spanish did not make them respect the rights of the various Caddoan-speaking groups.

Somehow, in the midst of all these disputes, the tribes found their settlements on the Spanish west bank of the Mississippi River to be more to their liking than life under the English. Concern over shoddy merchandise, the frustrations of a more frugal trade policy, and the menace of powerful, ancient enemies had been more than the tribal leaders could bear.

By 1802 Louisiana had been handed back to France, and rumors abounded that it would soon be American territory. Some of the Apalachee, Biloxi, Pascagoula, and Taensa had petitioned for, and had been granted, lands between the Sabine and Trinity rivers in Spanish Texas. Few, if any, of them moved there before 1805, some moved between 1805 and 1820, and most after 1820. The Opelousa, who were native to Louisiana, also sought to move and were given land, but whether they actually moved or not remains unclear. Apparently, some did, while others intermarried with free people of color in the settlements south of Natchitoches.

Spanish laws had treated the Indians generously, a circumstance they found fortunate as empires changed. *Las Recópilaciones de los Indios* had given Indians the right to settle the king's lands and had guaranteed them a square league around their villages for tribal use. The Spanish also had recognized tribal policy and the rights of chiefs to rule over their tribes. The French insisted that all such existing treaties, policies, and attitudes should, in general, be recognized by the Americans. The recognition of preexisting treaty rights was written into the negotiations for the Louisiana Purchase treaty, and Congress ratified the treaty with those articles included.

The tribes from east of the Mississippi thus were at least within their rights to be in what is now Louisiana. They were well established, and to this day the immigrant tribes remain Louisiana Indians. After the fog of international politics had lifted, two major groups of Louisiana tribes remained, those from east of the Mississippi River and the few resident tribes encountered by the whites when they first went west of the river. Of the latter, only the Atakapa, Caddo, Chitimacha, and Opelousa survived in any numbers.

The Americans quickly began the work of enumerating and describing tribes, establishing John Sibley of Massachusetts, a close friend of President Jefferson, as the first Indian agent at Natchitoches. Another observer, Simon Favre, was sent to the Choctaw east of the Mississippi. It was hoped that these men could evaluate conditions, recommend policy, and help control Indian behavior on the frontier. A new policy toward the tribes was in the making, different even from that of the British. Certain practices, however, had been institutionalized during the century of Latin rule, among them the annual congresses at New Orleans, Pensacola, Mobile, and Manchac; the use of gifts; and the appointment of medal chiefs. These policies continued into the 1820s.

The French and Spanish had licensed private traders to deal with the Indians. They had punished *gaboteurs*, or illicit traders, especially those dealing in guns and tafia. In spite of well-intentioned measures, numbers of these people, often *métis*, remained in the Indian communities. Those operating south of Natchitoches, near present-day Colfax and Boyce, were a notable problem.

To combat the unlawful practices and to consolidate their control of the tribes, the Americans soon put into operation a factory system based on trading posts administered by the government. This venture soon miscarried, and the Americans, like their predecessors, began issuing licenses to individuals. These private traders extended credit to Indians and began acquiring tracts of land in settlement of Indian debts. Losing hundreds of acres to the traders, the tribes often sought space in less settled and marginal areas, such as the Big Thicket of present-day east Texas, where the Alabama, Biloxi, Pascagoula, Pacana, and others found temporary refuge.

The tribes, by the end of the nineteenth century, had begun to find comparatively permanent homes. The Koasati, with a few Pascagoula and some of the Yowani Choctaw, moved north from villages near Colfax and modern Boyce and settled in the Caddo country north of Natchitoches, near the present Arkansas boundary. The Biloxi, Chatot, and other Pascagoula and Yowani began moving to lands along Bayou Rapides and Bayou Boeuf. The Ala-

bama and some Choctaw had established settlements near Chicot
or Cocodrie, in present-day south central Louisiana, and the Pacana
settled near present-day Elizabeth, on the headwaters of the Calcasieu River. The Apalachee and Taensa clung fiercely to their
lands at the mouth of Cane River, adjacent to the Pascagoula and
Biloxi, most of whom were already moving north to the Caddo
area or south to the banks of Bayou Boeuf.

The Houma, having absorbed the Acolapissa and perhaps the
Bayougoula and other minor tribes from the lower Mississippi,
moved across the river onto former Chitimacha lands near Bayou
Lafourche. Later, they seem to have split into two groups—one on
Lafourche, the other on bayous Dularge and Dulac—and even-
tually to have subdivided still further.

The Chitimacha moved deeper into the interior of Louisiana,
around Grand Lake and Bayou Plaquemine, even abandoning their
prosperous villages on Bayou Teche. They thus became the occupants of the Atchafalaya Basin proper, leaving the marshes to the
Houma. The banks of Bayou Lafourche (La Rivière des Chitima-
chas) shortly had only one Chitimacha village, and later only the
Houma and a few Choctaw interlopers remained. By approximately 1820, a few Taensa had been allowed to settle in the northern portion of the Chitimacha area, soon becoming closely associated with the Chitimacha themselves.

Crossing the Mississippi River westward to villages near Pointe
Coupee (New Roads), the Tunica and Ofo, after 1780, moved to a
village on Bayou Rouge Prairie and then to other locations along
the Coulee des Grues on the Avoyelles Prairie. The coulee thus became a boundary between them and the Biloxi. In all these areas,
the Tunica, Biloxi, Ofo, and a few Choctaw and Alabama lived in
close interaction. On the prairie they absorbed the older residents,
the Avoyel. The Atakapa and Opelousa held their old territories
along Lake Charles and Bayou Queue de Tortue, respectively. The
void left in the Florida parishes by the Acolapissa, Tangipahoa, and
others was soon filled with Choctaw from the southern part of what
is now Mississippi.

Some tribes, like the Mugulasha, were noted on Red River near
Rapides in the Spanish period of the 1780s, but are not mentioned
again after that and may have been absorbed by others. Many

other tribes mentioned in the interval from 1770 to 1789, among them the Bayougoula, Quinapisa, Tangipahoa, Chawasha, and Washa, dropped from sight. Although it is convenient to conjecture that they fell victim to disease, intertribal strife, Indian slavery, and absorption by other Indian or European communities, it is not prudent to do so. Other small tribes including the Avoyel and Ofo have retained their identities well into the 1980s, even in the midst of dominant Tunica and Biloxi. Some apparently lost tribal memories still may exist in the minds of older Louisiana Indians now living isolated lives in other tribes or non-Indian communities.

The Choctaw displaced some native tribes, such as the Adai west of Natchitoches, and moved into the empty lands along the Ouachita River, on Catahoula Prairie, along Bayou Nezpique, and south of Bayou Boeuf near Indian Creek at Woodworth and Glenmora. By 1807, they were known to be scattered across present-day north Louisiana from the Ouachita River to the Sabine.

The Lipan Apache, or Connechi, who had been introduced by the French and Spanish as slaves, became well established near Natchitoches among the Hispanic and Choctaw families at Spanish Lake, along the Sabine River, and among the free people of color near Cane River. The Kadohadacho had shifted to the west end of Caddo Lake, bringing with them the Upper Natchitoches and probably the Nasoni. By 1790 these northern Caddo were the dominant tribes, and they were one of the original Louisiana Caddoan-speaking groups. South of the Kadohadacho, the Yatasi were settled near present Logansport, and the Adai remnant clung tenaciously to a village on Rocks Bayou in what is now Natchitoches Parish. The Natchitoches proper resettled on the west bank of Red River across from Campti, north of the white settlement at Natchitoches.

Most of the Louisiana groups held their ground, but some tribes and portions of tribes moved westward to what is now Texas. The Caddoan speakers occupied most of northwestern Louisiana until they ceded the land to the United States in 1835 and attempted to move into Texas. After 1840 they moved en masse to the banks of the Blue River in the Kiamichi Mountains and into Texas and Mexico, leaving the area that had been their home for well over a thousand years. No settlements remain today. The Caddo had tried to accommodate the Quapaw in their Louisiana villages along Bayou

Treache on the Red River, but the latter had moved back to Arkansas, also leaving no communities behind. Floods and disease had driven them north.

Shaken by their experiences, the tribes remaining in Louisiana were ravaged by sickness. Smallpox took its toll, as did measles and respiratory ailments. Most of the groups, however, were still large enough to be considered viable communities as late as the 1890s.

A large new Indian population had begun to develop in southwestern Louisiana in the mid-nineteenth century. Apparently, immigrants from the Carolinas and Georgia sought areas where there were Indian or mixed Indian and black-and-white families. Today, these early Carolinians and Georgians would nearly all be from families bearing surnames associated with the nontribal groups in those states with the strongest Indian identities, such as the Lumbee, Haliwa, and Westoes. These were the people who came to be identified as "Red Bones." That pejorative evidently came from the West Indies, where *Red Ibo* was a label for any mixture of races. According to Joey Dillard, a recognized authority on black English, the West Indian term, pronounced "Reddy Bone," may well have been pronounced "Red Bone" in Louisiana and the Carolinas.

A scattering of Louisiana Indians, including Biloxi, Choctaw, and Pacana, sometimes called "Seminole" in error, was clearly associated with the Carolina and Georgia immigrants, reinforcing Indian genetics. Whites and blacks, in some instances, are said to have become part of this mixture of races and cultures. Indian identity remained strong in the Red Bone communities, and cultural behavior reflected Indian roots. Artifacts were placed on graves, fires were often lighted for the dead, matrilocal residence was common, and a forest economy with such material traits as basketry and blowguns persisted. Anthropologists and historians have neglected these communities even more than the Louisiana Indian communities with traditional tribal identities. Perhaps some of the many lost tribes of the colonial period can be accounted for in the oral traditions of these groups.

Among the Houma, referred to by local whites as the Sabine, from the Spanish word for cypress tree, or "red-and-white–spotted," French admixture was common. Like the Red Bones, they were suspected of absorbing blacks and once were rigidly segregated by the local white power-structure.

Both Indians and Red Bones long have been marginal to the plantation areas of Louisiana. The Indian settlements were in the swamps, pine woods, and marshes, and their closest non-Indian neighbors most often were white yeoman farmers, Acadians, and Scotch-Irish, who owned no slaves. If Indians lived near a plantation, the owner became their patron, offering them credit and protection from exploitation, at least by others. In exchange, they were required to hunt, entertain guests with ball games and dances, make baskets, tan hides, and perform other services that might, on occasion, include the recovery of runaway slaves.

Some Indians and the *métis* moved as far from whites as they could so as to avoid conflicts. Finally, however, the Red Bone groups lashed out in the 1880s and 1890s, and armed clashes between them and their neighbors were common. The most famous engagement occurred near Westport, where old-timers still recall the "Westport Fight." Even today, the Red Bones often prefer social isolation to interaction with outsiders.

Near the old Rapides and Avoyelles posts in central Louisiana, near Natchitoches in northwestern Louisiana, and in the lower Ouachita River area of Franklin and Richland parishes, populations of *métis* comparable to the mixed Indian-Scotch-Irish-French families of western Canada developed prior to the Civil War. Numbers of these families retained their Indian identities, and some even their tribal affiliations. As among the Red Bones in southwestern Louisiana, many communities became isolated, both geographically and socially. Many excluded blacks, owned no slaves, and wished no association with either group, and in so doing invited discrimination from powerful land-holding whites.

Indians had been tolerant of blacks in the early colonial period, but as early as the 1720s, Governor Bienville gave the black slaves a two-week furlough for killing large numbers of Chawasha near his post at New Orleans. Blacks near Lake Pontchartrain in 1850 were amazed when their masters punished them for abusing the Chaouche (Chawasha), or *sauvages*, as they were called.

The use of Indians to track runaway slaves and the instigation of racially linked conflict between blacks and Indians forestalled union of the two races throughout the colonial and early American periods. Slave rebellions took place, but Indians were never involved. After 1870, conflict between Indians and whites intensified, and interaction of blacks and Indians became increasingly strained. In most tribes, some degree of white mixture was tolerated, but those who mixed with blacks generally were excluded from the Indian tribal communities. The Indians scorned both blacks and the institution of slavery. Like blacks, Indians had been held as chattels until 1794, when Governor Carondelet freed all Louisiana Indian slaves except the Natchez, who were required to purchase their freedom as punishment for their war against the French. At that time, many of the eastern remnants of immigrant tribes, long harassed by Chickasaw and Talapoosa slavers, probably crossed into Spanish territory and joined the majority of their people. Slavery remained a powerful institution, however. Indians were revolted to learn that, even though they were free, they had no rights outside tribal areas. Isolation became a way of life; only seclusion insured security and the preservation of Indian traditions.

The Spanish declaration had freed the large numbers of Connechi (Lipan Apache) slaves held in northwestern Louisiana, who eventually intermarried with Spanish and mestizo families from the old capital of Texas, San Miguel de Los Adaes. John Sibley noted that they had also mixed with the French at nearby Natchitoches. The Bidai, Caddo, and Towakoni intermarried with Choctaw in the vicinity of the Sabine River, Spanish mixed with Nahuatl became their lingua franca, and a new pantribal Indian community came into being.

The Choctaw became the most widespread Indian population in Louisiana. Small groups of them were to be found in the Florida parishes, on lower Bayou Lafourche, from the Chicot settlement to the banks of the upper Calcasieu River in central Louisiana, in the Bayou Boeuf drainage, and scattered across the hills of northern Louisiana from the Ouachita River to the Sabine. They had villages on Bayou Nezpique and the German Coast along the Mississippi. Gradually, they filled the Florida parishes.

When John Sibley became Indian agent in 1807, he summoned the north Louisiana Choctaw to Natchitoches and directed them to select a chief. Displeased with their choice, Sibley eventually managed to replace him with a friendlier chief. Still, these kin-based band leaders had no control over their people or, at least, were not equal in authority to the traditional Choctaw chiefs east of the Mississippi.

During the half-century from 1780 to 1830, the Choctaw prospered and grew, even at the expense of other tribes like the Adai and Biloxi, until *Choctaw* became nearly synonymous with *Indian* in much of Louisiana. Their influence had been almost universal among the southeastern tribes for years by the time the Treaty of Choctaw Removal, in effect from 1828 to 1835, had been signed with the federal government.

The Choctaw had become so entrenched that those offered a chance to leave refused to go, and some of the eminent Louisiana chiefs, like Tuscahoma, who had signed the early Hopewell Treaty in Mississippi, declined to move their constituents to the newly designated Indian Territory in present-day Oklahoma. Dominique Rouquette, a friend of the Louisiana Choctaw, has left a lively description of the situation in 1850.

> They [the Choctaw] obstinately refuse to abandon the different parishes of Louisiana, where they are grouped in small family tribes, and live in rough huts in the vicinity of plantations, and hunt for the planters, who trade for the game they kill all they need: powder, lead, corn, woolen covers, etc. Their huts are generally [surrounded] by a fence. In this enclosure their families plant corn, pumpkins and potatoes, and raise chickens. The women use a kind of cane, which they knew how to dye different colors, to make baskets: *lottes* [baskets carried on the back], *vans* [winnowing baskets] and sieves, from which they derived a good profit. They also sold medicinal plants which they gathered from the forests: Virginia snake-root, sage, plantain, tarragon, wild fruit, *pommetes* [medlars] blue bottle, persimmons, and scuppernongs; also roots of *sequiena*, sarsaparilla and sassafras. They also do a little trading in ground turtles, which they find on the prairies. They dispose of these wares at the plantations, in country towns, and at New Orleans.

This description fits closely the people from the Florida parishes, Indian Creek, and Natchitoches, and even matches the oral traditions of aged contemporary Louisiana Choctaw. It could characterize other immigrants as well. There is some evidence that it describes most of the Louisiana Indians in the first half of the nineteenth century.

Rosa Jackson Pierite, a Choctaw-Biloxi from Indian Creek, has described how, in the 1920s, her mother and sisters put their baskets in a sheet, bundled it over a pole, and walked twelve miles from their homes near Indian Creek to Alexandria: "We spread them on street corners and sold them to passers-by." Rouquette has described a similar scene from nineteenth-century New Orleans.

> Nothing is more interesting to the tourists than to see them [the Choctaw] wandering along the streets of *La Reine du Sud* (the Queen of the South), *La Cité du Croissant* (Crescent City) with their *pauvres pacotilles* (small, cheap wares), in their picturesque costumes, half savages and half civilized, followed by a number of children of all ages, half naked, and carrying on their backs a papoose snugly wrapped in the blanket, with which they envelope themselves, like a squirrel in moss. Sometimes they squat in a circle, at the big market place, on the banks of the old river, patiently waiting with downcast eyes, for the *chalandes* [customers] who buy what they offer, more for the sake of charity than from necessity.

It is probable that Rouquette was in error about the charitable purchase of Indian wares. A Natchitoches resident, Major Cosgrove, noted many of the same circumstances that Rouquette did, but he added some notable details. His description suggests how important the Indian trade was. Silver ornaments, trade beads, and pipe tomahawks were still standard items in Natchitoches stores from 1820 to 1830. Cosgrove observed that clerks in Natchitoches had learned the "Indian language" and that stores actually closed after the "Indian Removal," probably referring to the Caddo. He further noted a "town" of "rich Indians" near present-day Fort Jesup, probably Choctaw or Apache. From New Orleans to Natchitoches, the Indians were a ready source of trade. Furs, basketry, wild honey, beeswax, and herbs were negotiable items until the 1930s.

The nineteenth-century Indian population, dominated by Biloxi, Chitimacha, Choctaw, and Tunica, was relatively large and important. At some point after the Americans assumed control, these people apparently had been relegated to such ecological niches as swamps, marshes, and infertile pine woods, and the whites, with their black slaves and intensive agriculture, took over the rich alluvial bottomlands.

The Indians eventually became dependent on the market economy. Lead, powder, axes, firearms, and European-style clothing began to replace traditional technology and costumes. Some Indians, like the Choctaw, rejected the white man's wages, identifying them with institutionalized slavery. Hunting and the preparation and administration of herbal medicines were considered honorable activities, and were not to be confused with the labors of *Yuka*, slaves. Freedom became a symbol of resistance, and Indians fought silently to maintain it.

The "Indian language," as some called the Mobilian Jargon, spread widely in Louisiana. As Cosgrove noted, it was used by clerks, plantation owners, and others. Indians sometimes referred to it as *Yama*, a hyperpolite word for "yes," much the same as "yes sir, boss." Mobilian Jargon was used with non-Indians because one had to be careful in one's relations with them, and its use minimized the risk of being misunderstood. Decimated by disease and war, and fearful of slavery and of losing land and legal rights, the tribes slowly began to deal with the dominant whites in ways increasingly circumspect and guarded.

Artists such as basket makers were considered to be peddling, a low-status occupation in the eyes of non-Indians. Hunters were considered unreliable, almost objects of ridicule. Social contacts with non-Indians were largely restricted to practically momentary encounters, so the ball games, dances, and the sacred rituals of religion became matters of curiosity and sources of entertainment for white planters' families and friends. Offered removal to Indian Territory and an alternative way of life, most Indian people rejected the chance, not once but twice.

Apparently, the Indians took little interest in the Civil War. Most chose not to fight. They did not wish to defend slavery, which was repugnant to them, and they had no rights to defend, states' or other. A mixed Biloxi-Choctaw-French man near Catahoula Lake stated it succinctly in a sentence so familiar to poor southern whites: "It's a rich man's war and a poor man's fight."

A second Indian removal occurred when the Choctaw nation and others in Indian Territory became fearful that they would lose their lands to whites. The Bureau of Indian Affairs in 1900 began to seek Indians, especially full bloods, eligible for enrollment and tribal allotments in Oklahoma. Both government and private agents went to Louisiana and Mississippi to recruit emigrants, and soon the Louisiana Indians were boarding steamboats. Even here misfortune pursued them. One boat carrying Choctaw from the Florida parishes sank in Lake Pontchartrain. Another group, the Jena

Band of Choctaw, walked up the railroad tracks to the vicinity of Idabel and Broken Bow in Indian Territory. There they were told that no allotments were left in the territory, and they had to walk back to Louisiana. Once returned, they had no recourse except to live as sharecroppers on the lands of white and mixed-blood neighbors to whom they had lost their traditional village areas.

Still others, including Biloxi, Koasati, and Tunica, actually moved to areas in Indian Territory. The majority eventually returned to their homes in Louisiana, but some remained in Oklahoma, most near the former Choctaw nation. Once word of the twentieth-century removal had spread, even some of the conservative Mississippi Choctaw fled to Louisiana communities after seeing Choctaw in Scott and Newton counties loaded into boxcars.

By this time the Louisiana Indians had become "invisible people." Most simply kept to themselves and were either ignored or harassed by whites. Albert Gatschet, a linguist with the Bureau of American Ethnology, reported how difficult it was to locate the Indian people. Their beloved French priest, Father Rouquette, whom they called Chahta Ima, was warning Indians in the Florida parishes and as far away as Barataria that a "government agent" was in Louisiana. He was referring to Gatschet. Even after this misunderstanding was straightened out, Gatschet had great difficulty. Although he eventually found most of the groups, nearly all of them remained fearful of his intentions. Until 1925, when American Indians were accorded citizenship, minimum contact was the preferred approach in relations between Indians and whites. One by one, the tribes have asserted themselves. Only since 1960 have some of the communities had recourse to outside aid and study.

The troubled immigrant tribes, gathered from far and wide, found homes in Louisiana. They are still there, living in company with descendants of people from many other parts of the world, who have given Louisiana its amazing mosaic of cultures.

REFERENCES

Most ethnographic material compiled by John R. Swanton deals with the tribes after 1700. His synthesis of southeastern Indian life contains much on the Louisiana immigrant tribes.

Swanton, John R.
1911   Indian Tribes of the Lower Mississippi Valley and Adjacent Coast of the Gulf of Mexico. *Bureau of American Ethnology Bulletin* 43: 318–26, Washington, D.C.
1931   Source Material for the Social and Ceremonial Life of the Choctaw Indians. *Bureau of American Ethnology Bulletin* 103, Washington, D.C.
1942   Source Material on the History and Ethnology of the Caddo Indians. *Bureau of American Ethnology Bulletin* 132, Washington, D.C.
1946   The Indians of the Southeastern United States. *Bureau of American Ethnology Bulletin* 137, Washington, D.C.

Most specific references to the cultures of the tribes after 1700 are scattered. Often they are thoroughly mixed with materials synthesized from earlier accounts. Two works deal with this period, but neither is in print.

Gregory, Hiram F.
1981   On the Road to Recognition: Louisiana Indians Since 1900. MS at Jean Lafitte National Park, New Orleans.

Drechsel, Emanuel, and T. Haunani Makuakane
1982   An Ethnohistory of the 19th Century Louisiana Indians. MS at Jean Lafitte National Park, New Orleans.

Before his 1981 work, Gregory, with James McCorkle and Kim Curry, had written another manuscript summarizing the history of the post-eighteenth-century Indians of Natchitoches Parish. It remains unpublished.

Gregory, Hiram F., James McCorkle, and Hugh K. Curry
1979   The Historic Indians of Natchitoches Parish and Significance. *Natchitoches Parish Cultural and Historical Resources*, Natchitoches Parish Planning Commission, Natchitoches.

Regional accounts written earlier give details on the Choctaw in southeastern Louisiana.

Bremer, Cora
1907   *The Chata Indians of Lower Pearl River.* New Orleans.

Bushnell, David I., Jr.
1909   The Choctaw of Bayou Lacombe, St. Tammany Parish, Louisiana. *Bureau of American Ethnology Bulletin* 48, Washington, D.C.

Dagmar LeBreton described the lives of these Choctaw and their missionary, L'Abbe Rouquette, or Chahta Ima.

LeBreton, Dagmar Renshaw
1947   *Chahta-Ima, The Life of Adrien-Emmanuel Rouquette.* Baton Rouge.

A relative of Chahta Ima, Dominique Rouquette, was editor of a Fort Smith newspaper in 1850. Both at Fort Smith and at Bonfouca on Lake Pontchartrain he was in contact with the Choctaw. His wonderful source, if a bit romantic, is filled with data.

Rouquette, Dominique (Olivia Blanchard, trans.)
n.d.   *The Choctaw.* Survey of Federal Archives in Louisiana, Louisiana State University, Baton Rouge.

Tixier, an early French traveler, pictured early nineteenth-century Choctaw on the lower Mississippi.

McDermott, Francis, ed.
1940   *Tixier's Travels on the Osage Prairies.* Norman, Okla.

An American traveler wrote of the Alabama and Choctaw living in southwestern Louisiana.

Olmstead, Frederick L.
1857   *A Journey Through Texas, or, A Saddle Trip on the Southwestern Frontier.* New York.

Gregory's brief overview of the central Louisiana Choctaw deals specifically with those in LaSalle Parish.

Gregory, Hiram F.
1977   Jena Band of Louisiana Choctaw. *American Indian Journal* 3: 2–16.

Some accounts of the Chitimacha were written in the nineteenth and early twentieth centuries.

Bushnell, David I.
1917   The Chitimacha of Bayou Lafourche, Louisiana. *Journal of the Washington Academy of Sciences* 7: 301–307.
1922   Some New Ethnological Data from Louisiana. *Journal of the Washington Academy of Sciences* 12: 303–307.

Gatschet, Albert
1983   The Shetimasha Indians of St. Mary's Parish, Southern Louisiana. *Transactions of the Anthropological Society of Washington* 2: 148–58.

A recent account on the Chitimacha is available.

Hoover, Herbert
1975   *The Chitimacha People.* Indian Tribal Series, Phoenix.

M. R. Harrington visited several tribes in the early 1900s and left an admirable collection of photographs, which can be found at the Heye Foundation, Museum of the American Indian, New York. He also left some letters that pertain to the Chitimacha, located at the National Anthropological Archives, Smithsonian Institution, Washington, D.C.

In a newspaper article printed about 1900, an old-timer reminisced about the Indians around Natchitoches and discussed an "Indian Removal."

Cosgrove, J. H.
n.d.   Indians at Natchitoches. *Texas Magazine* 3(1): 72–75.

A rare, detailed source exists on the Atakapa.

Dyer, J. O.
1917   *The Lake Charles Attakapas (Cannibals), Period of 1817 to 1820.* Galveston.

The small groups that lived in Grant Parish, including the Apalachee and Choctaw, have been described.

Ethridge, Adele
1940   The Indians of Grant Parish. *Louisiana Historical Quarterly* 23: 1107–31.

An early history of the Caddo in Louisiana remains a classic.

Glover, William B.
1935   A History of the Caddo Indians. *Louisiana Historical Quarterly* 18: 872–946.

Additional material on the Caddo recently was synthesized.

Webb, Clarence H., and Hiram F. Gregory
1978   The Caddo Indians of Louisiana. *Anthropological Study* 2, Louisiana Antiquities Commission, Department of Culture, Recreation, and Tourism, Baton Rouge.

The Caddo land cession has been described in detail.

McGinty, G. W.
1963   Valuating the Caddo Land Cession of 1835. *Louisiana Studies* 2: 59–73.

Dan Jacobson's work on the Koasati must be considered a primary source.

Jacobson, Dan
1960   The Origin of the Koasati Community of Louisiana. *Ethnohistory* 7: 97–120.

This has been updated by a historian.

Johnson, Bobby H.
1976   *The Coushatta People.* Indian Tribal Series, Phoenix.

Swanton's work remains the oldest, most basic material on the Koasati.

Swanton, John R.
1922   Early History of the Creek Indians and Their Neighbors. *Bureau of American Ethnology Bulletin* 73, Washington, D.C.

The Tunica were visited by both Swanton and Frank Speck; however, Speck left few references to them. Swanton remains the best early source. Recent fieldwork, from 1970 to 1980, has yielded some information on tribal ethnography.

Brain, Jeffrey P.
1977   On the Tunica Trail. *Anthropological Study* 1, Louisiana Archaeological Survey, Department of Culture, Recreation, and Tourism, Baton Rouge.

Downs, Ernest C.
1979   The Struggle of the Louisiana Tunica Indians for Recognition. In *Southeastern Indians Since the Removal Era* (Walter L. Williams, ed.), Athens, Ga., 72–89.

Still another approach to the Tunica is available.

Juneau, Donald
1980   The Judicial Extinguishment of the Tunica Indian Tribe. *Southern University Law Review* 7: 43–99.

The Biloxi and Pascagoula, both closely associated with the Tunica, have been described in great detail along with the Caddo, Koasati, and Alabama in an edited version of an early account of eastern Texas.

Berlandier, Jean Louis (John Ewers, ed.)
1969   *The Indians of Texas in 1830*. Washington, D.C.

James Dorsey wrote of the Biloxi in Louisiana at a slightly later period.

Dorsey, James Owen
1894   The Biloxi Indians of Louisiana. *Proceedings of the American Association for the Advancement of Science* 42: 267–87.

This was followed shortly by another fine work.

Mooney, James
1894   The Siouan Tribes of the East. *Bureau of American Ethnology Bulletin* 22, Washington, D.C.

The most extensive literature on the migrant tribes stems from recent attempts by the Tunica and others to secure federal recognition.

1944   Survey of Federal Archives: Louisiana Indian Miscellany. MS in Louisiana Collection, Louisiana State University, Baton Rouge.

Baudier, Roger
1939   *The Catholic Church in Louisiana*. New Orleans.

Brain, Jeffrey
1970   Tunica Treasure. *Peabody Museum Bulletin* No. 70, Harvard University, Cambridge.

1973   The Tunica. In *Handbook of North American Indians*, Washington, D.C.

1973   Trudeau: An 18th Century Tunica Village. *Lower Mississippi Survey Bulletin* 3, Peabody Museum of Archaeology and Ethnology, Harvard University, Cambridge.

1976   From the Words of the Living: The Indian Speaks. In *Clues to America's Past*, National Geographic Society, Washington, D.C.

1977   On the Tunica Trail. *Anthropological Study* 1, Louisiana Archaeological Survey, Department of Culture, Recreation, and Tourism, Baton Rouge.

Darby, William
1818   *Emmigrant's Guide to the Western and Southwestern States and Territories*. New York.

Downs, Ernest C.
1976   Tunicas and Biloxis: Indian Policy Versus Indian Survival. MS at Institute for the Development of Indian Law, Washington, D.C.

1978   Draft Petition for Recognition: The Tunica-Biloxi Indian Tribe. Native American Rights Fund, Washington, D.C.

Ford, James A.
1936   An Analysis of Indian Village Site Collections from Louisiana and Mississippi. *Anthropological Study* 2, Louisiana Geological Survey, Department of Conservation, New Orleans.

Gregory, Hiram F., and Clarence H. Webb
1965   Trade Beads from Six Sites in Natchitoches Parish, Louisiana. *Florida Anthropologist* 18(3): 15–44.

Haas, Mary R.
1942   The Solar Deity of the Tunica. *Papers of the Michigan Academy of Arts and Letters* 28: 531–35.

1950   Tunica Texts. *University of California Publications in Linguistics* 6(2): 1–174.

1953   Tunica Dictionary. *University of California Publications in Linguistics* 6(2): 175–332.

Hsu, Dick Ping
1969   The Arthur Patterson Site, A Mid-Nineteenth Century Site, San Jacinto County, Texas. *Archaeological Survey Report* 3, Austin.

Hutchins, Thomas (Joseph G. Tregle, Jr., ed.)
1968   *A Historical Narrative and Topographical Description of Louisiana and West Florida.* Facsimile ed., Gainesville.

Saucier, Corinne
1943   *The History of Avoyelles Parish, Louisiana.* Baton Rouge.

Dorsey, James Owen, and John B. Swanton
1912   A Dictionary of the Biloxi and Ofo Languages. *Bureau of American Ethnology Bulletin* 47, Washington, D.C.

Webb, Clarence H.
1962   Early 19th-Century Trade Material from the Colfax Ferry Site, Natchitoches Parish, Louisiana. *Southeastern Archaeological Conference Newsletter* 8: 3–33, Cambridge.

Williams, Stephen
1962   Historic Archaeology in the Lower Mississippi Valley. *Papers Presented at the 1st and 2nd Conferences on Historic Site Archaeology,* Cambridge, 55–63.

The Houma have been discussed a number of times as the great debate about their identity has kept them in the anthropological spotlight.

Speck, Frank G.
1943   A Social Reconaissance of the Creole Houma Indian Trappers of the Louisiana Bayous. *America Indigena* 3: 135–46.
1976   (rpr.) The Houma Indians in 1940. *American Indian Journal* 2: 4–15.

In the 1950s, the Houma were discovered by sociologists. After two decades of anthropological work, the question of their identity became even more confused.

Parenton, Vernon J., and Roland J. Pellegrini
1950   The "Sabine": A Study of Racial Hybrids in a Louisiana Coastal Parish. *Social Forces* 29: 148–54.

Roy, Edison
1959   The Indians of Dulac: A Descriptive Study of a Racial Hybrid Community in Terrebonne Parish, Louisiana. M.A. thesis, Louisiana State University.

The civil rights movement extended down the bayous in the 1960s, and the events there were chronicled by an anthropologist.

Fischer, Ann
1968   History and Current Status of the Houma Indians. In *The American Indian Today* (Nancy Lurie, ed.), Baltimore, 212–35.

By 1980 Mennonite volunteers had moved among the Houma. Their goal was federal recognition of the tribe. Their work is summarized by Greg Bowman and Jan Roper-Curry.

Bowman, Greg, and Janel Roper-Curry
1982　*The Forgotten Tribe: The Houma People of Louisiana.* Mennonite Central Committee, Akron, Pa.

VII

TRIBAL SETTLEMENTS

The Indian people of Louisiana, though varied in life-styles, generally preferred to live in villages. Scattered across Louisiana, these settlements ranged in size from a few families to hundreds of people and differed considerably in the length of their existence. Some of the large tribes occupied several villages, while smaller ones might have occupied only a few dwellings. All the settlements, however, offered some measure of safety, social life, and economic advantage.

Archaeological evidence indicates that the prehistoric tribes moved freely and that this mobility was heightened by the appearance of the Europeans. Much inquiry into the lives of the Indians centers on the search for their village sites. Sometimes the history of a tribe can be deciphered through a study of the succession of places occupied, abandoned, and, sometimes, reoccupied. When such evidence corroborates tribal legends, the latter accounts become more credible.

Some settlement sites were occupied early and were held continuously for long periods of time by successive tribes. Such places offered natural advantages like freedom from flooding, easily worked good soils, and abundant fresh water, game, fish, or salt. Land already cleared was attractive, as were places considered aesthetically pleasing. Sometimes, the appeal of a particular spot stemmed in part from such cultural factors as its suitability for defense or trade, and its spiritual qualities and associations.

The Houma site at present-day Angola; the settlement at Jonesville, at the junction of the Ouachita, Black, and Little rivers; and Bayougoula on the banks of the Mississippi were long occupied. The same is true of Marksville and many other places, though not all of them were continuously held before historic times. The ex-

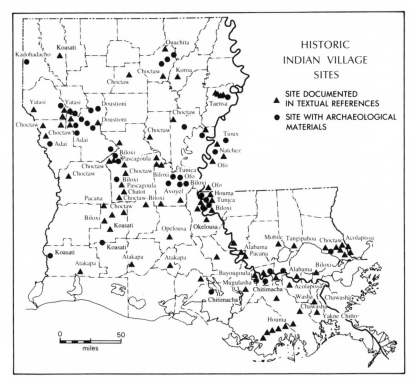

Courtesy of the Louisiana State University Cartographic Section

tended occupation of places defies the suggestion that locations were abandoned because of the exhaustion of game, firewood supplies, or soils. The Koasati were driven from one site by ants and from another by rattlesnakes—a phenomenon culturally perplexing to modern Americans.

Indian settlements lacked the regularity of plan found in most modern towns. In the absence of draft animals and wheeled vehicles, there was no requirement for wide, regularly oriented streets. The structure of the aboriginal settlement reflected the fundamental place of agriculture in the economy and the absence of a mechanical technology.

Each major settlement contained a central nucleus within which were located the temple and the house of the chief, on opposite sides of a plaza. Such a plaza may have served as the ceremonial ground and as the playing field for the common chunkey game. A few houses of those who served the chief and performed religious duties and some minor structures completed the central assemblage. About it there may have stood a protective stockade. In later times, replacing the chunk yards, there appeared a large, level clearing in which were located the goalposts used in the Indian stick-ball game.

Little clusters of dwellings and individual houses of the general populace were dispersed widely and linked to the nucleus by irregular footpaths, as the spokes in a wheel are joined to the hub. The seeming disorientation of the houses actually afforded the farmers proximity to the family-controlled cultivated fields which were not usually contiguous. The cornfields were at some distance, extending a mile or more from the center of the settlement. At most dwellings there was a small "kitchen" garden. All this cultivated ground lay within the acknowledged boundaries of the settlement, giving the community a sense of unity somewhat at variance with its dispersed arrangement.

Among the individual tribes, there was both conformity to and variation from this general pattern of Indian settlement. The so-called "towns" of the Natchez actually were neighborhoods scattered through the forest and interspersed with fields over an area of some thirty-five square miles. The house of the great chief stood on a mound ten feet high and faced a temple on another mound. Between these elevations lay a plaza, around which several other dwellings were arranged. A single Taensa village is said to have extended approximately three miles along Lake St. Joseph. Centrally situated were the house of the chief, the temple, and eight other houses, the whole surrounded by a stockade. The principal Houma village, standing on a hill, was somewhat different. Houses there were set about the edge of a large, level, centrally located plaza, and cornfields stood in valleys and on other hills.

An eighteenth-century Bayougoula town was built on the level floodplain near the Mississippi River. A stockade enclosed the temple, the house of the chief, and a number of large dwellings. Outside, close by, lay the cultivated fields. Early references to Caddo settlements yield only incomplete pictures of scattered dwellings, not grouped in towns, in loose associaton with temple centers and well-tended fields. Early Spanish maps of Red River indicate a mound center near present-day Texarkana.

The Atakapa, who were primarily gatherers of shellfish, fishers, and hunters, and to whom agriculture was of minor importance, did not conform to the usual pattern. Their economy required seasonal shifts of residence, and at times in their annual cycle they lived in quite compact settlements.

In the time of de Soto there existed heavily populated, compact, fortified towns in which flat-topped mounds were being raised, at least among the Tunica and Natchez. By 1700 the large towns with their truncated mounds had generally begun to disapppear, and the dispersed settlements became an even more common pattern. Fortified temple centers with plazas remained in some places, surrounded by smaller clusters of houses or even by individual dwellings set in cleared fields scattered through the forest. The large towns, such as the eastern Choctaw towns on the Creek border and the Ouachita settlement on the Caddo eastern flank, often stood as buffers against unfriendly tribes.

Some evidence suggests that these changes in settlement form were in progress prior to de Soto's journey through the Southeast. There may well have been a pervasive atmosphere of restlessness, not ascribable to European contact, that contributed to deterioration of the settlements and territorial shifting, especially among the small tribes.

The Indians of Louisiana developed several types of buildings, each intended to serve a particular purpose. The most common structure was the simple family dwelling, and others were granaries, storage places for game and equipment, and mortuaries. There were also dance houses, sweathouses for purification, temples, and simple, flat-roofed, open arbors to shelter people guarding the planted fields.

Louisiana Indians developed no building that has come to be as well known as the tepee of northern and western tribes. In coastal Louisiana palmetto-thatched houses could be seen, which surely were descended from Indian construction techniques though they did not always reflect Indian form. Few have heard of the beehive-shaped grass houses once built by the more northerly of Louisiana's Red River Caddo, and the complicated wattle-and-daub dwellings and temples of most Louisiana tribes have disappeared without trace or memory. Knowledge of them comes only from the early accounts.

House plans and methods of construction varied, primarily over broad regions, but more minor differences were to be seen even from town to town. In northern Louisiana, from the lands of the Caddo eastward, two kinds of dwellings were erected, one tightly constructed as a winter house and another built as a more open, airy summer residence. Both temples and chiefs' houses were usually only larger, more elaborate varieties of the square winter houses, though among the Natchez and Taensa, temples were round and houses were square in ground plan, their shapes clearly differentiating the structures by function.

The main dwellings, or winter houses, of the Avoyel, Houma, Natchez, and Taensa were square and measured from fifteen to thirty feet on each side. In their construction, the four corners were first marked by four long hickory saplings set upright in the ground, and smaller poles were similarly set between them about fifteen inches apart. Then the standing poles of each side were bound to an inside horizontal pole placed at a height of about six feet, thus determining the height of the walls. Next, the four large corner poles were bent inward to a dome shape and securely bound. The smaller poles were treated similarly. Flexible canes were placed horizontally across the upright poles about eight inches apart and bound to them, forming gridlike walls. This grid, or frame, was plastered with approximately four inches of clay mixed with Spanish moss. This was the precursor of the *bousillage* technique adopted by the French. Then both inside and outside were lined with cane mats securely tied in place. The entire exterior was thatched with bundles of grass four to five feet in length and, finally, was covered with cane mats laced tightly in place with vines.

This simple but substantial structure had neither windows nor smoke holes; it had only a small entrance facing the east, which was the sacred, or "good luck," direction. During winter, a fire in the middle of the house kept it very warm. Although the smoke must have been disagreeable to the occupants, they probably preferred it to the mosquitoes. Raised platforms around the walls served as benches and beds. They were made of pole frames resting on forked sticks and covered with mats. According to the Choctaw and Caddo, such shelves and beds should be built "higher than a flea can hop." Stored under them was a hodgepodge of articles ranging from harvested crops to baskets, pots, spare moccasins, and clothing.

Downriver from the Houma, the other Muskogean speakers built houses that were round rather than square. Unlike the houses of the Choctaw proper, these houses had walls that stood straight up and down, so that the cone-shaped roofs rested upon and extended

Fig. 3
PALMETTO HOUSE, BAYOU LACOMBE, *ca.* 1881
National Anthropological Archives, Smithsonian Institution

Fig. 4
PALMETTO HOUSE, TERREBONNE PARISH, 1950s
Photograph by William Knipmeyer, Courtesy of the Williamson Museum, Northwestern State University, Natchitoches

Fig. 5
CADDO WATTLE-AND-DAUB HOUSE, WPA RECONSTRUCTION
Photograph by Douglas Raymond, Courtesy of H. F. Gregory

Fig. 6
CADDO GRASS HOUSE AT BINGER, OKLAHOMA, WPA RECONSTRUCTION
Photograph by Douglas Raymond, Courtesy of H. F. Gregory

Fig. 7
CHOCTAW-APACHE LOG HOUSE NEAR CONVERSE, LOUISIANA
Courtesy of Don Sepulvado

beyond them to form eaves—a departure from the ordinary smooth, flowing meeting of roof and wall. The houses appear to have had entrance rooms or passageways like those of their northern neighbors, the Chickasaw, and at least some of them had smoke holes that could be opened or covered. The passageways might be curved to handicap an intruder, while the entrance rooms could be used for storage.

The summer house of the Choctaw in northern Louisiana is described as a rectangular gabled structure with a framework of wooden posts set in the ground. Vines were twined about the posts, which were plastered with mud and then covered with bark or palmetto fronds. The house lacked windows and was entered through a low opening facing south, and a hole at each gable end allowed smoke to escape from the fire built in the center. Far simpler as summer shelters were the arbors, with flat roofs and open sides, used by the Choctaw speakers of south Louisiana.

Temples and the houses of chiefs were set on earth mounds in de Soto's time. By 1700, however, mound construction had generally ceased, being retained only by the Natchez and the Taensa. Stuffed animals, and carved, colored figures, animal and human, of wood or clay, might be placed within a temple and in front of a chief's house. Along the lower Mississippi River, temples were covered with mats, and some bore on their roofs wooden figures of birds. Before them stood colored images of people, frogs and other animals, and imaginary beings of clay and wood. Human heads impaled on lances were positioned before one temple. Carved, decorated figures were placed in the vestibule, which also might have held collections of weapons. Interior walls were decorated, and carvings in wood and moldings in earth occupied open spaces. Perennial fires burned in the temples of the Bayougoula, Caddo, Natchez, Taensa, and perhaps others. These temples sometimes served as charnel areas where the bones of chiefs were stored.

While the structures described above, with the variations noted, were prevalent along the Mississippi River and in adjacent areas, there were departures among the Red River Caddo and in the coastal areas occupied by the Chitimacha and Atakapa. Of all Louisiana tribes, only the Atakapa, nonconformists in so many respects, had a mobile house. Composed of poles and mat coverings, it could be disassembled and hauled to another site. The basic house structure of all the Caddo was round, with poles set in the ground and pulled together at the top. Farthest downstream on Red River, the houses apparently had walls composed of mud-daubed wattle, giving rise northward to the beehive-shaped Wichita grass house. Arrangement of houses in settlements, the enclosing of perpetual fires in temples, and the setting of chiefs' houses on low mounds were like practices along the Mississippi. Simple arbors with outdoor hearths for summer cooking also related Caddo practices to those nearer the Mississippi River. The Caddo built temporary shelters in their hunting camps, and French records suggest that skin tents were seen near Natchitoches. In one major respect, the lack of stockades, Caddo settlements differed from those of all eastern tribes. The marginal Ouachita River Caddo may have been an exception, but little is known of their sites.

The Chitimacha, isolated about Grand Lake along Bayou Teche and along the network of streams in the Atchafalaya Basin, built dwellings of palmetto thatched over pole frameworks, with small entrances and smoke holes in the roofs. The probable rectangular ground plans of Chitimacha, Chawasha, and Washa houses were in marked contrast to the round winter homes of the Choctaw and may have been related to the square Natchez houses. The Chitimacha chief's house was simply a larger version of the common dwelling.

A dance house, or temple, with a pointed roof was found in every large Chitimacha village. Unlike the temples to the east and north, the Chitimacha dance house lacked idols, stuffed animals, and similar sacred objects. A specialized structure was the isolated bone, or charnel, house, where the dead were left until their flesh was sufficiently decayed to be picked off the bones by the bone pickers, or Turkey Buzzard men. The bones were interred in low mounds, or were kept in small baskets. These morticians, who were also present among the Choctaw, lived apart, near the charnel houses. The sweathouse, not a common building, was a low pole or cane structure placed over a hole in the ground large enough to hold a single person. Some tribes used sweathouses for healing and purification. Steam was produced by throwing water on stones heated in an outdoor fireplace or, in stoneless south Louisiana, by quenching open fires with water. "Sweats" were common medicine, and the houses built for that medical treatment seem to have been temporary.

Granaries to secure corn, squash, and other harvested crops against animal predators, in the lower Mississippi Valley, were generally round buildings raised as much as fifteen feet on one or more peeled, polished posts. Caddo houses were built with compartments near their entrances that served as storage places, but other bins, both square and round, were located outside on posts. Harvested foods and other crops were sometimes buried in the ground until needed, or they were simply pushed under the benches that lined the walls of the secure winter houses.

Security of the settlement was always a concern, and in Louisiana, as elsewhere, village planners sought protection in various ways. A measure of safety might be gained by locating the houses on a hill or bluff. In some instances a stockade was considered essential to any plan of defense. The stockade walls were laid out so as to shield the heart, or nucleus, of the settlement with its grouping of public buildings. The walls themselves were made of great posts, standing upright, with ends buried five or six feet in the ground. Narrow spaces might be left between some of the posts so that arrows could be discharged between them, or the walls might be pierced with loopholes for that purpose. A banquette of earth was built up along the interior base of the upright logs, and watchtowers were raised on posts spaced at intervals along the walls, providing platforms from which an attacking force could be resisted. The Bayougoula stockade, according to Iberville, was ten feet high and made of canes set one inch apart. It seems that most stockades were little more than large fences intended to retard intruders rather than bar them completely.

The indistinct picture of aboriginal Indian settlements in Louisiana that has been pieced together from early accounts and physical remains implies a sedentary mode of living, which in turn reflects an economy primarily based on the exploitation of local resources. It was a substantial, secure way of life, but the legacy it left was largely one of the spirit and heart rather than of tangible relics.

The simple Indian habitations of the past are gone, their former sites betrayed by darkened zones in the soil and by shreds of decaying wood in ancient postholes. The huts of thatch and wattle-and-daub have been replaced by modern structures of wood, glass, and brick veneer. Even so, Indian communities of today reflect the older forms by maintaining their traditional dispersed format, as the Koasati have done. Their church–ball field complex became the center of this dispersed population, later giving way in part to a tribal center–ball field complex. These centers clearly correspond to the traditional hothouses of the Creeks and their neighbors; the Koasati have maintained traditional values while modifying the architectural forms. The symbolic value of a socioreligious center, with a public building and a ball field to the west, has persisted.

Palmetto-thatch construction survives among the Houma, and several groups build summer houses, or shades, of pine boughs or willow limbs. These forms, however, are increasingly rare, and one who seeks Indian patterns has to learn to look for log mortars in yards, basketry hanging on walls, and moss, palmetto, and cane hanging in carports and sheds—the sure marks of craftsmen.

The older Indian people still prefer to "live in the woods," almost hidden away. Each household usually has its own garden patch, and those who know the communities well still hear of houses being ceremonially washed with sacred herbs or smoked with cedar smoke to purify them. Even in public housing tracts, practices from former times persist. Axes can sometimes be seen planted in yards to split clouds, and certain plants found near the houses have medicinal or other special properties. Perhaps, as the French say, "The more things change, the more they remain the same."

REFERENCES

Studies of Louisiana Indian settlements have only recently been undertaken. Few of the data are systematic, but at least some information has been made available. John Swanton discussed architecture and some details of village size and plan, basing his work entirely on eighteenth-century and earlier primary sources.

Swanton, John R.
1911   Indian Tribes of the Lower Mississippi Valley and Adjacent Coast

of the Gulf of Mexico. *Bureau of American Ethnology Bulletin*
43: 318–26, Washington, D.C.

An attempt at comparative settlement pattern studies can be seen as early
as 1919. David Bushnell of the Bureau of American Ethnology attempted
to synthesize the types of villages east of the Mississippi.

Bushnell, David I.
1919   Native Villages and Village Sites East of the Mississippi. *Bureau
of American Ethnology Bulletin* 69, Washington, D.C.

The historian Marcel Giraud, in his work on French Louisiana, probably
achieved the best recent synthesis of eighteenth-century settlement patterns and their natural environs.

Giraud, Marcel
1974   *A History of French Louisiana, Volume I: The Reign of Louis XIV,
1698–1715.* Baton Rouge.

Another important source is on the Natchez.

Albrecht, Andrew C.
1948   The Location of the Historic Natchez Villages. *Journal of Mississippi History* 6: 67–88.

For further information, one must turn to archaeological studies that rely
on only partially ordered data with limited cultural or chronological control. The best overview of any portion of the state is William McIntire's
work on coastal Louisiana.

McIntire, William
1958   Prehistoric Indian Settlements of the Changing Mississippi River
Delta. *Louisiana State University Coastal Studies Series* 1, Baton Rouge.

Another general synthesis of archaeological site distributions appears in
the review by Phillips, Ford, and Griffin of the lower Mississippi Valley.
This remains the best short source on the settlements as they appeared in
de Soto's time.

Phillips, Philip, James A. Ford, and James B. Griffin
1951   Archaeological Survey in the Lower Mississippi Alluvial Valley,
1940–1947. *Papers of the Peabody Museum of Archaeology and
Ethnology* 25: 347–90, Harvard University, Cambridge.

Phillips and his students expanded their earlier work in a more recent
study of Tensas Basin archaeology.

Phillips, Philip
1970 Archaeological Surveys in the Lower Yazoo Basin, Mississippi, 1949–1955. *Papers of the Peabody Museum of Archaeology and Ethnology* 60, Harvard University, Cambridge.

John Peterson's synthesis of Choctaw settlement and life in the swamps of southeastern Louisiana is notable.

Peterson, John
1975 Louisiana Choctaw Life at the End of the Nineteenth Century. In *Four Centuries of Southern Indians* (Charles Hudson, ed.), Athens, Ga., 101–31.

Also see Cora Bremer's earlier work on the Louisiana Choctaw.

Bremer, Cora
1907 *The Chata Indians of Lower Pearl River.* New Orleans.

Fewer contemporary-settlement studies have been accomplished than either archaeological or historical studies. Only two exist at present. Donald Hunter's study of the Koasati settlement at Bayou Blue near Elton summarizes the Koasati's maintenance of traditional values in a modern setting.

Hunter, Donald G.
1973 The Settlement Pattern and Toponymy of the Koasati Indians of Bayou Blue. *Florida Anthropologist* 26(2): 79–88.

Malcolm Comeaux's study of swamp dwellers in the Atchafalaya Basin, as John Peterson suggests, contains much of use on contemporary settlements.

Comeaux, Malcolm
1972 *Atchafalaya Swamp Life, Settlement and Folk Occupations.* School of Geoscience, Baton Rouge.

Studies are under way to determine the development of Houma settlements along the natural levees of the relict delta systems between Houma and the Mississippi River. Relevant to such marsh settlement studies is the early archaeological and ecological work on the delta of the Mississippi.

Brown, Clair B.
1936 The Vegetation of the Indian Mounds, Middens and Marshes in Plaquemines and St. Bernard Parishes. *Louisiana Geological Survey Bulletin* 8: 407–22, Louisiana Department of Conservation, New Orleans.

Kniffen, Fred B.
1936 Preliminary Report on the Indian Mounds and Middens of Plaquemines and St. Bernard Parishes. H. V. Howe, ed., *Louisiana*

Geological Survey Bulletin 8: 407–22, Louisiana Department of Conservation, New Orleans.

Gatschet, Alfred
> Field Notes on the Shetimasha Indians, Charenton, Louisiana. National Anthropological Archives, Smithsonian Institution, Washington, D.C.

Fred B. Kniffen's early efforts to secure data on folk housing in south Louisiana yielded information not only on the Choctaw palmetto houses of southeastern Louisiana but also on the Europeanized gable-end palmetto dwellings of the Houma and so delineated continuity in change.

Kniffen, Fred B.
> 1936 Louisiana House Types. *Annals of the Association of American Geographers* 26: 179–93.
>
> 1965 Folk Housing: Key to Diffusion. *Annals of the Association of American Geographers* 55: 549–77.

Jeffrey P. Brain has presented eighteenth-century map and settlement data on the early Tunica sites on the Mississippi.

Brain, Jeffrey P.
> 1973 Trudeau: An 18th Century Tunica Village. *Lower Mississippi Survey Bulletin* 3, Peabody Museum of Archaeology and Ethnology, Harvard University, Cambridge.
>
> 1977 On the Tunica Trail. *Anthropological Study* 1, Louisiana Archaeological Survey, Department of Culture, Recreation, and Tourism, Baton Rouge.
>
> 1979 Tunica Treasure. *Peabody Museum Bulletin* No. 70, Harvard University, Cambridge.

Hiram F. Gregory has presented an ethnographic map of the nineteenth- and twentieth-century Tunica settlement in Avoyelles Parish.

Gregory, Hiram F.
> 1978 A Historic Tunica Burial at the Coulee de Grues Site in Avoyelles Parish, Louisiana. In *Texas Archaeology* (Kurt D. House, ed.), Dallas, 146–64.

These later studies, which combine archaeology, ethnohistory, ethnology, and geography, suggest a future research trend. Their relationship to land claims and tribal sovereignty moves them into the forensic arena and gives them added relevance in understanding contemporary Indian culture. No groups show this more clearly than the Caddo and Koasati.

Wedel, Mildred Mott
1978 La Harpe's 1715 Post on Red River and Nearby Caddoan Settlements. *Texas Memorial Museum Bulletin* 30, Austin.

Williams, Stephen
1964 The Aboriginal Location of the Kadohadacho and Related Tribes. In *Explorations in Cultural Anthropology* (Ward H. Goodenough, ed.), Princeton, 545–70.

Wilmsen, Edwin N.
1961 A Suggested Developmental Sequence for House Forms in the Caddoan Area. *Bulletin of the Texas Archaeological Society* 30: 35–40.

VIII

LANGUAGES

The aborigines of North America spoke a surprising variety of languages. In present-day Louisiana alone, European observers between 1690 and 1794 reported the presence of more than twenty-two tongues. At least eleven more were imported by immigrant tribes moving west near the close of the eighteenth century, making a total of more than thirty mutually unintelligible languages that were spoken, or had been spoken, in the present-day state. Most of the native Louisiana languages are considered isolates; that is, they are unrelated to others. Too little is known about them and how they related to neighboring Indian languages to bring them into an orderly linguistic classification of established Indian language families.

The pattern of Indian language distribution in Louisiana is therefore far from complete and is much more complex than might be imagined. Even so, this language pattern serves as a guide to the identities and placement of the tribes. Differences and similarities in language are commonly employed as criteria according to which basic tribal divisions might be arranged, just as the tribes might be set apart on the basis of shared economies or other traits.

The Louisiana Indian dialects and variants, when grouped together, at about 1700 comprised six families. Caddoan languages dominated the upper Red River valley lands eastward to the Ouachita River and the general area of what is now northwestern Louisiana; Atakapa prevailed in the southwestern part of the present-day state; Chitimacha was predominant in the central southern section; Tunica and Koroa languages held sway in the northeast; Natchez ruled in a limited space along the Mississippi River and lower Red River opposite modern Natchez; and Choctaw-related, or Muskogean, tongues prevailed in what is now southeastern

TRIBES
AND
THEIR LANGUAGES
1730s

*—LANGUAGE ISOLATES
+—SIOUAN LANGUAGES

OSAGE

KADOHADACHO
NABITI

QUAPAW

CHICKASAW

TUNICA

NADARKO

CADDOAN

KORDA*

YATASI

DOUSTIONI

OUACHITA

TAENSA

HAINAI

ADAI
NATCHITOCHES

AIS

NATCHEZ

NACOGDOCHES

GRIGRA*

MUSKOGEAN

AVOYEL*

NATCHEZ*

OFO+

CHOCTAW

OKELOUSA*

TUNICA*

ATAKAPA

OPELOUSA*

CHITIMACHA*

QUINAPISA
ACOLAPISSA

BILOXI+

BIDAI

ATAKAPA*

BAYOUGOULA

PASCAGOULA*

CHITIMACHA

CHITIMACHA*

HOUMA

CHAWASHA*

YAKNE CHITTO*

WASHA*

0   50
miles

Courtesy of the Louisiana State University Cartographic Section

Louisiana. No doubt other languages, now long forgotten, were also once spoken there.

Some of the six language groups named are thought to be clearly related, as are English, Greek, and Russian. Atakapa, Chitimacha, and Tunica have been grouped as members of the Gulf stock of languages, yet to their speakers, other languages in the Gulf stock were completely foreign tongues. The Choctaw dialects spoken in southeastern Louisiana belonged to the Muskogean family, as Natchez may have, but Choctaw and Natchez were far from being mutually intelligible. Tunica was different from these others. The Siouans—Biloxi and Ofo—moved to Louisiana after 1764, raising the number of families to seven.

In former times, the communications gap between Indian groups speaking mutually unintelligible tongues was bridged by the Mobilian Jargon, a contact, or pidgin, language based principally on Choctaw loanwords and basic grammar. Mobilian Jargon apparently had been developed and used at the old conjunction of small tribal groups near Mobile Bay. Once the jargon had reached present-day Louisiana, it may have been spread rapidly by part-Indian traders from Canada, some of whom were *métis*, and others who had had social dealings with many tribes by the late seventeenth century. Some linguists believe that the jargon became significant in the course of trade under French auspices. The increase in the complexity of the language pattern that resulted from the in-migration of multilingual populations would have been even more intense and confusing had Mobilian not been widely spoken in Louisiana.

The *coureurs de bois*, many of whom were *métis*, had an affinity for living with Indians, and in the same fashion as Indians, throughout the eighteenth century, though priests and lay officials alike opposed the practice. Frenchmen and *métis* lived in open concubinage with Indian women, often abandoning Christianity, and their children usually spoke only Indian languages. This acculturative situation led to the rapid flow of northern Algonkian language influences into both Louisiana French and Mobilian, probably deriving from Ojibway brought south by the *métis*. The basic language, or jargon, however, seems a composite of Choctaw and Creek dialects with an abridged grammar.

The Houma may have learned Mobilian, since in the 1840s the Choctaw in Oklahoma made overtures to them and the Chitimacha, urging them to come to Oklahoma because they knew the Mobilian Jargon. Only a few Houma or Mobilian words have survived. Le Page du Pratz noted that the Natchitoches and the Kadohadacho used the jargon in the eighteenth century. In its stead, or along with Mobilian Jargon, most of the Caddo and Lipan substituted a Spanish dialect heavily laced with Nahuatl words, the trade jargon of the Mexican Indians. Most Lipan slaves sold in Louisiana were women and children aged from three to twelve; their isolation in Spanish-speaking communities soon forced upon them a linguistic shift to Spanish, French, or some Caddoan language.

The Mobilian Jargon did not replace the more traditional languages, but it was learned by whites, blacks, and tribal language speakers and served as a lingua franca in trade and social situations involving these groups. It remained in use in Louisiana until the 1930s. Even now, quite extensive vocabularies of the jargon are known by the elderly of several Louisiana Indian communities.

Many of the Indian place names and even accepted tribal names heard outside of the old Choctaw-speaking area are Choctaw or Mobilian Jargon, probably resulting from an approach from the east by Europeans employing guides who spoke these tongues. Tribes west of the Mississippi, other than the Caddo, who were shielded by distance, were given Choctaw or Mobilian names before the French saw them. *Atakapa* and *Chitimacha* are examples of names that originated outside the tribes.

With the passage of time, which is almost always a generator of change, the native tongues of Louisiana and the people who spoke them were transformed in many ways. Migrants from the Mobile area brought an entire series of new languages into contact with the more traditional Louisiana tongues. By the 1760s the migrations had given rise to pantribal communities in various parts of the state, such as the community that developed on Bayou Rouge in present-day Avoyelles Parish about 1780. Although predominantly Tunica, the group included a few Ofo, some Biloxi and Alabama, and a handful of Frenchmen.

Other gatherings of this sort were established in what is today southern Natchitoches Parish, along Bayou Boeuf on the Red River, near Bayou Chicot in Evangeline Parish, and on the prairie near present Opelousas. Still others appeared along the Mississippi River and Bayou Lafourche, comprising the Bayougoula, Houma, and Acolapissa. By 1800, the Mobilian Jargon was widely spoken among these diverse populations.

The impact of European languages wrought further changes in the aboriginal tongues. From the time of the coming of the first white men, the speakers of the Indian languages incorporated Spanish and French words into their vocabularies: *wak* (Choctaw for *cow*) from *vaca* (Spanish); *caouaille* (Caddo for *horse*) from *caballo* (Spanish); *shapo* (Choctaw for *hat*) from *chapeau* (French); *sonak* (Choctaw-Mobilian) possibly from *sunak* (Algonkian-French); *scully* (Choctaw for *money*) from *escalin* (French, meaning a silver coin).

Some languages, like Tunica, absorbed a long list of French loanwords, some remodeled phonetically and others somewhat resembling Tunica words. Mary Haas, probably the leading authority on Louisiana's Indian tongues, has found a number of such words.

Today, English is the new lingua franca, and pantribal gatherings are almost wholly conducted in that language. Alabama, Choctaw, and Koasati, all of which originated in areas east of Louisiana, are still viable languages in the state. The tongues that developed within Louisiana or in other areas nearby have virtually disappeared, though Atakapa, Chitimacha, and Tunica were still spoken in the 1930s. The Spanish-Nahuatl dialect of northwest Louisiana now is spoken conversationally only by people more than sixty years of age. Although English has been stressed in Louisiana's school systems, recent efforts to eliminate the state's unique French dialects have not been successful. Rather, French has all but replaced Houma, Chitimacha, Tunica, and Atakapa. The Houma are now the most conservative of all Louisiana French speakers.

Although some Louisiana Indian languages of 1700 are no longer spoken, some of their elements have been preserved. Reasonably complete vocabularies in the Atakapa, Chitimacha, Natchez, and Tunica tongues have been recorded. The linguistic affiliations of several extinct tribes, such as the Chawasha, Okelousa, Taensa, and Washa are in doubt, but some languages of later migrants have been studied and portions of them have been recorded. Among these are Apalachee, Choctaw, Koasati, and Pascagoula. The Biloxi and Ofo of the migrant tribes were also studied, but only for a brief time and only after a meager handful of speakers, mostly older people, remained as tutors. The ethnologist John Swanton located a few Natchez speakers among the Oklahoma Creek, and Ana and Jack Kilpatrick found others there among the Cherokee.

While most classifiable languages in Louisiana were Muskogean, others were in the Caddoan family. Its representatives had left the state by 1840 and now mostly live between Binger and Fort Cobb in Oklahoma. There, too, the Caddoan tongues are in peril of being replaced by English. A few octogenarians there recall songs in the Natchitoches language, and at Binger and in the mountains to the northwest, the Caddo sometimes gather at dance grounds to sing in Hasinai, Kadohadacho, and, rarely, Natchitoches or some other Caddoan language from the south.

Other languages, isolates, usually persist only as word or phrase retentions. All the Atakapa speakers in Louisiana have disappeared. In the 1930s a few were located at Vidor, near Beaumont, Texas, but no attempt was made to gain imformation during the encounter or to follow it up, and no additional linguistic work was done.

Even though languages are culture traits requiring much time for development, history has shown that they may vanish with remarkable speed. Such was the case with most of the Indian tongues of Louisiana. A number of factors contributed to their quick demise, and only a few were able to survive European contact for any length of time. None of the languages existed in written form, a deficiency certain to attenuate the life of any language subjected to extreme pressures. In Louisiana, some language groups were wiped out as Indians were killed by diseases of European origin. Tribal interactions were intensified, sometimes escalating into hostilities as the political rivalries of the Old World were extended into the New. Indian people of the Southeast were set in motion, and the constant coming and going of various groups, many of whom were newcomers to Louisiana, further weakened the native language base.

Marriage with non-Indians made its contribution to the difficulties opposing the retention of Indian languages, and it seems likely that slavery was another highly erosive factor. Living in culturally alien communities from an early age, with little or no opportunity to communicate with others in one's own language, coupled with needing to please one's master to endure, has a devastating effect on language survival.

An especially crushing blow was dealt the aboriginal languages by the Indians' experience with public education. Unfortunately, education in Louisiana included among its goals the eradication of French, Spanish, and all the Indian languages. Since the aboriginal tongues had no written systems, they had no chance to match the English literary tradition.

For generations, Indian children were totally excluded from schools, even from those otherwise integrated. With white schools closed to them, they declined in most cases to attend black, segregated schools. Ruth Underhill, a representative of the Bureau of Indian Affairs' education office, actually recommended to the Tunica in the 1930s that they abandon their traditional land base and move to Texas, where their children could attend public schools. Some followed her advice and remain there today, going back to Louisiana on special occasions.

Other attempts at providing education for the Indian children had the same harmful effect on the tribal tongues. Federally funded schools for Indian young people were established among the Jena Choctaw and Koasati, but only a day school at the Chitimacha tribal area remains of that effort to educate Indians in an Indian environment. Koasati and Houma schools, supported by the Congregationalist and Methodist churches, respectively, used an assimilative model of education with the Anglo-American mode of living as their goal. This approach stressed the exclusive use of English, and even the speaking of French and Spanish was often punished.

In northwest Louisiana, where Spanish had remained unchanged since the eighteenth century, that language persisted only as verbal communication. The first public schools, with Anglo-Saxon teachers, appeared there in the late nineteenth or early twentieth century. Parochial schools of the time, taught by Irish nuns, offered little or no choice of languages. Even family names were transliterated. *Ybarbo* became *Ebarb*, *Prosela* became *Procell*, *Castillo* became *Castie*, and *Ramirez* became *Remedies*. Spanish became a stigma, almost a mark of low caste. Indian in race and Spanish in language, the population became socially isolated and developed its own schools and churches. Today, Spanish is nowhere taught as a formal language, even in schools where Indian-Spanish populations predominate. In consequence, Spanish is becoming a lost language among Louisiana Indians, soon to be forgotten like the Indian tongues it replaced.

Among the Houma, French had almost completely replaced the tribal language, and after English became the ideal language of public educationalists, the Houma were left as one of the larger linguistic islands of Louisiana French. Locally called by the derogatory name "Sabines," the Houma were markedly illiterate and still experience discrimination, despite recent efforts to preserve Louisiana's French heritage.

Non-Indians have undertaken the study of aboriginal languages in Louisiana, but many of their efforts have contributed little to an understanding of the ancient people, their history, and their way of life. In the 1930s, the students of Edward Sapir, noted linguist of Columbia University, went to Louisiana to study Indian languages. Sapir was a close associate of Swanton, and both had been influenced by Franz Boas's descriptive approach to field ethnology.

The linguists combed the state searching for Indian language groups. Most of their work was historical, that is, oriented toward the classification of languages into families, which in turn was expected to yield information on their origin and development. This phylogenetic, or family-tree, approach to language development led to a concentration of effort on description and classification, and largely left untouched the processes of language maintenance and change. Although the work preserved much linguistic data, it did not always yield answers to questions about why or how the languages were being kept or lost. It also led students of Indian tongues to look for purely aboriginal languages and, with few exceptions, to ignore the complicating factors of social interaction and the widespread use of the Mobilian Jargon.

Languages, once located or relocated, were pinned down and written about like butterflies impaled on mounting boards. Often the informants were erroneously described as "last speakers," and no efforts to sample linguistic variety were made. Louisiana Indians marvel at the way the linguists, despite their best intentions, seem to have appeared just as languages were threatened with extinction.

Few non-Indians have attempted to learn the native languages, though some have acquired Mobilian. Tribal elders show surprise when non-Indians know even portions of their languages. One needs only to read the early recorded and translated speeches of the Caddo, Choctaw, Natchez, Tunica, and others to realize the high quality of these tongues. Lost with them must have been a priceless store of tribal lore, history, and thought.

Oratory was prized among the tribes, and many chiefs were noted for their eloquence. Even today, the tribal leaders are esteemed as public speakers. Most are as articulate in English as in their native tongues; several have mastered French, Spanish, and even some other Indian language as well.

The Indians themselves must make the main effort if their languages are to survive. Community involvement in Bible translation at the Koasati center and in a language retention program among the Jena Choctaw are recent efforts to preserve the native tongues. At the Koasati community center, children are now learning to read in their primary language, Koasati. Adult reading, with the help of an applied linguist, and the use of the Koasati and Choctaw languages in a mental health program have created a new awareness of, and appreciation for, their native language. Although similar undertakings elsewhere have not been encouraging, perhaps such efforts will help maintain the three surviving language groups: the Choctaw, Koasati, and Spanish-Nahuatl.

Indian languages have not all been preserved, but words from various tongues have come into the vocabulary and heritage of every Louisianian: *bayuk* (Choctaw or Mobilian Jargon) became *bayou; filé* (Choctaw) came to refer to the thickening spice of typical gumbos; *babiche* (Algonkian) was adopted in Louisiana French to mean rawhide thongs, or strips; *chaoui* (Choctaw) became *raccoon* to French speakers as well as to speakers of Choctaw or Mobilian Jargon. Numerous streams bear Indian names, among them the Atchafalaya, Bogue Chitto, Bon Fouca, Catahoula, Shongaloo, Tchefuncte, and Whiskey Chitto. Alabama Bayou, Coushatta Chute, and Kisatchie Creek bear Indian names reflecting Alabama and Koasati (Coushatta) influences. Many parishes have names of Indian origin, among them Avoyelles, Caddo, Catahoula, Calcasieu, Natchitoches, Ouachita, Tangipahoa, and Tensas.

An observant visitor to Louisiana soon learns that the truly exotic words heard as place names and in French, Spanish, and English dialects are usually of Indian origin. It has been well said that "if you can pronounce Tchoupitoulas, Tchefuncte, Atchafalaya, Tangipahoa, and Natchitoches, you're a native." All these are Indian words that have survived.

REFERENCES

Louisiana Indian languages have been studied rather extensively, certainly more than other aspects of Indian life in the region. Just after the Louisiana Purchase, which occurred between 1803 and 1807, President Jefferson directed his agents at Natchitoches to begin the collecting of local languages. John Sibley and his successors undertook the work. Adaes, a Caddoan language, and other Caddoan tongues attracted their attention. Efforts to study and classify these languages have been summarized.

Taylor, Alan
1963   Comparative Caddoan. *International Journal of American Linguistics* 29: 113–31.
1963   The Classification of the Caddoan Languages. *Proceedings of the American Philosophical Society* 107(1): 51–57.

Lesser, Alexander, and Gene Weltfish
1932   Composition of the Caddoan Linguistic Stock. *Smithsonian Miscellaneous Collections* 87(6): 1–15, Washington, D.C.

Two early agents, Sibley and George Gray, noted in their reports that they might secure Apalachee texts and other lexical items. However, they seem not to have done so. Only the historical study of the linguist Mary Haas has given ideas about the Apalachee language.

Haas, Mary
1949   The Position of Apalachee in the Muskoghean Family. *International Journal of American Linguistics* 15: 121–27.

Unfortunately, President Jefferson's lead was not picked up by linguists for nearly a century. The first academic linguist to go to Louisiana, Albert Gatschet, made a number of attempts to locate Indian languages there. His fieldwork, beginning in 1886, continued, with interruptions, for almost a decade. Gatschet located speakers of Alabama, Biloxi, Chitimacha, Choctaw, Koasati, Pascagoula, and Tunica. Even then, the languages were eroding, and Indians in increasing numbers were turning to English and French.

Gatschet, Albert
1879–1880 -Caddo. *American Antiquarian* 2: 236–37.
1907   Chitimacha. *Bureau of American Ethnology Bulletin* 30(1), Washington, D.C.

Gatschet, Albert (John R. Swanton, ed.)
1932   A Dictionary of the Attakapa Language, Accompanied by Text Material. *Bureau of American Ethnology Bulletin* 108, Washington, D.C.

James Owen Dorsey also collaborated with Swanton, who published a dictionary of Biloxi and Ofo based on Dorsey's work.

Dorsey, James Owen, and John R. Swanton
1912   A Dictionary of the Biloxi and Ofo Languages. *Bureau of American Ethnology Bulletin* 47, Washington, D.C.

Dorsey early extended his interest to the southern Siouan speakers.

Dorsey, James Owen

1886   Migrations of Siouan Tribes. *American Naturalist* 20: 211–22.

1894   The Biloxi Indians of Louisiana. *Proceedings of the American Association for the Advancement of Science* 42: 267–87.

Gatschet's work, though largely unpublished, served as a catalyst for other linguistic fieldwork, most notably by Swanton. Gatschet's field notes are in the National Anthropological Archives, the Smithsonian Institution, Washington, D.C. Swanton's linguistic notes are mixed with his general ethnographic observations.

Swanton, John R.

1908   The Language of the Taensa. *American Anthropologist* 10: 24–32.

1919   A Structural and Lexical Comparison of the Tunica, Chitimacha, and Attakapa Languages. *Bureau of American Ethnology Bulletin* 68, Washington, D.C.

1924   The Muskoghean Connection of the Natchez Language. *International Journal of American Linguistics* 3: 46–75.

1909   A New Siouan Dialect. In *Putnam Anniversary Volume, Anthropological Essays Presented to Frederick Ward Putnam in Honor of His 70th Birthday*, New York, 477–86.

1910   Ofogoula. *Bureau of American Ethnology Bulletin* 30, Washington, D.C.

1911   Indian Tribes of the Lower Mississippi Valley and Adjacent Coast of the Gulf of Mexico. *Bureau of American Ethnology Bulletin* 43: 318–26, Washington, D.C.

1921–1923   The Tunica Language. *International Journal of American Linguistics* 2: 1–39.

1929   A Sketch of the Attakapan Language. *International Journal of American Linguistics* 5: 121–49.

Swanton also reworked some of the Gatschet material and published much of it.

Mary Haas has given considerable attention to Swanton's interpretation of Gatschet's texts.

Haas, Mary

1948   A Review of John R. Swanton's Indians of Southeastern United States. *Journal of American Folklore* (Jan.–Mar.): 89–90.

Since the 1930s, she has been the unheralded dean of the students of Louisiana Indian languages. She published her classic work on Tunica.

Haas, Mary

1946   A Grammatical Sketch of Tunica. In *Linguistic Structures of Native America* (Harry Hoijer, ed.), Washington, D.C., 336–37.

1953 Tunica Dictionary. *University of California Publications in Linguistics* 6(2): 175–332.

She also visited the last Biloxi speakers.

1968 The Last Words of Biloxi. *International Journal of American Linguistics* 34: 77–84.

Haas also wrote several papers on French-Tunica loanwords and myth.

1947 Some French Loan Words in Tunica. *Romance Philology* 1: 145–48.

1969 A Lexical Comparison of the Attakapa, Chitimacha and Tunican Languages. *International Journal of American Linguistics* 35: 83–101.

George Trager reviewed Haas's work on Tunica and noted French accentuations in the language texts.

Trager, George L.

1941 Review of Tunica, by Mary R. Haas. *Handbook of American Indian Languages* 4: 143.

More recently, Haas published a brief overview of Mobilian usage among the Koasati and others.

Haas, Mary R.

1975 What Is Mobilian? In *Studies in Southeastern Indian Languages* (James M. Crawford, ed.), Athens, Ga., 257–63.

Haas's works on regional language classification are still the definitive sources.

1971 Southeastern Indian Linguistics. Red, White, and Black: Symposium on Indians in the Old South. *Southern Anthropological Society Proceedings* 5: 44–54.

Franz Boas and Edward Sapir, at Swanton's insistence, sent students to salvage the linguistic data available in Louisiana. Haas, Vic Riste, Morris Swadesh, and Gene Weltfish all went to Louisiana in the 1930s. Haas went to the Tunica. Swadesh (Haas's husband), went to the Chitimacha, and Vic Riste went to the Natchez already in Indian Territory in eastern Oklahoma. Riste's field notes are in the National Anthropological Archives, Smithsonian Institution. After World War II, when the economic situation had improved, Haas and Swadesh managed to publish most of their findings. Swadesh's work on Chitimacha and related languages remains the outstanding study.

Swadesh, Morris

1933 Chitimacha Verbs of Derogatory or Abusive Connotation with Parallels from European Languages. *Language* 9: 192–201.

1934   The Phonetics of Chitimacha. *Language* 10: 345–62.
1946   Chitimacha. Linguistic Structures of Native America. In (Harry Hoijer, ed.) *Viking Fund Publications in Anthropology* 6: 312–36.

This work has been supplemented.

Haas, Mary R.
1939   Natchez and Chitimacha Clans and Kinship Terminology. *American Anthropologist* 41: 597–610.

Since 1950, Tulane University has maintained an active program in native American linguistics, concentrating on the Koasati languages. Much has been accomplished there under the direction of John Fischer, and it is probable that much remains to be done. Although the Tulane fieldwork findings are for the most part unpublished, the material will serve, like Gatschet's, as a focus for future efforts.

Pavie, David
1963   Notes on the Semantics of Koasati Kinship Usage. MS at Department of Anthropology, Tulane University, New Orleans.

In the early 1970s, Claude Medford, Jr., and Rosaline Langley, a Koasati, discovered some Mobilian speakers. Learning of this find, Haas dispatched students to Louisiana. Among them was James Crawford of the University of Georgia.

Crawford, James M.
1978   *The Mobilian Trade Language.* Knoxville.

At about the same time, Emanuel Drechsel, then a graduate student at the University of Wisconsin, Madison, traversed Louisiana, identifying and recording Mobilian wherever he found it.

Drechsel, Emanuel
1979   Mobilian Jargon: Linguistic, Sociocultural, and Historical Aspects of an American Indian *Lingua Franca.* Ph.D. dissertation, University of Wisconsin, Madison.

Applied linguistics appeared in Louisiana Indian communities in the 1970s. After having gone without linguistic attention since Gatschet's visit at the turn of the century, the Jena Band of Choctaw began a language maintenance program with the help of a grant from the Center for Applied Linguistics. Paul Cissna, a student at American University, was employed, and efforts were begun to train native speakers to organize classes for non-Choctaw speakers. Dale Nicklas, linguist for the Choctaw bilingual programs, had published a number of basic grammars, which came into use in Louisiana.

Nicklas, Thurston Dale

1974   The Elements of Choctaw. Ph.D. dissertation, University of Michigan, Ann Arbor.

1975   Choctaw Morphophonemics. In *Studies in Southeastern Indian Languages* (James M. Crawford, ed.), Athens, Ga., 237–49.

Nicklas, Thurston Dale, Betty Jacob, and Betty Spencer

1977   *Introduction to Choctaw.* Durant, Okla.

Nicklas, Thurston Dale

1979   *Reference Grammar to the Choctaw Language.* Durant, Okla.

A number of studies have been published on the Koasati and Alabama languages, which are related.

Haas, Mary R.

1944   Men's and Women's Speech in Koasati. *Language* 20: 142–49.

Rand, Earl

1968   The Structural Phonology of Alabaman, a Muskogean Language. *International Journal of American Linguistics* 34: 94–103.

Living among the modern Koasati, Gene Burnham of the Wycliffe Bible Translators not only began translation of the Bible into Koasati but undertook with the tribe the preparation of a series of childrens' books and teenagers' books. For the first time, Koasati children could see their language in print and with pictures.

Burnham, Gene

1979   *Naas Mathaali and Naas Onapa.* Koasati tribe, Elton.

1981   *Innakaathohe Thoiliichit Hiichachi.* Koasati tribe, Elton.

Most recent is a complete, unpublished dictionary of Koasati compiled by Jeffrey Kimball of Tulane University in 1982.

In northwestern Louisiana, Hiram F. Gregory and Louisa Stark collected a series of lexical materials from the Spanish-Indian communities along the Sabine River. Samuel Armistead of the University of California—Davis and Hiram Gregory have continued that fieldwork. Armistead has published a brief report on the relationship between the Spanish-Indian dialect, heavily laced with Nahuatl words, and colonial Spanish in Louisiana. Recently, a few Choctaw or Mobilian words have appeared in the dialect. It may be too late to adequately assess the impact of culture change on the language.

Stark, Louisa

1979   Notes on a Dialect of Spanish Spoken in Northern Louisiana. Typescript in H. F. Gregory's files, Natchitoches.

Armistead, Samuel G.
1980   Notes on Three Spanish-Speaking Communities in Louisiana. MS at Jean Lafitte National Park, New Orleans.
1982   Three Spanish Dialects in Louisiana. Paper read at the 9th Convocation in Romance Philology, University of California—Davis.

Atakapa was recorded by Swanton in 1911 and by his Louisiana colleague Caroline Dorman at Vidor, Texas, in the 1930s. A few of her field notes are in the Dorman Papers, Fieldnotes 1935–1937, Special Collections, Eugene P. Watson Library, Northwestern State University, Natchitoches.

Remnants of languages—fragments of elaborate systems maintained for centuries—exist. Now linguists, like their archaeological colleagues, find themselves trying to salvage even the rare bits and pieces. Some texts and songs have been recorded among the Tunica-Biloxi by Hiram F. Gregory, Claude Medford, Jr., and Emanuel Drechsel. Drechsel also found a few isolated speakers of Mobilian. Greg Bowman, Janel Curry, and other Mennonite volunteers collected song fragments among the Houma.

Curry, Janel M.
1980   The Forgotten Tribe: The History and Culture of the Houma Tribe of South Louisiana. MS in Mennonite Central Committee files, Akron.

Gregory found fragments of Indian vocabularies, as yet unidentified, mixed with Mobilian at the Clifton Choctaw community. What remains of Apalachee, Chatot, and most other languages, if anything, is unknown.

Koasati, and a little Alabama and Choctaw, are left as the only viable Indian tongues in Louisiana. It is hoped that they will survive and that the numbers of their speakers will increase. For the linguists of the future, there must be preserved an opportunity to aid in language maintenance and preservation. This is not a field to be relegated to history.

IX

<hr>

ARTS AND CRAFTS

The everlasting struggle to survive and prosper is a relentless but effective school. During ancient times, the Indian people of Louisiana learned many lessons, among which were the arts and crafts associated with the making and use of tools, weapons, and the other artifacts that life required. Many were needed because of their utility while others, no less essential, gave only pleasure. Some of the aboriginal articles have managed to survive, as have certain beliefs, attitudes, techniques, and bits of knowledge that are still useful, though their origins may be obscure.

WOODEN OBJECTS

Louisiana is largely a forest state, and Indian cultures there long have featured an elaborate body of learning derived from thousands of years of forest experience with the various woods and their uses. Articles of wood, among them tools, weapons, and even toys, were common in pre-European Indian households, and many still can be seen in Indian and non-Indian contexts in Louisiana. The Indians understood that a specific kind of wood was usually preferred for each type of tool The relationship of the tool to the wood of which it was to be made was well established, and the form of the implement was determined by tradition and experimentation.

In order to traverse Louisiana's thick maze of waterways, the aborigines turned to the dugout canoe, the antecedent of the famous French pirogue. The canoes were most often made of cypress (*Taxodium distichum*), cottonwood (*Populus deltoides*), or black walnut (*Juglans niger*). As Acadian craftsmen still remark, "The tree has a boat in him; you have to get it out." Immense trees of all these species stood in swamps and along the sandy river battures of Louisiana as late as the 1940s, when most of them fell as casualties in World War II. Any that survived are threatened by land clearing for the expansion of rice and soybean farms in north Louisiana and the Atchafalaya Basin.

The boatbuilders viewed the cypress with awe and respect. Apart from the tree's superior qualities as a raw material, the seasoned cypress was red, a sacred color. The Chitimacha believed that specific cypress trees were sacred, the last one being grown in Lake Portage. Once others stood on lower Bayou Lafourche, near Vermilion Bay, and along Bayou Teche. If touched, it was said, these holy trees produced rain, and they were trusted as guardians of tribal territory. The *Isti Houma*, a red pole, probably of cypress, stood on the bank of the Mississippi River marking the boundary dividing Houma and Bayougoula lands. The name of Louisiana's capital city, Baton Rouge, was inspired by this ancient tree.

The Indian's stone axe was a serviceable implement, and he was an efficient woodsman. A key ingredient in his method was patience. The tree to be felled was girdled; that is, a notch was cut around the tree near its base all the way through the bark. This killed the tree, and it began to dry. Later, a thick belt of mud was applied around the tree trunk, leaving a space next to the ground uncovered. A fire was kept burning around the tree at ground level, burning through the trunk below the mud shield. Eventually, the tree fell. Felling timber by burning was best accomplished in the fall because the trunk was drier in that season.

A log to be worked into a boat was first marked and shaped into a blunt-ended, boatlike form and then was moved closer to the village for convenience. Logs could be floated and towed or moved along the ground by being slid over beds of dry leaves piled underneath. Once at the working site, the cypress log was split lengthwise with stone or hardwood wedges. Each half of the log would yield a boat. The hull was shaped externally by careful burning at places where the wood was to be removed and then chipping and scraping away the charred wood with chisels of wood, stone, or shell.

When the exterior of the boat's hull had taken shape, the log was rolled over and the laborious process of hollowing it out was begun. Burning was the principal technique. Layers of wet mud were piled on the flat log surface, and fires were built in spots left exposed. Hollow canes served as bellows, and air was blown through them to direct the fire into the log. The scrapers again were used to remove the charred wood and reduce the hull to the desired thickness. The hulls were square-ended rather than pointed like their European and African counterparts.

The boats the Indians made ranged from one- or two-man size to forty feet long, two to three feet wide, and capable of carrying a dozen people. Unconfirmed reports describe dugouts with capacities of from sixty to eighty passengers.

Maintenance of the dugout canoe was a simple matter, chiefly requiring that the boat be prevented from drying out and splitting. When not in use, dugouts were sometimes carried ashore, placed in the shade, and stuffed with wet Spanish moss. More often they were simply sunk in shallow water. In later times, boats occasionally were painted on both the interior and exterior. Although dugouts may seem clumsy, they were surprisingly graceful, sturdy, and long-lived. Their great value for travel in wetlands of all types more than justified the work of building and the precautions taken for their care and preservation. The dugout cypress canoe is still useful and can even be regarded as a pleasure craft.

Among the Indians, wood filled important needs in the work of food preparation. Cooks ground their corn by pounding it in wooden mortars made by the burning and scraping process, preferably of bald cypress. The mortars were adopted by early Acadians and Creoles for pounding corn and rice, and though other methods are at hand, old women, both Indian and French, still prefer their mortar, or *pilon*, to other implements. In Indian usage, at least two women pounded in a mortar at the same time, so two to four pestles were kept with each mortar.

Mortars were usually made from sections of log some fifteen inches wide and about twice that long. Two styles of mortar were in general use, one of them straight and the other with a narrow waist. Gum, tupelo, hickory, oak, beech, and even cedar might be used instead of the prized cypress, but maple was taboo since it imparted a bad taste to cornmeal. The pestle, or *pile*, was about three inches in diameter, five or six feet in length, and narrowed at the middle to make grasping easier. Sometimes the upper end was the heaviest portion.

Mortar and pestle were implements sacred to women, and as such they were carefully guarded. New ones were put into use by

Fig. 8
EMERICK SANSON, FRENCH CHOCTAW, BUILDING A CYPRESS DUGOUT, 1935
Courtesy of H. F. Gregory

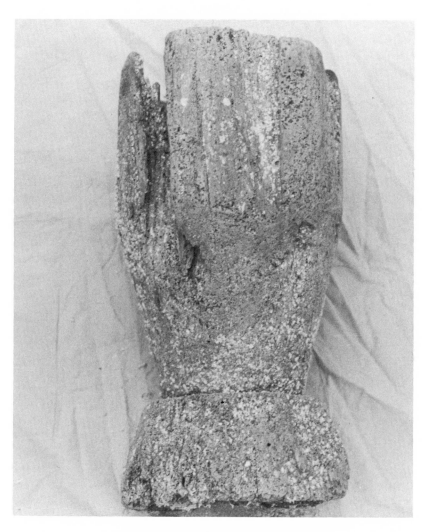

Fig. 9
CYPRESS MORTAR, HOUMA TRIBE
Courtesy of the Williamson Museum, Northwestern State University, Natchitoches

four women who represented the sacred number of cardinal directions and who sang a special song as they pounded together. The Choctaw sometimes crushed grain in mortars burned and chipped into logs, several in a row being common. Pestles and techniques of use were about the same as those of other Indians.

Wooden implements resembling paddles found varied uses in Indian culture. Many of these objects were made of hickory because of its fine grain, resilience, and resistance to decay and wear. Smoothed to shape and hardened in the smoke of a slow fire, the tough wood could hold an edge sharp enough to cut.

One type of paddle, approximately two feet long, double-bladed, and with a bit, or blades, three to four inches wide, was used in tanning hides. The hide was soaked in water until some of the hair "slipped" off. Then all the remaining hair was removed by beaming the hide on a log set in the ground at an angle. After soaking overnight in a tanning solution, the hide was laced tightly on a rack and then scraped dry with the paddle. The scraping forced the solution throughout the skin, making it soft and pliable.

A slightly larger paddle was used for stirring pots of corn soup, called *sofke*, or *chawaka*. The paddle was sometimes made of cedar (*Cyperus* sp.), but hickory was generally preferred. John Swanton in 1911 illustrated that a Chitimacha stirring paddle and similar ones were made to stir roasting coffee and, probably, to stir boiling yaupon leaves.

The dibble, a stick five or six feet long with a fire-hardened point at one end, was used to plant corn, beans, and squash, and to gather roots and tubers. A favorite tool of early Europeans, it remained in use for generations. The Natchez made a wide-bladed hickory hoe with a short handle for cultivating their fields. This implement is not mentioned in reference to other tribes, but its use probably was not confined to a single tribe. Spears and darts were made of cane, hickory, and dogwood. Harpoon shafts were fashioned of ash, cypress, and willow poles, which floated and created resistance when being pulled through the water, thus tiring the fish or other game.

A weapon far older in human prehistory than the bow was seen in Louisiana by de Soto's party. This device, a spear and dart thrower known to the Mexicans as an atlatl, was shaped somewhat like an enlarged crocheting hook. The shaft was carved from wood and often had an antlerlike hook at one end. In use, the atlatl was held by one end in the hunter's hand, with the hooked end extended away from his body. The hook was seated in a socket or hole at the base of the spear shaft, so that the atlatl served as an extension of the thrower's arm. The throw was made in a motion resembling the tennis overhand stroke, the arm coming forward and the shaft leaving the atlatl as the arc of the throw passed its peak. The atlatl had the effect of increasing the length of the thrower's arm and thus increased the thrust imparted to the weapon. A dart or spear cast in this way could be driven with surprising velocity and force. In one instance, a dart, or long arrow, cast with an atlatl passed entirely through a man wearing a coat of mail. As a hunting tool, the atlatl was effective in taking both large and small game. The Indians' preference for wood of which atlatls were to be made is not known, but hickory or cypress is the most probable choice.

The weapon often referred to as a club sometimes had an unusual shape. It was often like a cutlass, with a sharp edge and blunt back, and bore a ball about three inches in diameter near the back. Overall, the club was about eighteen inches long and two and one-half inches wide. It could be used in striking blows or thrown. Among the Natchez, the club was elevated to use as a figure in their symbolism and was quite likely a survival from the employment of monolithic axes as status symbols. What is known of the clubs is derived largely from contemporary sketches. In many of the eastern states, Indian clubs were made of maple or of the boles of black walnut, red maple, or oak trees. The Louisiana Indians could have made them of any hardwood.

The craftsmanship displayed in the manufacture of some wooden implements was often of a high order. The hickory rackets with which the stickball game was played were elaborately made, each having a cup bent on one end, which was tied in place and laced with deer- or squirrelskin strips. Rackets varied in length, and there were tribal variations. Tunica sticks, a Creole version of bitter pecan or hickory, were much lighter than those of other tribes. Similar pains were taken in making the curved or notched hickory sticks thrown as spears in the chunkey game.

Boat paddles were made with special care, for an implement so utilitarian and likely to be used for hours at a time had to be properly fashioned. Ash was the wood preferred, since it did not seem to become heavier when saturated with water. To increase dexterity and minimize fatigue, the Indians carved the paddle to a very thin configuration.

Hickory was a wood popular in Indian technology. Clear, or knotless, wood was made into mortars, pestles, and many other items. Bows, always interesting artifacts, were usually of some kind of hickory or pecan but were sometimes made of Osage orange (*Maclura pomifera*), called *bois d'arc* by the French. This term was corrupted by the Anglo-Saxons into *bodark*.

Bow construction varied from tribe to tribe. Koasati bows were quite straight, while those of the Chitimacha had markedly curved ends. All were made of a single stave. Bowstrings were of twisted deerskin thongs, fiber, or even bark. Bow pull seldom exceeded forty or fifty pounds, but penetration was sufficient to kill reptiles and other animals, birds, fish, and men. According to one account, an Indian wounded one of de Soto's men by shooting an arrow with a sharpened, fire-hardened wooden tip through the mounted Spaniard's armored leg and into his horse's body. Other reports state that a skilled archer could shoot arrows with good effect at ranges as great as 120 yards.

Arrow shafts were made of dogwood switches, switch cane, and hickory. The tips were sharpened and hardened in fire, or they carried points made of gar scales, split bone, or chipped bone. The projectiles were fletched with hawk, duck, goose, or turkey feathers, sometimes cemented to the shafts with a glue made by boiling fish bones, deer horn or bison hoof. More often, the feathers were bound to the shaft with wet sinew. Fire arrows were made by wrapping dry Spanish moss around the shafts.

Some accounts mention canoes made of elm (*Ulmus* sp.) and cypress bark, but they found extremely limited use and little is known about them. Boxes and chests were made of boards split from logs with stone or wooden wedges. Corners of these containers were drilled and sewn together with bison or deerskin thongs. Other everyday items fashioned from wood included four-legged stools, each made from a single piece of wood; dishes and bowls of oak and tupelo gum; cypress spoons; persimmon-root combs; frames for cradle boards; and musical instruments. Cedar flutes were especially popular.

Drums were made from hollow cypress knees. These pneumatophores of the root were cut off and tuned by thinning the walls. The larger end was covered with skin and beaten with a stick, usually of dogwood. Cypress-knee drums were sometimes partially filled with water so that the tone could be changed by varying the water level. Shards of pottery were placed in the drum to yield additional vibration against the bottom. Some authorities suggest that the cypress-knee drums are the functional equivalents of some types of pottery and even metal containers, which also were used as water drums. Another kind of drum featured pegs driven into its sides. Reminiscent of some drums from West Africa, this instrument may have been borrowed from black slaves in America. It seems to have been made only by the Bayou LaCombe Choctaw.

Black-gum twigs, cut, peeled, and chewed vigorously on the ends, were used to scrub the teeth and gums. This practice was borrowed by Anglo-Americans, who also used the brushes to spread snuff.

Wood-splint basketry was made, and still is, by the Houma and, to a lesser extent, by the Koasati. White oak was so widely used by the Indians for making splint baskets that the wood is still called "basket oak" in north Louisiana. Such splint baskets are usually European forms, but both tribes manufacture such traditional forms as square-bottomed carrying baskets, large storage baskets, egg baskets, wall-hanging baskets for the storage of small items, and gizzard baskets. The pliant white oak, rived into thin splints, was the ideal medium for this craft, which was shared with newcomers, both white and black. It persists today in all three communities. Far from white-oak forests, the Houma quickly adopted splints made from the *gros bec* ("grow back"), or second-growth, cypress trees. Some of the fine-grained woods, persimmon, and some of the oaks, were the materials from which spacers and the needles used in net making were fashioned. Gauges and spacers, perhaps borrowed by the Indians from Europeans but doubtless ancient and almost universal, were sometimes made of cedar.

The Spanish introduced the Spanish spinner, or *tarabi*, a simple, carved wooden spinning device of hickory or red oak used for making horsehair rope. The Alabama, Choctaw, Koasati, and Houma quickly adapted the spinner to the twisting of the inner fiber of Spanish moss. It was used for twisting rawhide ropes by the Apache and Choctaw at Ebarb, probably its original function.

It is plain, even at this distance in time, that the Indian had a knowledge and perception of woods and woodlands so intimate and accurate that his use of the forest was gentle, effective, and efficient. Europeans coming into Louisiana were also forest users and were quick to borrow from the woods lore the Indians had gathered. Log mortars were put to use in making grits and hominy. For their part, the Indians were equally ready to try new things and seized upon the *tarabi* and other items, particularly the steel axe.

CANE OBJECTS

In Indian times the great curving natural levees supported the canes, the native grasses *Arundinaria tecta* and *Arundinaria gigantica*. To the aborigines, the canebrakes were almost sacred places. They furnished blowguns, darts, arrow shafts, shields, knives, and spears. Apart from supplying this arsenal, the cane was used in rafts, baskets, bedding, roofing, floor and wall coverings, and as containers for everything from the bones of the dead to the plant seeds to be used as food during famines. Duck calls, whistles and flutes, tubes for bubbling medicines, and even beads were of cane. The brakes of river cane, as the Indians and others called it, have been compared to a supermarket that offered something for almost every purpose.

One traditional cane product was the blowgun, called *Sabracane* by the Creoles. This weapon was much more restricted in time and areal distribution than either the atlatl or the bow. It was used throughout what is now Louisiana and the Southeast in hunting small game. The blowgun was made of river cane with an outside diameter of about one inch and was usually from seven to ten feet long. It is speculated that in ancient times slender hardwood rods were inserted into the cane and shaken to clear the joints, but the Indians must have had a more effective way to accomplish this. Joe Langley, a Koasati, used the hard root of the cane to punch out the dividing sections. Today, a rasp is made by punching holes in the top taken from a tin can. The rasp is wrapped around one end of a wooden dowel and thrust through the cane. The dowel is moved back and forth and twisted so that the rasp smooths the joints and other irregularities inside the cane tube. One straightens the tube by heating it, then grasping it in the teeth and tensing it to straighten curved lengths. Finally, one decorates the blowgun by wrapping it with strips of bark and exposing it to a fire, creating a ribbonlike effect. According to Frank Sylestine of the Alabama and Claude Medford, Jr., Barber-Pole and Diamond patterns were preferred.

Darts, six to ten inches long, were made of sharpened strips of cane or hard pine. These could be decorated like the blowgun tube and were usually twisted to impart a rifling effect. Three to five inches of each dart's length was wrapped with thistledown so that when the missile was inserted in the blowgun tube, sharp end forward, it became a piston and could be propelled through the tube by a single explosive puff of breath. Darts were driven with force sufficient to kill birds, squirrels, and even rabbits.

A part of the blowgun's ability to survive has been the sheer fun of its use. Long after adult hunters had turned to guns, Indian boys maintained the ancient skills with bow and blowgun by hunting small game with them. Blowguns became popular with rural whites throughout Louisiana, and copper wire wrapped with cotton gradually replaced the cane sliver bound with thistledown. Some Koasati have adopted plastic tubing and bicycle spokes as blowgun and dart, surely the ultimate in acculturation.

On the coast, the Houma developed a blowgun made of two grooved half-round cypress rods wrapped together with cord or woven palmetto strips. They also made shorter tubes of marsh elder (*Iva frotescens*) branches, which are the only forms of the blowgun remaining today. These substitutes for cane blowguns show a remarkable similarity to the composite blowguns used in South America.

The Indians mastered a variety of skills, but nothing in their repertoire matches the excellence and utility of their basketry. The lightness, strength, durability, and beauty of the baskets has insured the survival of basketry while other useful Indian crafts have been forgotten. Fragile pottery was almost totally replaced by mass-produced European ceramics, but native baskets, beautiful and serviceable, serve everywhere as both utensils and objets d'art.

The Koasati, Chitimacha, and a few Choctaw still weave. Tunica-Biloxi cane basketry has finally disappeared. For a time it seemed that the art might be entirely lost, and its continuance still depends on the survival of the cane. Robert S. Neitzel, long a student

Fig. 10
DENNIS WILSON, KOASATI, IN CANEBRAKE, ALLEN PARISH
*Photograph by Donald G. Hunter, Courtesy of the Williamson Museum, Northwestern State University,
Natchitoches*

of the arts and crafts of his Biloxi, Ofo, and Tunica neighbors, commented on the painful efforts of the older women to preserve the art they loved. They even resorted to "bad" cane, which had stems or had hybridized with bamboo. In some cases, wisteria, honeysuckle, and rattan strips were used as a filler.

Swanton felt that cane basketry reached its peak of excellence in the lower Mississippi Valley, where this invaluable art has been preserved by the Chitimacha. The women cut the cane and, while it was still green, snapped it sharply across the thigh, breaking it into four or eight strips. Each strip was then held in the teeth and peeled once or twice. The cortical strips were bundled for storing or dyeing. The Chitimacha, and probably others, made vivid red, yellow, and black dyes from various plants, particularly dock (*Rumex crispus*) and black walnut. The beautiful baskets incorporated the properties of the cane. The profound understanding of

Fig. 11
WOODEN BLOWGUN, HOUMA TRIBE
Courtesy of the Museum of Geoscience, Louisiana State University

medium demonstrated by the Chitimacha suggests that their basketry involved not only artistry but ritual as well.

Beautiful cane matting in designs much like the abstract patterns the Chitimacha call "blackbird's eyes" was unearthed at a prehistoric site dated A.D. 1050, north of Shreveport. The Choctaw basket maker Claude Medford has observed that the eyes in the bird motif of the matting found at that site, Mounds Plantation, are the simple crosses seen in contemporary Chitimachan basketry. Robert Scott, an Appalachian weaver of wool and cotton fabrics, has identified similar designs and names in southern white crafts, and suggests that they were borrowed by whites from southern Indians. The design displayed in the Mounds Plantation matting seems to support this idea, as does the fact that the bird's-eye design was used by the Indians before the white men went to Louisiana.

Recently, artists have recognized corresponding designs on Caddoan pottery vessels from northwest Louisiana. The checkerboard, or diaper-dot, design of Chitimachan basketry—called "little-trout"—similarly can be seen on the Coles Creek period ceramics of the lower Mississippi Valley, and both are dated at about A.D. 800 to 1000. In Louisiana, as around the world, it seems that basketry is an art more ancient than ceramics.

The designs and plaiting techniques varied among the tribes, all of whom made cane baskets. Caroline Dormon, probably the best-informed local student of Louisiana Indian art, reported that she could identify the plain baskets of the Chitimacha, Choctaw, Koasati, and Tunica by subtle variations in the plaiting. The most notable differences to be seen in contemporary cane baskets occur in the hem found around the rim and in the ways that the bottoms are twilled. All the single-weave basket forms are made in southeastern Oklahoma today. The excellent basket makers there are the descendants of central Louisiana Choctaw who moved to Indian Territory around 1900. The Chitimacha, especially Ada Thomas, still make the double-weave baskets. Some of these double-walled containers are so tightly fabricated that they will hold water.

Basket forms, too, were highly varied. Conical baskets, used in harvesting corn and other crops and in various other tasks, were made in two forms. One, called the elbow basket, was made in the shape of a *V*. Its many uses ranged from mixing herbs to holding wine bottles. The other was a simple heart-shaped receptacle that, in its modern form, is called a friendship basket and is frequently given as a wedding gift in southeastern Oklahoma. Once, in southeastern Louisiana, it always contained a gift. Wall-hanging baskets, sometimes called spoon baskets, were used to store items above the reach of children. These and other basic baskets, such as the fanner (for winnowing corn), egg basket, sifter, and tray, were common throughout the eastern part of the country. Chitimacha weavers made miniature baskets, as difficult to weave as larger forms, to train young weavers. Hiram Gregory and Clarence Webb used the Dormon notes of the 1930s to illustrate examples of most Chitimachan forms.

Large burden baskets, carried with tumplines of soft, tanned deerskin, were widely made and used, for the Indian had no beasts of burden other than slavès. At the time of early European contact, Indian people, particularly the Choctaw, were frequently on the move and carried most of their belongings in such containers. A single basket of this kind could sometimes hold several bushels of corn or a child.

From time to time, anthropologists have, perhaps correctly, forecast the demise of Indian culture, particularly of the arts and crafts. The Indians were quick to turn to the white man's guns, axes, iron pots, and other trade items. Indian artifacts often were made only for sale to staring strangers in a degrading sort of exchange. Women and children made trinkets and sold them on street corners, from door to door, and even in the New Orleans French market. Under these circumstances, selling baskets was a humiliating activity and was little better than begging in the minds of many Indians.

The experiences, in which both the Indian and his art were debased, are reflected in a measure of resistance in the Indian communities to efforts to preserve and perpetuate items and arts that non-Indians have come to view as both beautiful and valuable. Today, Indian craftsmen and craftswomen operate on two disparate themes: revitalization and commercialization. It would be best to advance both causes, but recently the sale of baskets, blowguns, dolls, and filé came to be a sort of "penny capitalism" for Indians. Highly developed crafts, linked to mythology and religion, and integral to the home arts of the tribes, became sources of income.

By the late nineteenth and, especially, the early twentieth century, white collectors who wanted baskets demanded concessions that Indian artisans did not want to make. Negative emotions brought conflicts to the tribal artisans. Young people, in search of identity and self-respect, began to discard their ancestral ways.

Basketry did not disappear, but the marketplace began to influence the artisans. Handles, or bails, were added to the baskets, and new forms appeared. Place mats, lunch baskets, trash cans, cigar and cigarette holders, needle cases, and sewing baskets all reflect the non-Indian interests and functions the Indians had to accommodate. By World War II, Chitimacha weavers were even placing tinfoil between the layers of double-woven cigarette cases.

Colors, too, underwent change. Aniline dyes, commercially avail-

Fig. 12
KOASATI AND CHOCTAW STYLES OF CANE BASKETRY
Photograph by H. F. Gregory, Courtesy of the Williamson Museum, Northwestern State University, Natchitoches

Fig. 13
KOASATI INDIANS MAKING CANE BASKETS, 1980
Courtesy of Don Sepulvado

able, were easier to use than plant dyes and yielded vivid reds, greens, oranges, and purples that began to replace the more subdued organic reds, yellows, and blacks of former times. The bulk of what the craftsmen and craftswomen produce is still marketed directly by its makers.

By 1900 most of the giant canebrakes were destroyed by burning, cattle grazing, and clearing. Further damage was done by logging. Today, weavers must search farther and farther afield to find cane. Negative connotations, for example, the low status assigned to artisans in the Indian community and the oppressive drudgery the women experience in selling on street corners and from door to door, along with the decline in the quality and availability of cane, have nearly obliterated what was once one of the most sophisticated arts of the Louisiana tribes.

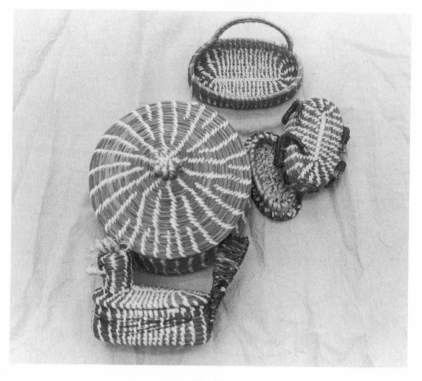

Fig. 14
TUNICA-BILOXI PINESTRAW BASKETRY
made by Ana Juneau and Rosa Pierite
Photograph by H. F. Gregory, Courtesy of the Williamson Museum, Northwestern State University, Natchitoches

PALMETTO AND OTHER BASKETS

Palmetto (*Sabal* sp.), like river cane, was widely used by the Louisiana Indians. Among the Choctaw and Houma it served as a house covering, and palmetto-thatched houses still exist in the Houma country near Golden Meadow, Montague, and Dulac, Louisiana. As an emergency measure, the Choctaw of southeastern Louisiana, and other tribes, peeled the stalk of the palmetto to secure the cortex, with which they plaited baskets. Immature palmetto fronds, bleached in the sun, were cut into thin strips, plaited into flat tubes, and sewn together with needles and thread to make baskets. The Houma made baskets using a simple checkerboard pattern,

Fig. 15
PART OF A PINESTRAW BASKET, *ca.* 1940
Courtesy of Don Sepulvado and Donald Hunter

and one specimen, collected near the city of Houma, is a square-bottomed, double-thick receptacle. Houma cypress-splint baskets are still used for carrying shrimp by both the Houma and their non-Indian neighbors. Some Houma coiled-grass baskets are of a unique style found only in Louisiana and Tierra del Fuego. Tied with palmetto, they were made as late as the 1930s but now appear only in museum collections.

A regional innovation, the weaving of pinestraw baskets, appears as one enters the hill country. The straw of the longleaf pine (*Pinus palustris*) is bundled, coiled, and sewn in place with the inner bark of dogwood or slippery elm. Some anthropologists believe that pinestraw baskets are later European imports. The Koasati, however, point to baskets coiled from wire grass (*Pahe*) and tied with elm (*Bataco*) or dogwood bark as the antecedents of their contemporary pinestraw basketry. Such baskets were also made farther east by other Muskogean speakers.

The Koasati, seeking to supplement their incomes by selling baskets, have introduced new styles sewn with commercially dyed raffia, which was introduced by home demonstration agents in the 1930s. Claude Medford reported that older Koasati said they adopted raffia after having seen it used to tie bundles of onion sets. Scrolls, zoomorphic forms, and geometric stitching echo ancient tribal art and mythology, but camels and elephants now appear along with the more traditional frog, bear, raccoon, armadillo, crayfish, duck, and turkey. Although baskets are now generally bought by non-Indians for nonutilitarian purposes, their prices are still based on size, just as if they were functional items—a tradition started with plaited-cane basketry. Baskets are still serviceable items among modern Indian communities and are used to hold everything from toys to hair rollers. It is not surprising to find that some traditional modes of behavior remain widespread in association with an item as significant in Indian culture as the basket. According to one taboo, one should never put a pinestraw basket over one's head, since to do so will cause one's hair to fall out.

Elderly Koasati Indians say that they made baskets of coiled wire grass (*Spartina* sp.) prior to the 1930s, but now the baskets are increasingly rare. Coiled-grass basketry similar to specimens found at Spiro, Oklahoma and in the dry caves of northern Arkansas may be considered part of the Louisiana Indians' store of crafts. Koasati basketry is rapidly becoming the showpiece of Louisiana Indian art. Some Koasati have joined the Chitimacha as artists, and their work is to be seen in crafts stores and museums throughout the eastern United States.

The story of basketry well demonstrates the strength and resilience of Indian culture. Basketmaking has persisted as both a functional household skill and as a commercial enterprise in a national society. Although ancient traditions have had to make some adjustments to accommodate non-Indian elements, they have never given way to tawdriness like that of much of the tourist art so widely sold. With much conscious effort, some Chitimacha, Choctaw, Tunica, and Biloxi have maintained their integrity as artists throughout more than 250 years of contact with non-Indian material cultures.

ASSORTED HANDIWORK

It is most regrettable that the Indian technique of making feather mantles and blankets has disappeared from Louisiana. The base of a feather garment was usually a net made from the roots of bull nettles, a special silk grass, mulberry-bark fibers, or, rarely, deer sinew. Sometimes a fishnet was used.

Knots utilized in this netting were of a common type, and there is no indication that a shuttle was employed. Small turkey, Carolina paroquet, swan, or duck feathers overlapped one another on both sides of the netting. The product was a garment light, warm, and beautiful. Le Page du Pratz illustrated some examples of these capes, which he saw being worn by Natchez persons of high rank. Featherwork, once widespread in the Southeast, is now seen only among the Pamunkey of Virginia, where burlap sacking has replaced netting as a garment base. Efforts to revive this work in Louisiana have been unsuccessful.

Weaving has long been a significant element of Louisiana Indian culture. The work was done on upright frames, not true looms, with suspended loose warp. Twining, plaiting, and weaving were accomplished with the fingers. Such frames were in use among the Koasati of Louisiana well into the twentieth century and may still be used occasionally. Textiles, cord, rope, nets, and, more recently,

Fig. 16
CHITIMACHA WOMEN WITH CANE MAT, "LITTLE-TROUT" DESIGN
Courtesy of the Dormon Collection, Special Collections, Eugene P. Watson Library, Northwestern State University, Natchitoches

saddle blankets were woven from twisted Indian hemp, nettle fiber, mulberry bark, and hair from the bison and opossum. Saddle blankets were also woven of cured Spanish moss. It is not known how old the weaving of moss may be among the Indians, but it probably predates white contact.

The Houma and Koasati today make small dolls of Spanish moss, with shell buttons and glass beads. While the toys are limited in distribution to these communities, it is not known if they predate European contact or were introduced for Europeans.

Gourds were made into a wide range of artifacts. They were dried, scraped thin, and boiled several times to "sweeten" them by removing the bitter taste that they imparted to anything they touched. Gourds so treated made excellent containers for water

Fig. 17
CARVING A GOURD
Courtesy of Don Sepulvado and Donald Hunter

and other liquids, since their slight porosity served to cool the fluids they held. Cups, bowls, birdhouses, rattles for musical accompaniments, and ceremonial masks worn by dancers all seem to have been made of gourds. In making these items, the gourds were polished, carved, burned, and painted to give them artistic qualities far beyond the simple requirements of utilitarian functions.

The carvers of gourds often worked in spirals, making round orifices in the containers, in accord with the religious traditions of their tribes. The mixed-blood descendants of eastern tribes who moved to Louisiana in the nineteenth century retained the habit of carving square openings in their birdhouses, a trait Frank Speck observed only among tribes in Virginia. The long-stemmed gourds seem to have provided a number of forms that became prototypes for ceramic container shapes.

Toys whittled from wood often follow traditional forms. During the 1940s, the Jena Choctaw made toy mortars and pestles, as the Houma, Koasati, and Tunica-Biloxi do today. Families of mixed blood in Catahoula and Concordia parishes once carved toy dugouts for small boys, and cruder ones are still made by the Houma as tourist art. Wooden bowls burned and scraped from tupelo gum became a standard trade item for several Choctaw groups.

Small "limber men" are made by the Houma and, rarely, by the Koasati. These seem analogous to the "limber jacks" of Anglo-American culture. The Indian figures, however, are of little men with horns on their heads; tails; ornaments made from silver coins; and beads, often painted black. They do not dance on paddles as do the limber jacks. Koasati craftsmen have said that they represent the "tailed men" of their old myths.

That Chitimacha women made miniature baskets for toys was an almost magical device insuring that girls learned to plait baskets. It seems probable that such scaled-down versions of adult-sized artifacts were traditional. Small boats, bows, and similar items were models of life-sustaining tools, and the sooner they could be made comfortable in the hands and minds of their future users, the better. The Koasati still occasionally make toys to be placed near newborn infants. These are axes and knives for boys, and pots and pans for girls, defining traditional roles early in life.

A peculiar trap made of shredded palmetto fronds attached to a wooden base is used to capture drill conchs. The traps are weighted with four or five vacant conch shells and sunk in oyster beds. The shellfish attach themselves to the traps when they come to eat oysters. The traps full of conchs are pulled up and left on shore, where the stranded conchs soon die.

Conchs were, and still are, used as dippers. In precontact times, they were especially important in rituals where the Black Drink, *La Cassine*, was taken from a common pot. Sacred conch dippers were elaborately engraved with mythic symbols. Everyone made gourd dippers, and the Koasati made medicine dippers of tortoise shells.

In coastal areas of Louisiana, as in all the states on the Gulf of Mexico, more utilitarian uses were made of conch shells. The scarcity of stone led to local adaptations; gouges, adzes, and scrapers

Fig. 18
TUNICA-BILOXI HORN SPOONS
Courtesy of Don Sepulvado

were made from shell. Even in the hill country of northern and central Louisiana, the Caddoan speakers made hoes and picks from large perforated conchs.

The common freshwater mussel (*unio*) was eaten, and its shell was perforated for hoe blades and, among the Caddoan groups, used as a spoon. Today, in Koasati and at least one Caddoan dialect, the word for shell still means "spoon." In other dialects of Caddo, the word used for spoon is synonymous with the word for "horn." Horn spoons, made originally from bison horn and later from cow horn, were important utensils. Cut from the cores, the horns were boiled, scraped, and polished into scooplike shapes. Some older ones are so thin that they are translucent. Spoons of horn were also made by the Muskogean-speaking tribes and others. They have persisted in Louisiana longer than shell spoons. The Tunica-Biloxi, Choctaw, and a few Koasati still carve and scrape out such spoons, and Choctaw along the Sabine River decorate the utensils with elaborately carved birds' heads.

STONE OBJECTS

Of all these artifacts made from natural sources, stone tools and pottery can best be traced to prehistoric times. Stone tools were of two types: the chipped, or flaked, type and the ground, polished variety. Although the stone tools were replaced rapidly by iron and steel tools after the coming of Europeans, the Louisiana tribes made excellent stone arrow points, spear points, knives, scrapers, and drills. Most were made from large pebble gravels that were obtained from numerous outcrops in the Tertiary uplands of present-day northern and southeastern Louisiana. Some areas, such as the western edge of the Kisatchie Wold, yielded special materials, among them silicified palm wood and the snow white Catahoula sandstone, both of which were traded widely in prehistoric times. The Avoyel, or people of the rocks, were said to be the source of such raw materials.

Flint from what is now central Texas and novaculite from near present-day Hot Springs, Arkansas, were traded into Louisiana for hundreds of years, providing material for large knives and spear points that could not have been made of the smaller Louisiana gravels. European firearms rapidly replaced stone, bone, and gar scale–tipped arrows and the bow. Even with this rapid transition, however, the older patterns persisted until well into the twentieth century, and the blowgun and the bow continue to be produced as home crafts and, on occasion, tourist art.

Flint knapping is a lost art. Although periodic attempts have been made to revive the ancient work, no one has equaled the beautiful fishtail points found at eighteenth-century Natchez and Bayougoula sites. Not even the neat isosceles triangles chipped by the Caddoan groups have survived.

Metal points, often ground or cut from kettles, gun parts, and other European sources, were adequate for the Indians' use and rapidly filled the functional niche of arrow points. Some were cut into simple triangles while others were wrapped into cones and attached to shafts.

To grind or polish a piece of stone into a useful tool took time, so objects made in this way are more rare than those turned out by chipping. The most common ground tool was the celt, a wedge-shaped, ungrooved axe. For use, it was set in a hardwood handle and held in place with wet rawhide wrappings or glue.

Celts ranged in size from large ones thirteen to fifteen inches in length to miniature ones probably used by children. At the time of European contact—the Mississippian-Plaquemines period, A.D. 1200 to 1400 in the lower Mississippi Valley and Glendora Focus in the Caddoan area, *circa* A.D. 1400—small celts were more common, but a few large ones were carried at dances and on ceremonial occasions. For the most part, celts were made of dark gray to black greenstone or quartzite. Greenstones were imported from present-day southern Illinois, and quartzites were found in what is today the north Louisiana uplands. The latter stones were also used for hammers, abrasives, and, in prehistoric times, for mortars. Steel axes rapidly replaced the stone forms, which were pictured by A. De Batz in his drawings of Louisiana Indians. Since his sketches date to the eighteenth century, the stone tools evidently were not given up overnight, even when the metal tools were readily available. Glass slivers replaced stone flakes as the material favored for scraping both wood and horn.

Stone pipes were part of the culture of every tribe. They were made of clay stone, siltstone, sandstone, and, more rarely, of red pipestone (catlinite) imported from present-day Minnesota or some variety of black stone. The pipes were usually elbow or effigy forms. Some were inset with plugs of kaolin, and in later times, molten lead was added in imitation of silver. Both the French and the Spanish left descriptions of the pipe rituals. The Caddo offered smoke from the pipe to the cardinal directions before their meals, and most of the tribes held the calumet ceremony for visitors. In this ritual, the stem of the sacred peace pipe was of paramount importance. It was often made of cedar or cane.

Chunkey stones, polished stone disks ranging in size from two to six inches, were rolled along the ground, and poles were cast at them for scoring. Eventually, this game, still played when the French met the Natchez and Choctaw (*chunkey* is the Choctaw word for the game), was replaced by stickball, which spread across the Gulf Coastal Plain from the Catawba, Cherokee, and Tuscarora well after white contact. Round stones were saved for throwing at wild game, and others were used in the construction of fish weirs in the north Louisiana uplands. One man told of the use of prehistoric plummets, found widely in north Louisiana, as missiles for killing squirrels and rabbits.

POTTERY AND CEREMONIAL ART

Perhaps the highest level of artistry achieved by Louisiana Indians was in their pottery. Ceramics appeared in what is now Louisiana during the Poverty Point period, from 300 to 1000 B.C., in the form of fiber-tempered, mostly plain or rocker-stamped containers. By the time of European contact, these soft, simple wares had evolved into some of the most beautiful ceramics in North America. Shell, probably soaked in salt water, was ground for temper. After white contact, metal and mass-produced wares rapidly eroded the ceramic traditions of the tribes. In Louisiana, the Chitimacha parted with their last historic vessel in the early 1900s, when the late George Williamson placed it on exhibition at the St. Louis World's Fair. It was destroyed in a fire in 1965. Only one traditional Koasati potter maintained the craft. In that tribe, herbal medicines were deemed ineffective if brewed in metal containers, and one woman continued to make the needed shell-tempered utilitarian vessels.

In the 1980s, her grandniece still makes shell-tempered pottery, the only Louisiana Indian known to do so. Organic clays are preferred, and the vessels are black, the result of a reduced atmosphere in firing. For religious and magical reasons, they are not made in the spring.

From about 1000 B.C. to the present, clay vessels have been made by coiling and scraping. Occasionally, elaborately carved or cord-decorated paddles were used along the Gulf coast to decorate pots (paddling for decorative purposes reached its peak of popularity between A.D. 800 and 1000), but away from coastal areas incising, brushing, and engraving were the most popular forms of embellishment. Kaolin, or white-clay, pigment was sometimes used on pots. Rarely, red pigment, ocher, was washed or painted on the vessels. No true glazing was known, though some pieces were apparently filled with oil or fat and differentially fired.

Making pottery by hand called for considerable time and effort, and this probably had as much to do with the Indians' quick turn to items of European make as did the newer utensils' serviceability. The clay was pounded, impurities extracted, and temper added. Grog, made of crushed potsherds, fossils, or burned shell, was often used for temper. Once tempered, the clay was rolled into long ropes that were coiled, from the bottom up, into the desired size and shape of the vessel. A mussel shell, a smooth pebble, or the hand was used to smooth the surface and to insure the weld of the coils. Some small "pinch pots" were made by squeezing a ball of clay into the form of a container.

Decoration was usually added at this stage, but the Caddoan potters often preferred to engrave the surfaces of dried vessels. The Choctaw combed on decorations in elaborate geometric patterns. Chitimacha, Tunica, and Natchez favored pots ornamented with incised motifs. Once finished, the pieces "aged." The Koasati waited several days, at least, for drying. When thoroughly dry, the vessels usually were placed tops down on a thick layer of hardwood or cedar, and fired. Pine was never used for this purpose.

Clay vessels were of a number of types, including large, coarse bowls for making salt and capacious storage jars for nuts, corn, and oil. Some of the latter were capable of holding as many as fifty pints of bear oil. Other clay utensils included cooking pots, jars, bowls, plates, pitchers, and bottles. Even drums were made of clay.

Rare effigy vessels, toy pots, and figurines are included in the inventory. Clay pipes, usually in simple elbow forms, were common. Larger, more elaborate pipes were probably intended for the calumet.

The Indian enjoyed things of beauty and spent much time in artistic work and development. Wood carving, engraving on bone or shell, and statuary were excellently done. Much of the work was of a religious nature or significance. Acolapissa charnel houses displayed carvings of doves, their wings outstretched and heads pointing down, described by the French carpenter Penicaut "as if earnestly viewing or watching over the bones of the dead." Three carvings of birds on the roof of the Taensa temple were duplicated on the holy buildings of the Natchez and the Acolapissa. The vestibule of the Houma temple held idols of birds and four carved-wood statues, painted black, white, red, and yellow—the sacred colors associated with the winds and directions. The heads and hands of the statues were decorated with little animals and snakes. Stone images, especially those of frogs, were kept in temples and were seen at the temple in the Natchez Grand Village and among the Natchitoches. The Natchez temple also contained figurines of a rattlesnake, two hand-hewn planks with many minute carvings, little stone figures, and wooden beads.

The Taensa temple was "filled with idols," the figures of men and women made of stone or baked clay. That of the Tunica had images of frogs and women. The Bayougoula structure displayed figures of birds like cocks, painted red, and representations of bears, wolves, birds, and opossums, all painted red and black. The Natchitoches temple contained similar idols portraying a frog or toad and several *insectes*. The Acolapissa temples held idols representing dragons, serpents, and varieties of frogs.

In other places there appeared copper plates that, between A.D. 1000 and 1700, evolved into complicated art forms, some decorated with man-bird dancers or long-nosed gods. Plates decorated with the latter were used as ear ornaments. The Choctaw and possibly the Natchez made ritual masks of wood, gourds, and wasps' and hornets' nests.

This elaborate ceremonial art was the termination of a long evolutionary cycle. Mississippian Period Indians all over the Southeast had participated in a pantribal development sometimes called the Southeastern Ceremonial Complex, or the Buzzard Cult. Although it has disappeared for the most part, its influence is still seen in Louisiana's Indian artifacts. For example, the colors described for the Bayougoula and Houma temples are exactly the same as those used in Chitimacha basketry. The themes in that basketry also reflect older cult motifs, among them bird's eyes, rattlesnakes, and alligator entrails. The Houma still carve little esoteric idols from cypress—kneeling men, cats, and birds. Eclectic influences notwithstanding, the Indian ideas are still present.

Traditional patterns reflect religious influences more subtly than most non-Indians realize. In making a cane basket, the weavers must count splints in order to achieve symmetry, or harmony, within the design—to make the basket, as Louisiana Indian weavers say, "work out." It should not be surprising, then, how often the counts work out to four and six, the sacred numbers of the cardinal directions, up and down. Notes on Chitimacha dyeing suggest that these numbers structured the days on which materials were soaked, dried, and processed.

The cult motifs emphasized scrolls, circles divided into quadrants, other circles, crosses (pre-Christian elements representing the four directions), eyes, hands, and arrows. Certain elements can not only be found in archaeological specimens from Louisiana Indian sites but can still be seen in the basketry of the Chitimacha and other tribes.

Before the Europeans went to Louisiana, or as old Louisiana Indians say, "before the preachers taught us to pray," the Indian world was a sacred place. The Louisiana Indian has seen that sacred place assaulted. Indian art, replete with sacred designs and even sacred techniques, has been relegated to the secular realm of household function by the non-Indians, or worse, to art for art's sake. Some crafts are no longer practiced, but numbers of tribal Indians wish to have them restored and to revitalize other aspects of their culture. Revitalization seems a most logical step. It probably will not be easy, since the arts are sometimes so strongly identified with the negative white attitudes that developed between 1900 and 1940. Nevertheless, efforts have begun.

Craft workshops, where traditional artisans teach younger tribal members, have been held by the Koasati, Clifton Choctaw, Jena

Choctaw, and Chitimacha. Some of the Choctaw, Koasati, and Chitimacha have made presentations for non-Indians. A strong interest in tradition has thus manifested itself, and tribal and individual Indian crafts have prospered.

That so many crafts have survived and are the pride not only of Louisiana Indian communities but of the whole region stands as a testimonial to the strength of Indian character and culture. It seems likely that, though many Indian people prefer wrenches to stone tools and plastic to pottery, there will always be some who cherish and persist in keeping for later generations the best of Indian material culture.

REFERENCES

The material Indian culture of the entire southeastern United States awaits detailed study and analysis. That of the Louisiana Indians has attracted a measure of attention, especially the elaborate basketry of the Chitimacha.

Swanton, John R.
1911   Indian Tribes of the Lower Mississippi Valley and Adjacent Coast of the Gulf of Mexico. *Bureau of American Ethnology Bulletin* 43:318–26, Washington, D.C.

Merwin, B. W.
1919   Basketry of the Chitimacha Indians. *Museum Journal, University of Pennsylvania* 10(1):29–34.

Dormon, Caroline
1931   The Last of the Chitimacha Basketmakers. *Holland's Magazine* (Oct.):13–14.

Kniffen, Fred B.
1935   The Historic Indian Tribes of Louisiana. *Louisiana Conservation Review* 4(7):5–12.

Gregory, Hiram F., and Clarence H. Webb
1975   Chitimacha Basketry. *Louisiana Archaeology* 2:23–38.

Of all Louisiana Indian crafts and art, basketry, especially that kind called river-cane, or plaited, has undoubtedly received the most consideration.

Brandford, Joanne Segal
1982   *From the Tree Where the Bark Grows.* Peabody Museum of Archaeology and Ethnology, Harvard University, Cambridge.

Estes, James R., and Rahmana A. Thompson
1984   Cane: Its Characteristics and Identification in Baskets. In *Baske-*

try of the Southeastern United States (Marshall Gettys, ed.), Museum of the Red River, Idabel, Okla., 44–57.

Medford, Claude, Jr.
1984 Things of Cane. *Eagle Wing Press* (Fall):5, Naugatuck.

Williamson, George
1932 Utilization of Ancient Material by Primitive Man in Louisiana. *Proceedings of the Louisiana Academy of Sciences* 1(1):58–60.

Massoth, George W.
1964 Basket Making. *Louisiana Studies* 3(4):401–402.

Jacobson, Daniel
1954 Koasati Culture Change. Ph.D. dissertation, Louisiana State University.

James, George Wharton
1903 *Indian Basketry, and How to Make Indian and Other Baskets.* Boston, 15, 154–55.

Colvin, Thomas A. (Melba Colvin, ed.)
1978 *Cane and Palmetto Basketry of the Choctaws of St. Tammany Parish.* Mandeville, La.

Medford, Claude, Jr.
1967 A Choctaw Pack Basket. In *Material Culture Notes* (Norman Feder, ed.), Denver, 22–27.

Hunter, Donald
1975 Coushatta Basketry in the Rand Collection. *Florida Anthropologist* 28:27–37.

David Bushnell described the cane and palmetto basketry of the Bayou LaCombe Choctaw, as well as metallic ornaments, mortars, and other elements of their material culture.

Bushnell, David I.
1909 The Choctaw of Bayou Lacombe, St. Tammany Parish, Louisiana. *Bureau of American Ethnology Bulletin* 48, Washington, D.C.

Moreover, other authors have addressed coiled-pinestraw basketry, a recent craft in some communities but traditional to the Koasati.

Gregory, Hiram F.
1983 Pieces and Patches—A Whole from Many Parts. *Splittin' on the Grain, Louisiana Folklife* 8(1):9–11.
1981 *Passing It on and Getting It Right: North Louisiana Folk Art.* Alexandria Visual Arts Museum, Alexandria, Louisiana.

Johnson, Bobby H.
1976 *The Coushatta People.* Indian Tribal Series, Phoenix.

Cyril Billiot, a unique craftsman, has contributed to our knowledge of *gros bec* cypress-splint basketry. It is probable that the expertise of Claude Medford, Jr., is unmatched in the Southeast. His bibliography is virtually required reading on basketry.

Medford, Claude, Jr.
1984   Coushatta Baskets and Basketmakers. In *Basketry of the Southeastern United States* (Marshall Gettys, ed.), Museum of the Red River, Idabel, Okla., 51–56.
1974   The Tunica-Biloxi, Marksville, Avoyelles Parish and the Biloxi-Choctaw, Lecompte, Rapides Parish. Letter transmitted to Dr. Stanley, National Anthropological Archives, Smithsonian Institution.

Dion, Marie, Antoine Billiot, and Claude Medford, Jr.
1974   Palmetto and Spanish Moss Weaving. *American Indian Crafts and Culture* 8(2):14–17.

A revealing discussion of crafts in an isolated Indian group is available.

Miller, Shari, and Miriam Rich
1983   Folk Art in the Clifton Community. *Louisiana Folklife* 8(1):12–18.

Frank Speck's reports on blowguns and gourds are directly related to Louisiana crafts and their production.

Speck, Frank G.
1938   The Cane Blowgun in Catawba and Southeastern Ethnology. *American Anthropologist* 40(2):198–204.
1941   *Gourds of the Southeastern Indians.* Boston.

The palmetto weaving and solid wood, or marsh-alder, blowguns of the Houma await detailed description and are discussed here primarily on the basis of field notes, photographs, and specimens collected by Claude Medford, Jr., and Janel Curry-Roper in the 1970s. Antoine Billiot and his sister, Marie Dean, of Dulac have been particularly helpful. Roy Parfait, director of the Houma crafts group, helped collect and document a wide range of Houma crafts.

James A. Ford's classic study is probably the best overview of historic Indian ceramics of the Louisiana tribes.

Ford, James A.
1936   An Analysis of Indian Village Site Collections from Louisiana and Mississippi. *Anthropological Study* 2, Louisiana Geological Survey, Department of Conservation, New Orleans.

Ford defined Caddo, Choctaw, Natchez, and Tunica ceramic variation. His initial "marker types" remain valid, even to the ethnic groups to which he ascribed them. Claude Medford, Jr., has provided an account of contemporary Koasati pottery, especially that of Lorena Langley.

M. R. Harrington's 1908 visit to Louisiana left excellent photographs of material culture: Houma, Chitimacha, and Koasati-Alabama materials are included. The collection is available at the Heye Foundation, Museum of the American Indian, in New York. Other extensive collections of Louisiana Indian material culture were made by Harrington and Frank Speck and are now in the Denver Art Museum. The Peabody Museum of Archaeology and Ethnology at Harvard, the Williamson Museum of Northwestern State University, the Museum of Geoscience at Louisiana State University in Baton Rouge, and the Louisiana State Museum at the Cabildo, in New Orleans, all have large collections of material culture that are on exhibit or otherwise available to serious researchers. These holdings represent virtually all the tribes and cover at least a half-century of collected materials.

X

DRESS AND PERSONAL ADORNMENT

The human body is a frail thing at best, and people almost everywhere have sought to protect it with coverings of many kinds. The human ego is also fragile. To prop up his sagging self-image, man has often resorted to tiresome, costly, and even painful modes of personal ornamentation. The American Indians felt the need to enhance their feelings of self-worth, and among the tribes modes of dress and decoration were often highly significant, touching on matters of religion, politics, art, social status, and others. The study of dress and adornment is of great value in coming to understand aboriginal people and to know something of their achievements.

The manufacture and wearing of true tailored clothing, of materials cut and sewn together to fit the individual, is of comparatively recent emergence as a worldwide trait. It originated somewhere among the skin-using people of northern Asia and spread slowly to other areas. In the pre-Columbian Americas, tailored hide clothing was restricted to the Eskimo and a few of the northernmost Indian tribes. The culture trait of making and using semitailored clothing extended southward across the plains like a wedge thrusting into Texas. Only after the advent of the horse did semitailored skin clothing marginally intrude into Louisiana, reaching the Caddo of the northwestern part of the present state. Elsewhere in Louisiana, as in most of the Southeast, the people lacked tailored clothing, even though hides in quantity were at hand and provided the principal material for such garments as were worn.

The single item of apparel worn by many Indian men of Louisiana was the yard-long buckskin breechcloth, which passed between the legs and was held in place by a waist belt, usually made of woven bison hair. The ends of the cloth were passed over and under the belt so as to hang down in both front and rear, giving the appearance of aprons. Much of the time males wore no other garment. In cool weather and on special occasions, they draped the upper body with fur robes, feather mantles, or covers woven of the inner bark of the mulberry tree. Such coverings usually were worn over the left shoulder, leaving the right arm free.

When traveling, men wore full-length buckskin leggings resembling the cutoff legs of trousers but sewed some six inches from the edges, supported by the belt and garters below the knee. Moccasins were generally worn with the leggings. These were footgear made of a single piece of deer, bear, or bison hide, rather crudely shaped by a seam running on the top lengthwise from the top of the foot to the toe, puckered around the toe for better fit, and another seam up the back. The upper portion of the moccasin consisted of high flaps that were wrapped and tied about the leggings at the ankle. A crude shirt was sometimes worn, made of two dressed but untailored deer hides sewn together, face to face; it may have been pre-Columbian and certainly was rare.

Women wore a simple wraparound skirt that extended from waist to knee. It might have been of buckskin, bison hair, or the pounded inner bark of the mulberry tree, and most of the time it was their only garment. On occasion, they wore robes of woven cloth, bark, or fur, or they wore feather mantles like those of the men. Women's leggings were only half-length and were fastened by a garter, commonly of hair, worn just below the knee. Women wore moccasins even less than men did. Where leggings were generally absent, women's skirts were longer and their moccasins higher. Indian dress was far from uniform, and variations occurred from tribe to tribe, even within Louisiana. Caddo women, true to the Caddos' usual divergence from other Louisiana tribes, wore a poncholike garment of dressed skin draped over the shoulders with the wearer's head projecting through a slit in the middle.

Children dressed simply before reaching puberty. Among the Natchez, infants were adorned with strips of fur at their knees and ankles until one year old. Otherwise, their children went naked until the girls were eight to ten years old and the boys twelve to thirteen. Between then and puberty, when adult behavior was as-

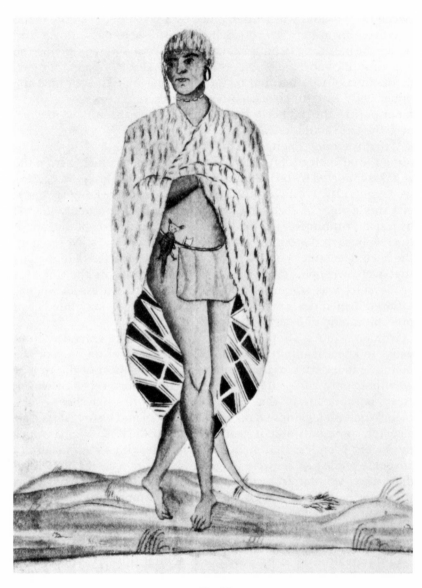

Fig. 19
EIGHTEENTH-CENTURY INDIAN IN WINTER ATTIRE
sketch by A. De Batz
National Anthropological Archives, Smithsonian Institution

sumed, there were tentative provisions for modesty, the girls wearing strings about their waists from which white shell beads dangled and boys covering themselves with breechclouts on some occasions.

Neither sex normally wore any distinctive form of headgear, though special offices and events called for different modes of head decoration. Old illustrations frequently portray Indian men wearing turbanlike headdresses. Prominent men, on occasion, wore silver headbands connected with netting so that similarity to a turban was even greater. The direct antecedents of the silver "crowns" may have been the crowns of feathers, higher in front than on the sides and displaying tufts of hair and a line of "fuzzies," or down feathers, described among the Natchez. After 1740, silver headbands were wrought from European coins, some of them highly ornate and identifying a chief. Many Indians made their own circlets by hammering silver coins together.

Prior to white contact, the Indians made thread of deer sinew split and chewed soft. Using a deer femur needle, the seamstresses hand-stitched beautiful clothes. Indian people were quick to adopt and adapt to their own uses the new materials and items of clothing made available by the Europeans. The result usually was a conglomerate of Indian and non-Indian items of apparel that considerably altered the wearer's appearance but left him unmistakably Indian.

Cloaks and other semitailored upper-body coverings for males were replaced by long, fringed buckskin hunting coats, of a style probably carried westward by the Creek, Cherokee, Delaware, and others. Solomon Northup, a black slave, described the long tailored and fringed coats worn by the men as being common before the Civil War. Shirts, pantaloons, buckles, and ribbons were affected by Indian men, betraying the influences of their European counterparts. Silver brooches, large crescent-shaped gorgets, bracelets, and headbands were used for decoration. Moccasins never were replaced by shoes, but it was color and coordination, not form, that distinguished Indian attire from European. For example, the early Europeans often borrowed the Indian's footwear.

Women's clothing changed too, as brightly colored fabrics and blankets began to replace deerskin and bark cloth. Patriotic ribbons had fallen from the favor of Europeans during the French

Fig. 20
SESOSTERIE YUCHIGANT, TUNICA, IN CEREMONIAL DANCE COSTUME, 1935
Photograph by Mary Haas, Courtesy of the Dormon Collection, Special Collections, Eugene P. Watson Library, Northwestern State University, Natchitoches

Fig. 21
EMIL JOHN, A BAYOU LACOMBE CHOCTAW, IN TRADITIONAL DRESS, 1909
National Anthropological Archives, Smithsonian Institution

Revolution, but Frenchmen entering the new trading areas among the Indians found the colored strips to be in great demand, especially to be worn with silver combs. "Moons," silver copies of ancient shell brooches and of European, especially Scotch-Irish forms, were pinned to ribbons or blouses. Moons often perpetuated

Fig. 22
TUNICA-BILOXI DOLLS DRESSED IN NINETEENTH-CENTURY STYLE
made by Ana Juneau
Courtesy of H. F. Gregory

circles divided into quadrants and other elements inherited from early times. Ankle-length skirts and long-sleeved blouses decorated with the silver moons gradually gained popularity. Although much like the severe styles worn by nineteenth-century European women, these clothes differed in color and ornamentation. Elaborate finger-woven sashes, descendants of those once made of bison hair, brightened the colorful clothes still further for dances and other special occasions.

Indian dress eventually became conservative. The topless, miniskirted ladies so attractive to eighteenth-century "woods runners"—traders and trappers—became the gentle maidens of the nineteenth-century Protestant ministers. Attire typical of the late eighteenth century was worn by Louisiana Indians as late as the 1850s and 1860s. M. R. Harrington found excellent examples of this pantribal expression still in use among the Alabama and Koasati he photographed early in the twentieth century. Both men and women continued to wear silver jewelry and sashes, or baldrics, showing elaborately beaded scrollwork. The Caddo are pictured in similar dress.

Among the Louisiana Indians, head hair was given careful attention since it had much meaning, both tribally and sexually. Body hair received more summary treatment. People of both sexes simply removed it entirely using tweezers made of clam shells.

Women wore their hair long except when in mourning. Natchez women sometimes cut bangs and worked the balance into a queue ornamented with strings of beads. Bayougoula women wrapped their hair around their heads, while plaits and tresses were fashionable among the Chitimacha. Caddo women parted their hair and fastened it behind the head, adding a special touch by putting in bear grease, a fashion not copied by the Mississippi tribes.

Even greater variety in hairdressing was found among men. Males among the Chitimacha, Choctaw, Houma, and Tunica usually left their hair uncut. Caddo men cut all but a few tresses, which were tied to or rolled around a small piece of wood worn at the side. All of them retained a little tuft of hair on top of the head, "like Turks," accoring to French sources. The Bayougoula males left a few tufts on top of the head and fastened feathers to them.

The Natchez, distinctive in so many ways, cut their hair around, forming a crown, "like the Capuchins." They left enough hair long to form a little tress hanging over the left ear, and in the middle of the crown, they retained a few long hairs for the attachment of feathers. Natchez males removed excess head hair by singeing it off with hot coals, a treatment probably administered with considerable care.

As if motivated by their scanty clothing, the Indians carried body ornamentation of various kinds to a high point. Conch shells were available only from distant sources along the Gulf coast but were widely used for personal adornment. Strangely enough, the shells were much neglected in the early literature dealing with the region. Archaeological evidence and meager accounts of the Natchez and Caddo indicate that the use of conch shells spread at least as far inland as the Great Lakes and the central Great Plains, possibly as articles in trade from the coastal tribes. These conchs were carefully curated and widely traded. Engraved with mythic animal and human motifs, such as winged serpents, half-men, dancing animals, eagles, and woodpeckers, they approached high levels of artistic achievement.

Buttons and long beads were ground and polished from the walls and columellae of the marine conch. Grinding and polishing was also employed to fashion a nail-shaped ornament to be worn in women's perforated earlobes. Among the Caddo, this ornament was pushed through a hole in the nasal septum or, as among the Bayougoula, thrust completely through the fleshy part of the nose. In later times, the Caddo wore a small, silver nose ornament, and the Plains Indian sign for *Caddo* was "pierced nose."

The Natchez made gorgets, which were ground-out oval or round pieces of the conch shell that were perforated and worn around the neck. The Caddo, like the Natchez, made magnificent gorgets. Pearls taken from Red and Pearl river mussels were perforated and strung as beads, as were crinoid stems and fish vertebrae. Copper beads from distant Lake Michigan were less common. Beads and other ornaments were worn for personal embellishment in necklaces, bracelets, armbands, and rings, and as ear and nose plugs. They were widely employed to decorate various articles of clothing such as garters and belts. They could also be found on skins and in strings used as media of exchange.

The introduction of European trade beads transformed Indian dress. Available to the Indians by the early 1700s, these colorful beads greatly broadened the limits of their already elaborate dress and ornamentation. Even drab moccasins took on a new look as aboriginal ornaments were supplanted by beaded woven sashes and similar decorative attire.

Nearly all the tribes seized upon the silver coins of the Europeans for the manufacture of unique silver jewelry. The native craftsmen competed with the traders for the dispersal of the moons, gorgets, bracelets, head- and hatbands, and other items of silver hammered cold and polished with ocher. One line of an old Tunica song told of their popularity—Tali hata pisa achokma, or "White rock, or silver, looks good." Even today, older Indians say of the full moon, "It has its silver on."

Indian modes of dress left much skin exposed, and it received its share of attention. Both sexes among the Caddo and the tribes along the Mississippi River used body paint. Preparation for war, ball games, and mourning, as well as social and economic standing, called for the application of pigments to the skin. Among males, a painted body was indicative of status or the advent of some special occasion.

Red, obtained from ocherous earth found in the White Bluffs near Natchez and in other places, was the most common paint color. Black, signifying mourning, was much used; blue was perhaps less used. White, yellow, and red pigments were derived from deposits in the bluffs marking the eastern wall of the Mississippi Valley, and blue and black were taken from organic sources. All of these colors could be produced organically when source earths were not available. Faces were often painted red or black, and designs were painted on the arms or torso.

The tattooing of the bodies of both sexes was almost universal among the Louisiana tribes. Like some other embellishments, this sort of body ornamentation was decorative and at the same time proclaimed the achievements and status of the wearer. The best accounts of the practice involve the Natchez, one of whose great war chiefs was named, appropriately enough, *Serpent Piqué*, or "Tattooed Serpent." Designs were traced on the skin with charcoal; then the pigments were pricked in with bone or thorn needles or, perhaps, a battery of needles set in wood. Tattoos on the arms, legs, face, and thighs carried no special significance, but representations of the sun, serpents, war clubs, and hieroglyphic signs on the torso were marks of special distinction reserved for those who had performed heroic deeds or were of high social rank.

Styles of tattooing differed somewhat between the sexes. All Natchez women were tattooed in their youth, some with a line across the highest part of the nose, some with a vertical line down the chin, and others in different places. Tunica women were sometimes tattooed over the entire upper body, even the breasts. Young males were tattooed on the nose, but not elsewhere until the right to wear distinguishing marks was earned by warlike deeds. Caddo of both sexes were elaborately tattooed with realistic designs of animals and flowers. Some Caddo women were tattooed from forehead to chin, with triangles at the corners of their eyes and even all over the lips. Mouths and lips were also tattooed among the Biloxi and Pascagoula. These people were often referred to as the "Blue Mouths," and as late as the early 1900s, their descendants were still said to have tattooed mouths.

The careful, deliberate shaping of the head was a general practice among the lower Mississippi River tribes. Although it seems to have had only one purpose, that of producing a cosmetic effect deemed highly desirable, it also reflected credit upon the mother who carried it out. The painful process of head deformation had to be accomplished in childhood while the bones were still plastic. The back of the infant's head rested on a little moss-filled pillow held in place by two deerskin bands over the forehead. Pressure was exerted until the infant turned black, and then was eased for a period of recovery. The treatment evidently continued until the child was nine or ten years of age.

William Bartram noted that all Choctaw males had flattened heads. Not all members of all Louisiana tribes were so deformed, though the practice extended to both sexes. Among the Caddo, the custom prevailed in late prehistoric and early historic times but was later abandoned. Tunica and Biloxi still mold an infant's head, massaging it with warm oil "to make it round."

Some modes of body adornment were of less significance. An example was the custom of Bayougoula and Natchez women to blacken their teeth by repeated applications of tobacco and wood ash or with an unidentified herb crushed in wax. This fashion was intended only to make the practitioner more attractive.

The Turkey Buzzard Men and women who performed their duties in the mortuaries of the eighteenth century were distinguished by the long nails on the thumb and first finger so essential to their work of picking decaying flesh off bones. The long nails probably were as indicative of status as they were of function.

Today, the traditional forms of Indian dress have been transformed. Indians who do beadwork are found in most communities, but the patterns they follow are usually pantribal Plains designs. The last baldrics, or beaded sashes, were made in the 1960s. Beads once were stitched singly or in groups to pieces of cloth, but now loom beadwork is most common.

Silverwork underwent a temporary renaissance among the Chitimacha and Koasati, and for a time brooches and gorgets were again popular. Now Indians are more likely to wear Puebloan or Navajo jewelry, further evidence of the new pantribalism. Only on very special occasions does the dress of the Louisiana Indians distinguish them from their non-Indian neighbors.

REFERENCES

Less has been written on the dress and adornment of Louisiana Indians than on any other aspect of their traditional culture. Swanton in 1911 and 1946 synthesized a number of seventeenth- and eighteenth-century sources on personal attire. The drawings left by A. De Batz provide graphic views of tribal people in the eighteenth century.

Bushnell, David I.
1927   Drawings of A. De Batz in Louisiana, 1713–1735. *Smithsonian Miscellaneous Collections* (35).

The French observer Jean Louis Berlandier left excellent nineteenth-century descriptions and watercolor sketches of Biloxi, Caddo, Choctaw, and other Louisiana tribes.

Ewers, John, ed.
1969   *The Indians of Texas in 1830 by Jean Louis Berlandier.* Washington, D.C.

Solomon Northup, a former slave, described the dress of the Alabama and Choctaw in what is now Rapides Parish during the antebellum period.

Northup, Solomon (Sue Eakin and Joseph Logsdon, eds.)
1968   *Seven Years a Slave.* Baton Rouge.

Excellent illustrations of late nineteenth- and early twentieth-century Choctaw clothing are to be found in:

Bushnell, David I., Jr.
1909   The Choctaw of Bayou Lacombe, St. Tammany Parish, Louisiana. *Bureau of American Ethnology Bulletin* 48, Washington, D.C.

A notable painting of a Choctaw nuclear family on the banks of Bayou

LaCombe dating from the nineteenth century provides an alternative view and has been reproduced.

Hudson, Charles
1976 *The Southeastern Indians.* Nashville.

Archaeological investigations at the Pascagoula and Tunica sites in central Louisiana have yielded further data.

Gregory, Hiram F.
1978 A Historic Tunica Burial at the Coulee des Grues Site in Avoyelles Parish, Louisiana. In *Texas Archaeology* (Kurt House, ed.), Dallas, 164.

Fieldwork among the Choctaw, Koasati, and Tunica helped flesh out these accounts. M. R. Harrington passed through Louisiana at the turn of the twentieth century. Despite the brevity of his stay, he left excellent photographs of a Koasati of that time in traditional clothing.

Pantribal dress has only recently become an important element in Indian communities in Louisiana, where Plains Indian stereotypes were introduced as early as the 1930s. The Jena Choctaw school featured above its door a painting of an Indian wearing a headdress. Although only a few people actually affected these styles, they gained popularity, like the powwows, in the 1970s, when urban Indian groups and hobbyists joined together in south Louisiana.

The best description of traditional silverwork deals with manufacture and techniques among the southeast Louisiana Choctaw.

Bremer, Cora
1907 *The Chata Indians of Lower Pearl River.* New Orleans.

Also at hand are other eminent studies of Indian silverwork.

Quimby, George I.
1958 Silver Ornaments and the Indians. *Miscellanea Paul Rivet,* Congreso Internacional de Americanistas, Mexico.

Medford, Claude, Jr.
1969 Southeastern Silverwork. *Singing Wire: Crafts and Culture of the American Indian* 3(6): 3–12.

The silverwork of the Biloxi and the Pascagoula has also been described.

Gregory, Hiram F.
1965 The Silver Crafts of the Louisiana Indians. *Louisiana Studies* 4(1): 80–82.

Gregory also reported on the silverwork found in a nineteenth-century Tunica burial at Marksville.

Gregory, Hiram F.
1978   A Historic Tunica Burial at the Coulee des Grues Site in Avoyelles
        Parish, Louisiana. In *Texas Archaeology* (Kurt House, ed.), Dal-
        las, 160–66.

Typical pieces of silverwork were described in a catalog.

Friends of the Cabildo
1966   *Louisiana Indians, 12,000 Years.* The Cabildo, New Orleans, 33.

Glass trade beads are discussed in a work by H. F. Gregory and Clarence H. Webb.

Gregory, Hiram F., and Clarence H. Webb
1965   European Trade Beads from Six Sites in Natchitoches Parish,
        Louisiana. *Florida Anthropologist* 18(3):15–44.

Jeffrey Brain has analyzed trade beads from the historic Tunica burials at
the Trudeau site in West Feliciana Parish, Louisiana.

Brain, Jeffrey
1979   *Tunica Treasure.* Peabody Museum of Archaeology and Ethnology,
        Harvard University, Cambridge.

The works cited discuss trade and chronology of the beads. Patterns and
techniques of using trade beads await discussion. A photograph of contemporary Alabama-Koasati beadwork is to be found in Jesse Burt and Robert
Ferguson's work *Indians of the Southeast: Then and Now* (Nashville).

XI

ECONOMIC ACTIVITIES

Like people of every time and place, the Indians of Louisiana have always faced the need to bring their human wants and ways of life into an effective relationship with the resources and restraints of the lands they have occupied. Unlike many people these aborigines have enjoyed the advantages of environments so rich that researchers sometimes find the exact circumstances of their association with their resource base difficult to uncover. This leads to misunderstandings.

Some have assumed, for example, that only agriculture could have sustained a thoroughly sedentary life-style such as that of most of Louisiana's prehistoric Indians. This assumption overlooks the carrying capacity of an endless supply of shellfish easily secured in the state's coastal waters. The enormous shell middens that once dotted Louisiana's shorelines were the work of Indians who collected and lived primarily on brackish-water *rangia* clams, crabs, conchs, and fish—a constantly replenished food store handy for the taking at all seasons. In addition, and probably most welcome, were great numbers of edible varieties of fish, mammals, reptiles, and birds of many kinds, both resident and migratory.

The late prehistoric introduction of hybrid corn, grown on extensive alluvial lands, seems to have led to the abandonment of coastal shell heaps, occupied since Archaic times, in favor of sites farther inland. To accept this as a possible course of events does not explain exactly why the change occurred. How, for example, might a preference for agricultural foods over shellfish evolve and how might it affect the move?

The basic economic activities of Louisiana's Indians once included farming, hunting, fishing, and the collecting of wild plants and animals. Also of importance in their economic life were the ac-

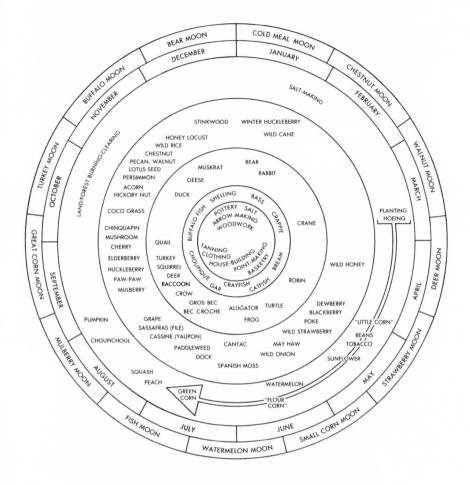

Fig. 23
ANNUAL CYCLE OF LOUISIANA INDIAN CULTURE
Courtesy of the authors and the Louisiana State University Cartographic Section

tivities associated with trade, food preparation and consumption, and the planning and accomplishment of the annual cycle of major economic pursuits.

People almost everywhere long have ordered their lives by the earth's annual cycle, and the Indians, too, devised a calendar. Months were counted by the changes of the moon, and years by the changes of the seasons. The months, or moons, were named by weather changes, the ripening of wild fruits, and other natural phenomena. Each season had its established activities in Indian life, and each sex had its prescribed duties. Women worked in the fields, collected wild fruit, and made the clothing. Among their main responsibilities men recognized hunting, fishing, engaging in sports, and making war.

With the advent of spring there were runs of fish, and fields were cleared for new crops. As the season advanced, the first wild fruits ripened, and Indians turned to communal planting. Summer brought the routine of attention to the crops, games, and the gathering of mussels and seeds. Sometimes there were the excitements of raids against enemies and the ensuing peace-making formalities. The new corn was marked everywhere by great ceremonies, the equivalent of New Year's celebrations. No one could eat corn without these most essential ceremonies, for it was a sacred plant staple and had to be respected.

The harvest festival occurred in the fall, along with the final harvest, the collecting of nuts, and the return of migratory waterfowl. Winter was a time of long hunts and journeys to distant lands for salt.

AGRICULTURE

It is probable that agriculture based on maize, various kinds of beans, and squash was the leading pursuit in the Indian economic order by the time of European contact. The harvest of one year normally did not carry over to the next, so other food sources were necessary. Perhaps, in the long run, hunting, fishing, and gathering were as significant as agriculture.

Despite the Indian's growing ability as a farmer, the older, non-agricultural skills were not lost. One large agricultural band, on the move for four years, lived well on harvests of wild plants and animals. Marginal communities occupied sites within the Mississippi River floodplain where agricultural production was curtailed by environmental factors, but where the hunting of waterfowl, fishing, and opportunities for harvesting freshwater plants like the lotus (*Nelumbo lutea*); nuts such as acorns and hickory nuts; and wild fruits, including mayhaws, blackberries, and dewberries, were extraordinarily good. There the emphasis in the economy reflected the prevailing natural conditions.

The Indians' knowledge of wild foods and the land suggests that the development of agriculture was comparatively recent and probably was not the original stimulus for a sedentary existence. This surmise finds support in certain attitudes toward the practice of the agricultural arts, especially on the part of Indian men. Agriculture, they seemed to feel, was useful when it supported their warring activities. It was convenient, for example, to carry a supply of cornmeal so that they might give undivided attention to fighting. However, farming was not always deemed a proper occupation for hunters and warriors. And, despite their fondness for green corn, the men seem to have agreed that no vegetable food had quite the toothsome appeal of bison or deer meat.

Regardless of the Indians' personal preferences, the growing of crops was a major source of sustenance, and it, more than any other factor, determined where a population of Indians would live. The requirement of deep riverine soils, reasonably free from flooding, eliminated some of the present state from consideration. The rich, well-drained natural levees of the major streams provided sites for fields and settlements. Narrow creek bottoms in uplands subject to flooding were naturally avoided, but the low-level inundations of the broad alluvial plains of the Mississippi and Red rivers were not serious impediments to aboriginal food production. The notable fertility of Louisiana's river deposits was so long lived that a site such as Jonesville in Catahoula Parish was occupied continuously from the remote prehistoric past almost until the historic arrival of the Europeans.

One may wonder why the sandy point bars of stream meanders, free of vegetation when the water receded, were not extensively cultivated. Swanton noted that the Natchez grew a crop they called *choupichoul*, a seed-bearing plant like millet, possibly cockspur grass, on sandy river bars. Recently, it was pointed out that the sandbars near New Orleans are exposed from mid-July to early February, affording ample time for a late corn crop. Deterrents include the aridity and infertility of the porous sand and the excessively high temperatures that prevail in the summer months.

The Natchez did not plant corn in the alluvial bottoms, preferring to cultivate the rich loess soils forming the blufflands east of the Mississippi. These soils were unusually thick, and Indian farming methods did them little harm. Cultivation was so shallow that little erosion occurred, and the emphasis placed on beans as a crop supplied nitrogen to the soil. The practice of planting squash, gourds, melons, and beans in the "hills" of corn virtually eliminated hoeing and weeding, and reduced erosion even further.

Even in the best of soils, however, the constant cultivation of corn, a heavy feeder, could bring about eventual soil exhaustion and could force abandonment of land. Shifting slash-and-burn, or swidden, agriculture could be discontinued if beans were planted as a major crop. Invasions by pyrophytic plants such as briars and palmettos presented further complications. In many places, occasional flooding left layers of silt to replenish the soil, and burning light coverings of ground litter every spring added potash. Otherwise, no fertilizer was added.

The natural levees of the major streams were thickly mantled with hardwood trees and cane. The latter could be readily knocked down with hickory hoes, dried, and burned; and small shrubs and grass could be dug or pulled out easily. But the great oaks, gum, magnolia, and other trees were quite a different matter. Chopping them down with a stone axe was practically impossible, so they were killed by girdling, that is, removing a belt of bark all the way around the trunk. With the foliage dead and fallen, sunlight could reach the ground and cause crops to grow. Eventually, the trunks rotted away, perhaps to be blown over by a storm wind. Rotting was sometimes encouraged by burning about the base and cutting out sprouts. The immense labor required to clear new land with primitive tools may have been one reason why lands, once cleared, were tilled for long periods and why great tracts of high agricultural potential were left unused.

Corn, beans, and squash, the great staples of historic Indian agriculture, all stemmed from domestication in Mexico, and each seems to have arrived in the Mississippi Valley independently. Squash went there long before the others and was possibly part of a presumed "pre-corn" agriculture that involved native plants: sunflowers (*Helianthus annus*); amaranth, or pigweed (*Amaranthus* sp.); goosefoot, or lamb's quarters (*Chenopodium album*); giant ragweed (*Ambrosia trifida*); marsh elder (*Iva annua*); and tobacco (*Nicotiana rustica*). With the introduction of the more productive corn and beans, most of the native plants became of minor importance, and squash joined the combination of corn and beans. Of the native plants, sunflowers and tobacco appeared most frequently as secondary crops in the gardens of historic Louisiana Indians.

Of all the edible roots, many of them heavily used, not one was cultivated. Included among the approximately 250 wild root plants utilized was the wild sweet potato (*Ipomoea pandurate*), which reached a size of twenty pounds. It may well be that, having received their major crop plants from remote sources, the Indians could not, or saw no reason to, bring wild plants under cultivation. Such cultivation would be particularly difficult if the root could not be propagated with seed, with which the Indians were familiar.

The earliest varieties of Indian corn (*Zea mays* L.) did not produce a high yield. Only with hybridization did maize produce abundantly. The effects were not felt in present-day Louisiana until late prehistoric times, when the yield of corn was so great that it produced revolutionary changes in Indian life. Not until the twentieth century has there been produced a hybrid corn yielding more abundantly than the Indian domesticates. The historic Louisiana Indians had three major varieties of corn: a tropical flint corn that went to Louisiana early, a northern or eastern flint corn, and a dent corn that probably went to the Natchez from Mexico late in historic times and was preferred by them as the base for hominy. The flint corns had hard kernels colored white, red, blue, or yellow. The dent corn had corrugated kernels that were white with pink mottling. Indian corn grew tall, one variety reaching ten feet. Early, or "little," corn, tropical flint, needed ten to twelve weeks to produce small ears of green corn. Late, or "great," corn, eastern or northern flint, took about fourteen weeks to produce larger ears of mature corn.

Beans (*Phaseolus vulgaris*) occurred in almost innumerable cultivated varieties, among them navy, red kidney, and pinto beans, both bunch and climbing. They could be allowed to mature or eaten green as string, or snap, beans. The kidney beans seem to have been especially popular, as were smaller, rounder beans commonly called "pease." Summer squash and pumpkins were early domesticates, present by 1000 B.C., and widely grown. Both were *Cucurbito pepo* and were said to have occurred in two principal forms—one described as round and the other compared with the form of a horn, surely the familiar crookneck. Related to squash was the gourd (*Lagenaria siceraria*), a minor but most useful crop. Grown about the gardens were weed plants tolerated for their usefulness, such as seed-bearing grasses and berries.

The triumvirate of corn, beans, and squash was the mainstay of Louisiana Indian agriculture except in coastal areas. According to Swanton, there is no record of the growing of beans and squash among the Chitimacha in aboriginal times. Whether this reflects a faulty record or whether corn alone was a regular crop is not clear. It has been suggested that natural conditions somehow did not favor the growth of beans and squash in their area, a conjecture difficult to follow. Among the coastal Atakapa, agriculture, if practiced at all, was of decidedly minor importance in an economy that stressed collecting and fishing and in which even the hunting of large game was of only secondary interest.

Although fields were sometimes quite large, covering scores or hundreds of unfenced acres, the cultivation of them resembled the disordered cultivation of pioneers more than modern commercial agriculture. Large fields might be divided by uncultivated strips separating family holdings. They might have deadened trees and more weeds and shrubs than normally were found in European fields. Apart from the outfields, kitchen gardens were kept at each dwelling.

Planting was done when the spring weather was favorable, beginning normally in March as soon as the danger of frost was past. The "great" corn planting took place after the ripening of wild fruits drew the birds away. Prior to this, the fields to be used were cleared of the accumulated vegetable refuse that was piled, allowed to dry, then burned. The actual preparation of the ground and planting was a community affair, the whole group of men and women aiding first one family and then another. Men were equipped with hoes, or mattocks—heavy hickory poles with one end bent to serve as a blade. The use of bison shoulder bones, fish bones, stone, and shell as blades for hoes has been reported. Women used shorter, heavy sticks sharpened at one end.

With their hoes the men broke the ground into coarse fragments. The women made shallow holes four to six feet apart with their sharp sticks. In each hole they placed several grains of corn and a few beans. As the corn grew, the beans climbed the stalks. When the roots of the corn emerged from the ground, earth was heaped around them, producing a series of hills dotting the field. In at least some of the more recent practices, hills were hoed up first, and then the planting was done. Squash and beans were planted between the hills of corn and beans, and sometimes entire fields were given to squash. Tobacco, planted only in special fields, received less attention and was relegated to marginal locations, as were gourds and other minor crops. Among some tribes, taboos forbade the planting of corn with other crops, so certain fields were reserved solely for it.

As the crops crew, there was considerable cultivation in the early stages to remove the grass and other weedy growth. At later stages, less care was taken, so that to a European the general effect of bean vines hanging on corn, mingled with squash, sunflowers, and weeds, was hopeless confusion and extremely bad husbandry. Nevertheless, the growing crops were closely observed to ward off birds, deer, rabbits, and other marauders. Guards mounted scaffolding to observe the fields and lived in nearby temporary structures, keeping watch day and night. The responsibility for protecting the growing plants was commonly left to the women and children, while the men were engaged in summer raids, hunting, fishing, and ceremonial activities.

Plantings were staggered between March and June so that the crops matured at different periods. The first to ripen was the "little" corn, which was picked in July. As with the planting, the harvest involved all the people working together as a crew to reap in turn the fields of all, carrying the corn in the large baskets made expressly for that purpose. The harvest of the "great" corn, from which was made the fine white flour, occurred in September, or even later. Some of the matured "great" corn might be left in the fields until needed, with ears broken downward and left hanging on the stalk to shed rain.

Dried corn might be taken from the field and directly stored in raised granaries, corncribs, or even dwellings, much like the modern practice with field corn. An earth silo, somewhat like a potato hill, was another method of storage. Also, the dried corn might be ground and preserved as the *pinole* of the Spaniards and the "cold meal" of the English and the French. The "great" corn of the later harvest was sometimes half-boiled and dried over a fire or in the sun. Pumpkins were commonly cut in spiral slices to be dried on a frame over a slow fire. Sun drying, probably the most common method of preservation, was applied to such items as berries, persimmons, grapes, and plums. Much of the new crop might be consumed in the feasting that accompanied the harvest, thus reducing the amount that had to be stored.

An inedible but highly useful part of the harvest comprised the bottle gourds, so useful as dippers, ladles, cups, bowls, birdhouses, rattles, and masks. Gourds possess the fortunate quality of a slight porosity, so that liquids kept in them are cooled by surface evaporation.

WILD PLANT FOODS

Few Louisiana residents today appreciate the abundance of wild plant food, excellent for human consumption, that goes practically unused. There was even more at hand prior to the alteration of the natural habitat by European settlement. The supply was so large that, combined with game and fish, it actually delayed the acceptance of agriculture as a major economic activity. The use of wild plants, animals, and fish, as practiced by early Indians of the southeast United States, has been referred to as "maximum forest efficiency." Possibly the greatest argument in favor of agriculture was that it provided a backlog of stored food, notably corn, that brought periodic freedom from the daily search for something to eat, providing opportunities for trading trips, hunting, and warfare. Even so, hickory nuts were more easily stored and were as nutritious as Indian corn.

Wild plant foods were gathered at varying times and in different amounts. Occasionally, a single wild plant was the chief source of subsistence for a time. Swanton's informant, Volsin Chiki, reported that the Tunica lived for a month each year on wild persimmons alone. In present-day Texas and possibly Louisiana, the Atakapa went inland each harvest season to live for a time on *tuna*, the fruit of the prickly pear. Such fruits required immediate drying if they were to be stored and so were largely consumed as they ripened. Among some primarily gathering people, hickory nuts, acorns, and other nuts were a chief article of diet at fall harvesttime and could be easily stored. Agricultural tribes often found wild plant harvests to be welcome tasty supplements to staple crop foods.

The list of wild plant foods eaten by the Indians is long and attests to the luxuriance and variety of usable plants in the lower Mississippi Valley. Aside from those mentioned already, there are edible roots such as groundnuts, wild sweet potatoes, *kunti* (*Smilax*), arrowhead (*Sagittaria*), Jerusalem artichokes, and wild morning glory. The useful fruits and berries included maypops, plums, grapes, mulberries, dewberries, strawberries, blackberries, and pawpaws. Nuts other than acorns included chestnuts, chinquapins, walnuts, pecans, hickory nuts, pond-lily nuts, and the beans of the honey locust. The latter were sucked to obtain a molasseslike substance. The hickory nuts were crushd in containers of water, where the heavy shells sank and the oil and meats rose to the top. The meats were ground on stone mortars, boiled into oil, and used in cooking and sometimes drunk. Frequently, the nutmeats were used to make tasty breadstuffs, as were persimmons and other fruits. Seed-bearing plants included palmetto, cane, cockspur grass, wild rice, and many others. The heart of the palmetto was used as well as the seeds. Miscellaneous plants included the wild pea, mushroom (rarely), and puffball. Unquestionably, the list should be much longer, especially if it is to include all the seed-bearing plants used by the Indians.

Harvesting equipment was primarily that used for other purposes as well—baskets, digging sticks, and paddles. Baskets in a variety of shapes caught the seeds that were beaten off the grasses with paddles. They also carried the nuts and the roots secured with digging sticks, and held the berries and other fruits not consumed on the spot. Nuts, roots, and seeds were sometimes stored in the granaries for future preparation and use. Certain chosen seeds, usually of the best fruits, were saved to be planted in places where it was thought they would grow well, thus increasing the supply and quality of even wild plants.

HUNTING

Hunting was an essential part of Indian economy. Prior to agriculture, it was the principal source of food for the interior tribes. While domesticated animals were almost unknown to the Indians, the aborigines enjoyed a relationship with their wild fellow creatures that was more intimate and more compassionate than that between Europeans and their animals. Prior to the white man's coming, the Indians viewed all life as sacred and recognized their own interdependence with animals. Indian hunters thinned out weak and sick animals and burned the forest, thus killing ticks and vermin and increasing the browse. They even planted seeds of wild plants that animals ate. The Indian believed that the animal he killed died to help him live, and he was grateful. This attitude produced and sustained the purest kind of wildlife conservation. The Choctaw even had a chief who regulated the hunting of deer. After the arrival of the Europeans, some tribes neglected agriculture in favor of hunting. It, along with warfare, was a prestigious occupation for men.

Although there was some hunting at all times of the year, there were periods in the annual cycle of activities especially devoted to the pursuit of game. The "short hunt" occurred between the planting of crops and the harvest. Significant quantities of game were not to be found near heavily populated localities, so families dispersed to more remote hunting camps after the harvest season. More specialized were the "long hunts" that required extended marches over many days, with rations limited to cold cornmeal. The distinction between the truly excellent hunters and those of lesser skill was so great that the latter usually remained behind or served the hunters in a menial capacity.

As game country was approached, hunters carefully surveyed open ground for game and enemies before entering it. They climbed trees, using them as observation posts, and hid their presence by holding branches over themselves. On other occasions, hunters entered woods or canebrakes to stir up the several kinds of game. Although there are vague reports of dogs being used to hold game at bay, details are lacking.

The animal that held the dubious honor of being the Louisiana Indian's favorite quarry was the Virginia, or white-tailed, deer

(*Odocoileus virginia*), which was numerous in most areas of the present-day state. The animal was at times tracked and killed from stands. Sometimes a hunter found a deer's bed and slept there during the night while the deer fed. At dawn, the hunter killed the deer returning to sleep.

Deer were taken primarily by still-hunting, or stalking, with occasional use of a communal surround. Still-hunting involved the use of a disguise, such as the skinned-out head and shoulders of a deer, held open by means of cane hoops. The mask was held by one hand as game was approached, often near a watering place. Appropriate sounds and the disguise enabled the hunter to get close to his quarry, a major Indian hunting skill. When the hunter was close enough, the mask was dropped, and the deer was dispatched with bow and arrow. A deer call, employed in the rutting season to bring bucks to the hunter, was also used in the spring to emulate the sounds of a fawn and entice does within range. Few hunters could surpass the tribal men who had the advantage of certain "medicines" believed to attract the deer or to make the hunter less visible.

The communal hunt, or surround, common in parts of the Southeast, is described only in connection with the Natchez, among whom it took the form of a game or sport. When a deer was sighted, a hundred or so men formed an open crescent. The fugitive deer was driven from one side to the other until it fell exhausted to the ground and was captured. The practice of simply running deer to exhaustion was notable among the Atakapa, who also employed fire to bring game into the open.

The hunter thanked the animal he killed, the Choctaw dignifying the occasion with formal prayers. Then skinning began. A sharp instrument made a start, but soon the hand, with or without a sharp flint flake or metal blade, was used to pull the skin loose from the integument holding it to the flesh. Since sharp tools sometimes punctured the skin, leaving unwelcome holes that became larger when the hide was stretched for tanning, hands were better than knives. The hide was cut along the stomach to the base of the mandible and up the tail; then the legs were ringed and cut down the middle. Removal by pulling continued, and the hide eventually came away as a whole piece with little loss of flesh.

In handling the carcass, the Indians often made cuts that followed the muscle, rather than cutting across masses of tissue. Long strips of meat resulted, especially from the deer's back and shoulders. Roasts, rib cuts, and shoulder steaks were cut much as they are by modern hunters.

Carrying the meat to the home village often required much effort to overcome the weights and distances involved and the usual absence of a trail of any kind. Whenever possible, carrying in game was the work of women, to be done by men only when hunting at a great distance and not accompanied by women. Animals were field dressed, and the meat was often dried to reduce its weight. Two rawhide straps, each two inches wide, were employed for carrying the meat container, which was often the animal's hide. One strap was passed over the forehead of the bearer and the other over his chest.

The whole deer was consumed: meat, skeleton, brain, tongue, liver, and heart. This was the traditional practice, and deer were not wasted until Indian life went under the influence of European hide traders in the 1730s. The deer's fat, marrow, brains, and sinew all had special uses. The mandible, antlers, hoofs, toes, leg bones, scapulae, and ribs were carefully kept as stock for tools and jewelry. Only the backbone seems to have had no special application, though it was chopped out for stewing. Antlers provided projectile points, harpoons, hammers, beads, and tools for making flint items. Ribs were softened by boiling, then bent into circles to be polished and worn as bracelets. Some ribs were notched to serve as rasps for musical instruments. The radius, ulna, and femur served the greatest variety of purposes. Split by one or two blows with a stone or an axe, these long bones yielded quantities of highly valued marrow. The remaining bone was made into fishhooks, gorgets, beaming tools, awls, needles, and, rarely, knives. Sickles for cutting grass were made by tying mandibles at right angles to sticks, and with both proximal and distal ends snapped, they were usable for shelling corn.

The occipital bone of the deer was pulled loose and the brains removed. Rich in protein, they were eaten or used in tanning the deer's hide. Sometimes the top of the skull, with antlers attached, was drilled so that it could be worn by a hunter trying to move into a group of deer—an ancient hunting technique in which the stalker mimics the quarry's looks and movements. According to reports, Caddoan hunters, especially the Natchitoches, were using antler and hide disguises early in the eighteenth century.

The deerskins were scraped free of meat and the hair was removed. They were then soaked in a tanning solution, often of eggs or squirrel or rabbit brains. They were finally stretched and paddled dry. The process yielded a skin as soft as chamois and easily cut and sewn into a variety of clothing and other coverings. The skins could be cut into thongs for many uses, and when smoked a golden brown color over pits of smoldering bark or corncobs, they became virtually waterproof.

Until the 1970s, Tunica-Biloxi tanners were famous for their smoke tanning of deer hides, and this ancient method is still employed by the Choctaw in LaSalle and Rapides parishes. Many non-Indians have sought to learn this procedure, but few have matched the Indians' skill. Some Indian tanners have become well known, among them George Allen and Anderson Lewis of the Jena Choctaw, the late Joseph Pierite of the Tunica-Biloxi tribe, and Jim Thompson of the Bayou Boeuf Choctaw-Biloxi. Of these, only George Allen and Anderson Lewis still tan, and they may be among the last living traditional tanners in the Southeast.

Bears were hunted extensively for their hides, meat, and especially for their grease, or oil. Some accounts of bear hunting in Louisiana relate that when female bears were found denned with their young in hollow trees, fire was tossed into the opening to drive them out. As the bears emerged, they were killed with bows and arrows. It is unlikely that the small native dogs played any part in bear hunting, but the large wolflike dogs present in the eighteenth century may have been utilized. It is also reported that the deadfall, a primitive trap with a baited trigger that dropped a crushing log, was used in taking bear.

Evidence suggests that there were no bison in Louisiana at the time of de Soto. However, when La Salle descended the Mississippi River nearly a century and a half later, he saw Indians hunting them south of New Orleans along a bayou subsequently called Terre aux Boeufs. About 1705, a party of French killed twenty-three bison near Bayou Manchac. Bison were still hunted and highly regarded for their meat and hides in the nineteenth century. They were less abundant in Louisiana than they were farther north and west, though a regularly used bison trail extended across the northwestern corner of the state. The St. Francis Basin of Arkansas and

Fig. 24
ANDERSON LEWIS, JENA CHOCTAW, TANNING A DEERSKIN
Courtesy of the Williamson Museum, Northwestern State University, Natchitoches

Missouri was the favorite hunting ground for the lower Mississippi Valley. Among the Caddo of Northwestern Louisiana, the increasing importance of bison hunting reduced their dependence on agriculture, particularly after the advent of the horse.

The few accounts of bison hunting indicate that stalking was the preferred technique. After a cautious approach, the hunter discharged his arrow. Aiming at the shoulder, he hoped to cripple the big animal and avert a charge. The flesh of bison cows was preferred to that of bulls, and the latter was said to smell bad if glands were not promptly removed. Esteemed above any plant food, the meat not immediately consumed was preserved by smoking. In this process, the meat was cut into flat pieces and placed on a grill made of forked sticks and green cane set about three feet above the ground. There it remained over a fire until the exterior was roasted and very dry.

Other animals were taken in a variety of ways. Raccoons were sometimes caught in the deadfall, and rabbits running along their trails were captured in snares that lifted the catch into the air. Beavers, otters, other small animals, and birds were snared as well as shot. Traps also included the figure-four, which may have been introduced by Europeans. Squirrels, hunted chiefly with the bow and blowgun, were largely the hunting preserve of small boys. Alligators were killed by thrusting sharpened poles down their throats, then turning them over to expose their vulnerable undersides, much like techniques now in use.

The range of animal life taken and eaten by Louisiana's Indians knew few limits. They consumed muskrats, beavers, wasps, beetles, locusts, lizards, snakes, porpoises, turtles, and terrapins. The opossum was generally excluded from their diet, but its hair was used in weaving. All groups avoided totemic animals, including those readily available as food. The Houma, for example preferred not to eat crayfish, and animals like the deer and turkey were spared by the Koasati.

Turkey calls made of wing bones and rasps were used to lure turkeys within bow range. Passenger pigeons, roosting in trees in countless numbers, were secured at night when they could be blinded with torches. The temporarily sightless birds were simply knocked off the branches of the roosts with long poles. Quail were taken in a hole dug into the ground. A slanting runway was prepared leading down to the hole, above which sticks were laid. Corn was used as bait to lure the birds into the pit. When they attempted to escape, they flew straight into the sticks. Having failed, they sat and awaited capture.

The scarcity of references to the hunting of waterfowl is quite strange in view of their great numbers and highly edible quality. It is unlikely that the large, tasty birds were ignored. From limited descriptions, it seems that ducks and geese were caught in shallow water, especially when the birds were feeding on mast. Nets were stretched across sloughs, and the ducks were frightened into them. There they were killed with arrows or dispatched with clubs by the wading hunters, who sometimes used gourds or stuffed bird skins as decoys. At times, geese were caught with the hands by patient hunters who lay motionless in the marsh until the curious birds wandered over to them for a closer look. The ibis, or *gros bec*, was taken by using a wounded bird as a decoy or by clubbing at night.

All these hunting methods were still known among Indian and part-Indian families in central Louisiana as late as the 1960s. Only the strict enforcement of game laws has prevented their continued use.

The record is scant on the domestication of wild animals by the Indians of Louisiana; midden deposits usually do not distinguish between meals and pets. Some small animals must have been tamed, and birdhouses made from gourds have been found. Evidence shows that one or more native breeds of dogs existed and that their flesh was eaten, at least on some ceremonial occasions. The large savage Irish wolfhounds that de Soto introduced to chase and destroy fleeing Indians must have interbred with native dogs, soon changing their character. Wolflike dogs were reported among the Natchez at a time long after the coming of the Spanish. A small, fat dog, much prized by de Soto's men, was bred by the Indians for food. The "Catahoula cur," Louisiana's official state dog, may have descended from these early dogs.

FISHING

Louisiana, at the time of earliest human occupance, as now, provided fish and shellfish in abundance and of excellent quality. The aboriginal could take only limited advantage of saltwater fish living at depth and away from land because he lacked equipment suitable for that type of fishing. However, tales of capturing sharks are on record, and sharks' teeth were an important item offered in trade by the Atakapa. There is some evidence of the use of small whales, but it is likely that they were limited to an occasional one or two cast ashore. The shallow, more accessible coastal waters and saline embayments yielded fish of excellent quality, such as drum, croaker, speckled trout, redfish, flounder, and mullet.

Reports state that the Natchez descended the Mississippi to its mouth to gather oysters, which were smoke-dried for preservation and were abundant in the lakes adjacent to Lake Pontchartrain to the east. There is limited archaeological evidence to support the extensive consumption of oysters. Much more demonstrates the widespread heavy use of the brackish-water *rangia* clam. The clam's popularity must have been due, at least in part, to the fact that it can easily be picked up from the bottoms of lakes and bays, while the oyster must be pried away from the reef to which it is attached. Shrimp waters extended into Lake Pontchartrain, and one species inhabited the Mississippi. *Unio* mussels occurred in the freshwater interior streams and lakes, as did crayfish, which were caught with the leg of a frog. Crabs shared their time between saline and fresh waters. Kitchen middens yield few traces of crayfish, crab, and shrimp, but there is enough reference to them to suggest that they were popular food items.

Plentiful, excellent freshwater finfish were available and could be readily preserved for storage. Among the many kinds familiar to the Indians were the gar; *choupique*, or grindle; catfish; paddlefish; sunfish; bass; eel; pike; sac-a-lait (*Sakli* in Choctaw), or white crappie; sturgeon; the sardine, or gizzard shad, which ascends streams in spring runs; and the buffalofish.

The modern Louisiana fisherman would have been at home with the aborigines, who employed almost every method now commonly utilized in catching fish. Anglers took fish with hooks and lines; rabbit-vine hoop nets; cone-shaped traps made of wooden slats, trotlines (attributed to the Acolapissa), weirs (apparently built by the Natchez), and spears used in shallow water at night by the light from torches of dried cane or fat pine. Koasati fishermen attracted the fish with ritual songs. Dynamiting and fish shocking were unknown, but the Indian counterpart, fish poisoning, was effective. This technique was usually employed in summer when the small streams were low. Poison was obtained from the horse chestnut, or buckeye (*Aesculis* sp.); the root of the devil's shoestring, or catgut (*Tephrosia virginiana*); and from green hickory nut or walnut hulls. The crushed vegetable poison was stirred into a pool, where the fish, their gills paralyzed, floated to the surface. This technique was effective only in still ponds or pools. Conditions favorable for the employment of weirs did not exist on the large streams, but they could have been built on the smaller creeks. The remains of a weir dated A.D. 1460 were discovered just north of the Louisiana state line in Mississippi in association with split-cane netting thirty to forty feet long.

In small streams, fish sometimes occurred in such numbers that pools could be dragged with bundles of brush and the fish concentrated so thickly that they could be caught and tossed ashore with the bare hands. Old people recalled another fishing practice called the *bec croche*, after the wood ibis. They simply waded in shallow ponds or sloughs to muddy the water and then picked up the fish that had been deprived of oxygen. Even inland people such as the Caddo were ardent fishermen and consumers of the catch. The surplus fish were commonly smoked and dried on a grill over a low fire, a method of preservation generally applied to all animal flesh.

PREPARATION AND CONSUMPTION OF FOOD

All the common methods of preparing food, even frying, were employed by Louisiana's Indians. The pot was the cooking utensil used, but on occasion, the Caddo, and perhaps others, boiled food in water heated in suspended deerskins, the skin actually being exposed to the flames. A separate pot was used for each article cooked; the meat pot, for example, was not used for fish. Meat was thoroughly cooked and never eaten raw. Large game was dressed out before cooking, but small animals were cooked whole, the edible portions being separated from the refuse by the diner. Boiling, broiling, frying, roasting, baking, and parching were all familiar methods of food preparation. Soups, porridges, mush, and stews, often combining a number of ingredients, were daily items of the diet.

According to one early visitor, the Natchez had no less than forty-two ways of preparing corn. Green corn was roasted before the fire or, more commonly, boiled, and so few charred kernels are found in archaeological sites. Hominy was prepared by removing the husk from the grains with ash-derived lye. Highly regarded, hominy was eaten alone or cracked in soup. Fine and coarse grits were made, as was sagamite, a porridge or gruel of boiled, husked corn and bean flour. An unfermented drink of finely ground corn in water was appreciated by Indian and European alike. Cornmeal was used as a thickener of soups and stews of meat, squash, and beans, and in a boiled mixture of mussels and oysters. Parched, smoke-dried cornmeal mixed with water was a sustaining food used especially on long journeys. Green cornstalks were sucked for their sugar content.

Bread was made in a variety of forms from several ingredients, by a number of methods. Corn, pounded and sifted to fine meal, was the prime ingredient, but persimmons, acorns, wild sweet potatoes, cane seeds, sunflower seeds, chestnuts, boiled beans, and other substances, separately or mixed with corn, were baked, fried, or boiled into balls, cakes, pones, ashcakes, fritters, dumplings, and other forms. The Caddo and Choctaw sometimes boiled bread wrapped in corn husks, a practice reminiscent of the making of tamales. The dough could be made thick, and the resulting loaves, though unleavened, were substantial. Bread accompanied most meals and apparently would last for some time without spoiling.

Condiments were used with most foods and were significant elements in the diet. Most common was bear's oil, highly esteemed even by the early Europeans who were accustomed to olive oil. In addition, there was pigeon oil derived from the immense flocks of passenger pigeons, deer suet, and acorn oil. Salt, an essential ingredient in a diet high in vegetable foods, was obtained by expeditions to salt-producing areas in the Caddo country or near the gulf, or by trade with favorably situated tribes. Nuts of all kinds and sunflower seeds were also used to impart additional flavor to vegetable diets. Some were eaten raw, while others were parched, boiled, or roasted. Live-oak acorns were especially favored, since they could be eaten without the leaching necessary with other acorns containing more tannic acid. A reddish jelly made by boiling pulverized smilax root, called *kunti* by the Creeks, may have been a sort of condiment.

Eating habits depended to a large extent on the amount of food available at a time. Great feasts, involving almost continuous eat-

Fig. 25
CHOCTAW WOMAN POUNDING CORN, BAYOU LACOMBE
National Anthropological Archives, Smithsonian Institution

ing, marked the harvest. Late winter might be a time of dwindling food supplies when meals were skimpy and far apart. There was no regular schedule of daily meals. When communal work such as planting, harvesting, or the clearing of new land was in progress, a midmorning meal might be eaten after some tasks had been accomplished and another at night after the day's labor was done. The killing of game, or a good catch of fish, might result in its immediate preparation for feasting.

As a general rule, cooked food was served in common pots from which people ate whenever they were hungry. People ate together only on special occasions, such as feasts, or when engaged in group activities of some kind. Women prepared the food in the morning; one woman might do the cooking for several families. During general feasting, as on all other occasions, men and women ate separately. Men and boys were always served first, a practice paralleled by American pioneer families.

Despite the almost constant availability of prepared food, Louisiana's Indians did not suffer from overeating. Obesity and diabetes were rare before the Europeans introduced foods high in starch and sugar. Today, diabetes is a major health problem in every Indian community.

Even by modern standards, the diet of Louisiana's pre-Columbian Indians was excellent. Although corn, for example, is deficient in amino acids, this shortcoming is readily made up by beans. These two common items, in combination with meat, fresh fruit, seafood, and a variety of other foods, provided the desired balance of nutrients. The actual consumption of food employed largely the hands and fingers. Pottery, wooden bowls, and spoons of wood and horn were used with soups and similar foods.

TRADE AND COMMUNICATIONS

The exchange of goods was an established part of the economy of Louisiana Indians. Trade helped compensate for the unequal geographic distribution of essential resources such as shell, flint, salt, and choice bowwood. In part, it effected the distribution of what might be termed luxury items, such as stone beads, conch shells, pearls, copper, and galena, all important objects of exchange at one time or another. Trade also testified to the quality of superior goods produced by the skilled artisans of various tribes. Among these were the superb baskets of the Chitimacha and pottery of the Caddo.

Raw materials moved in trade between coast and interior and between plains and uplands. The average Indian never traveled far from his home territory, but there were native traders and those unusual individuals obsessed with the desire to see distant places and people. Much trade was carried on through middlemen, so that it was not necessary for the principals to travel far to effect an exchange involving the movement of goods over great distances. The Tunica and Avoyel were professional traders of this sort. After European contact, the Tunica were able to gain much wealth and power through horses and cattle imported from Mexico and Texas.

The coastal Atakapa and Chitimacha exchanged various products for articles from the interior of Louisiana. From the Atakapa went smoked fish; Spanish moss, of limited distribution in the hills; marine curios from the beaches; bitumen; and plumage for feather cloaks. In return, often indirectly, they secured Osage orange (*Maclura pomifera*), a form of bowwood, from the Caddo area; possibly projectile points and flint blanks from the Avoyel through the Opelousa middlemen; skins of the large animals not found in their area or not easily taken by them; and pottery, which they did not make extensively themselves. Some of their flint they traded with the Karankawa of Texas for globular and conical oil jugs. The Chitimacha similarly exchanged smoked fish for stone and obtained large skins in trade for their fine baskets and other products. They sought stone beads, projectile points, and bowwood from the Caddo and other interior tribes.

Recent finds suggest that the excellent Caddoan pottery was traded at least to Tunica and Natchez groups. The Caddo received turquoise and cotton blankets from the distant Southwest in exchange for bowwood, especially the Osage orange. Salt, another important trade item from the Caddo area, was not generally available to Louisiana's Indians, making its production and distribution important aspects of their trade relationships. Interior sources were limited to several salines in Caddo territory. The Natchitoches were major salt producers who made three-pound cakes of the prized mineral. Salt-encrusted earth from nearby salines was placed in suspended baskets, and water was poured through it to leach out the salt. Then the water was evaporated by boiling in large pots. Involved in the salt trade, acting as middlemen between the producers and river tribes such as the Taensa, were the Koroa, Tunica, and Ouachita. The salt domes of the coast, mined in both prehistoric and modern times, were not used by historic Indians. They preferred to secure their salt from seawater by evaporation. There is no mention of this salt as an article of trade.

Interior Louisiana tribes exported the bills of ivory-billed woodpeckers to distant northern tribes, who traded copper ornaments. From present-day Minnesota, catlinite for pipes found its way to Louisiana. The Natchez obtained pearls from upper Pearl River. *Marginella* shells for decorative purposes were traded to tribes along the Mississippi from those on the Atlantic coast.

Europeans altered ancient trade patterns by introducing a new store of strange, desirable goods: knives, axes, iron hoes, glass beads, needles, guns, bells, metal pots, and the like. The coming of the horse also altered trade practices. Horses were of limited advantage and service in wooded areas, but where the country was more open, as in the Caddoan territory, the effect of having horses was to give less importance to agriculture and more to hunting so that, in effect, the western Caddo became a marginal plains people rather than woodland agriculturists.

Not all trading could be direct, that is, object for object, so it was necessary to have various media with an accepted value—in effect, money. For this purpose, Indians used shells, pearls, vermilion coloring, and pieces of quartz. The best-established medium of exchange was the shell bead, commonly referred to collectively as wampum among northern tribes. The shells were of several species and origins. From the sea came conchs and *Marginella* shells, attractive marine shells that seem to have been favored over freshwater shells and were used far inland. Four deerskins were equated with a large conch-shell bead, according to John Adair.

Without writing or a developed mathematics, there was nevertheless a workable system of keeping count. As elsewhere, it began with counting the fingers. Consequently, the decimal system was in use. Bundles of small sticks were used to count the lapse of days before an appointed time. As each day passed, a stick was broken and discarded. Knotted strings, somewhat like the *quipu* of Peru, and notched sticks were employed to keep count of quantities and of time. There were mnemonic belts of shell beads of different colors arranged in varying patterns with which the principal events in the tribe's history were recorded. The Natchez, for example, preserved some knowledge of forty-five to fifty Great Sun rulers and the events of their reigns.

The Chickasaw, and perhaps others, recorded trade transactions by marking on the ground a short line for each unit, then with a cross setting off each group of ten. Ball game scores were kept by setting up sticks in the ground. Tribal markings were left behind for identification when an enemy was raided. Indians drew excellent, reliable maps that served as both planning aids and travel guides.

Le Page du Pratz records examples of pictographic messages that may well have been aboriginal. Meanings were also conveyed by the use of pantomime. Indians sometimes communicated with smoke signals, and some messages could be sent by intoned whoops or cries. Perhaps these survived among rural blacks and whites in each family's distinctive shout. Mobilian Jargon was a universal communications net, giving every tribe an intertribal communications capability.

The Indians were quick to recognize the newly arrived white men and their Old World kinsmen as potential buyers of Indian products. As the Indians moved to supply these demands, they made adjustments that were both pervasive and dynamic, many giving rise to still other changes in the aboriginal system of trade, and, indeed, in life itself.

One of the first major changes was a shift to the hunting of animals, particularly deer and bison, for skins rather than for subsistence and raw materials. The aboriginal hunter who had sought his quarry only to feed and clothe himself and his family now became a killer of game on a much larger scale. By the mid-eighteenth century many tribal men had become professional hide hunters. As late as the nineteenth century, one Koasati hunter sold nearly three hundred deerskins at Natchitoches. Villages of Caddoan speakers were devoid of young and middle-aged men for weeks at a time while they hunted far out on the southern plains. Hides were shipped to France, Spain, and England for the manufacture of hats and footwear.

The French rapidly adapted old Indian trade strategies. They lived in the villages, frequently raising families there and learning the native languages. As one traveler observed of the nineteenth-century Tunica and the French, it was difficult to determine who had influenced whom more.

The rise of commercial hunting led to territorial disputes, breakdowns in cropping cycles, and a dependence upon Europeans as sources of material culture. It also attracted non-Indians to the villages, bringing with them alcoholism and disease. By the beginning of the Spanish period, about 1682, the eastern tribes had begun their far-ranging slave raids. Forbidden by Spanish law, Indian slavery was an adjunct to the hide trade in the English colonies. The Choctaw poured across the Mississippi as hunting depleted their income sources east of the river, and intertribal conflict intensified.

The Caddoan tribes, especially the Natchitoches, and the Tunica became the middlemen in a horse and cattle trade toward the west. The Natchitoches and the Adai received livestock from their linguistic kinsmen, the Hasinai, Wichita, and others in present-day Texas. In the mid-eighteenth century, Athanase de Mézières, a French diplomat, forged a peace between the Wichita and Commanche that gave Louisiana Indians greater access to horses, cattle, and Apache slaves taken from the Spanish in present-day Texas and Mexico. These new items followed the ancient salt routes leading from what is now east Texas and northwest Louisiana southeast to the Mississippi River, southward to Opelousas, and northeast to St. Genevieve and St. Louis.

By the nineteenth century, the tribes had for the most part abandoned these strategies. They moved to isolated areas—swamps and pine woods—not in demand by the expanding plantation economy of the time. Planters used Indian hunters to augment their meat supplies, to track down runaway black slaves, and to provide entertainment. Stickball games and even traditional dances were held on the plantations to amuse the planters' guests. Planters in Natchitoches Parish gave Indians barrels of whiskey to dance and amuse their friends. The performers were also rewarded with gifts of food and other objects of material culture.

Even so, in the newly developing European centers of Natchitoches, Natchez, New Orleans, Opelousas, and Monroe (Fort Miro), the Indian trade was to remain important well into the second half

Fig. 26
CHOCTAW CATTLEMAN, LASALLE PARISH, *ca.* 1920
Courtesy of the Williamson Museum, Northwestern State University, Natchitoches

of the nineteenth century. Indian men sold blowguns, smoke-tanned skins, game, and wild honey, while the women sold plaited-cane baskets, herbs, and remedies. A market in New Orleans near Bayou St. John became known as the "Indian market," and Indians sold their wares in the French market as well. In Natchez and Alexandria, Choctaw women sold baskets from street corners. Stores required their clerks to speak Mobilian, and their stocks included pipe tomahawks, glass beads, and silver ornaments.

The bands of Choctaw and other Indians were permitted to live in the backswamp or in hill areas of plantations. Creole planters became patrons of these groups and frequently attempted to protect them from Anglo-American intruders.

Eventually, after the Americans had gradually extended their political control over all of Louisiana, the Indians of the state began to accept jobs as day laborers. The men preferred work in forest locations well removed from their white bosses, with whom they did not wish to interact. These jobs gradually came to an end under the "cut out and get out" policies of the lumber companies. Some Indians, like the Choctaw-Biloxi at Indian Creek in Rapides Parish, left their homes. These men and their families followed the sawmill from nearby Woodworth to its new location at Bessmae, Texas.

Some families found themselves sharecropping, an occupation that the Indians hated and equated with slavery. Living in poverty, working long hours, suffering from exposure, and often being in close contact with non-Indians, they suffered more terribly than ever from the ravages of disease and acculturative stress. Many died of tuberculosis, smallpox, measles, and influenza. Alcoholism and interpersonal violence intensified, and the tribes, one by one, had to find new ways of coping with a situation that could only be described as tragic.

The condition of tribes in the twentieth century is better. Wage income is far more common, and sharecropping is virtually unknown among the Indians. Increasingly, government program development and higher levels of educational achievement have provided the Louisiana communities with both means and incentives for improving their economic and social conditions. A few have fared well at traditional activities, among them the Houma and Chitimacha, who are now widely known for their skill as trappers and fishermen. The Lafitte skiffs of the Houma, used everywhere

Fig. 27
HOUMA MAN GATHERING WOOD, LAFITTE SKIFF IN BACKGROUND, 1930
Courtesy of the NSU News Bureau Staff and the Dormon Collection, Special Collections, Eugene P. Watson Library,
Northwestern State University, Natchitoches

along the Gulf coast, are generally recognized as one of their contributions to Louisiana culture. The selling of Christmas trees by the Koasati is a good example of how older adaptive strategies are being integrated into contemporary economic systems.

Koasati men are employed in the oil industry—as drillers, captains of crew boats, and offshore workers. Construction work in New Orleans and Texas has drawn many Tunica-Biloxi to urban areas. Boat building, trapping, and commercial fishing provide the Houma with a wide range of occupations. The Choctaw and Koasati also work in the forest industries, as do people of the many scattered smaller communities. The work is hard, but in the summer, there is dancing, storytelling, and the softball tournaments that have replaced the traditional games. Families gather on Christian holidays and, when possible, in the seasons they prefer—summer and fall. Somehow, the old days endure and are not forgotten.

REFERENCES

Serious investigation of the past and present relationships of Louisiana's Indians to the land was set in motion in the 1930s when a young geographer, Fred B. Kniffen, began his overviews.

Kniffen, Fred B.
1935   The Historic Indian Tribes of Louisiana. *Louisiana Conservation Review* 4(7):5–12.

Influenced by the classic work of A. L. Kroeber, Kniffen intensified his efforts to collect economic data as part of his synthesis of aboriginal American adaptations.

Kniffen, Fred B.
1947   *Cultural and Natural Areas of Native North America.* Berkeley.

Still, much of this information is scattered and hard to compile. Swanton, in his works of 1911 and 1946, probably cataloged more categories of economic activities than any other single researcher.

Excellent sources on Indian manufacture and uses of salt are available.

Keslin, Richard O.
1964   Archaeological Implications on the Role of Salt as an Element of Cultural Diffusion. *Missouri Archaeologist* 26.

Phillips, Yvonne
1962   Salt Production and Trade in North Louisiana Before 1870. *Louisiana Studies* 1(2):28–46.

The plant and wild animal resources of the southwestern part of the country have been dealt with in many works. Some treatments are especially sensitive.

Brown, Clair A.
1936   The Vegetation of the Indian Mounds, Middens and Marshes in Plaquemines and St. Bernard Parishes. *Louisiana Geological Survey Bulletin* 8:407–22, Louisiana Department of Conservation, New Orleans.

Dormon, Caroline
1934   *Wild Flowers of Louisiana*. Baton Rouge.

Gagliano, Sherwood
1967   Point Bar Agriculture. *Proceedings of the 22nd Southeastern Archaeological Conference, SEAC Bulletin* 5:13–14.

Gregory, Hiram F.
1968   Maximum Forest Efficiency: Swamp and Upland Potentials. *Proceedings of the 21st Southeastern Archaeological Conference, SEAC Bulletin* 3:52–59.

Hunter, Donald
1969   Koasati Uses of Wild Plants. Paper in Anthropology 311, Northwestern State University, Natchitoches.

Speck, Frank G.
1941   *Gourds of the Southeastern Indians*. Boston.
1941   A List of Plant Curatives Obtained from Houma Indians in Louisiana. *Primitive Man* 14(4):49–73.
1946   Molluscan Food Items of the Houma Indians. *Nautilus* 60(1):34.

Taylor, Lyda Averill
1940   *Plants Used as Curatives by Certain Southeastern Tribes*. Cambridge, Mass.

Some of this information was obtained by field observation among the Choctaw, Koasati, and Tunica-Biloxi. Fred Kniffen worked with the Koasati, particularly with their late chief Mark Robbins and with Jackson Langley. More recently, Hiram Gregory has continued to study Koasati culture. Virtually that entire community has been involved, and special thanks are due Bel Abbey, Nora Abbey, Joe Langley, Bertney Langley, Ruth and Jimmie Poncho, Ernest Sickey, and Sam and Marie Thompson, among others.

Kniffen worked with the Tunica chief Sesosterie Yuchigant, or Sam Young. Gregory later pursued the study with Earl Barbry, Sam Barbry, Clementine Broussard, Harry Broussard, Florence Jackson, Ana Juneau, Norma Kwajo, Horace Pierite, Joseph A. Pierite, Sr., Merlan Pierite, Rosa Jackson Pierite, Rosa Pierite White, and others.

Deerskins tanned in the traditional way can now be found only in Louisiana. The best descriptions of that craft appear in rather diverse sources.

Medford, Claude, Jr.
1971   Southeast Buckskin Making, 1971. *American Indian Crafts and Culture* 5(6):8–9.

Gregory, Hiram F.
1982   Hide Tanning: Jena Choctaw, La Salle Parish. Field notes, Jean Lafitte National Park, New Orleans.

Swanton, John R.
1946   (rpr. 1979) The Indians of the Southeastern United States. *Bureau of American Ethnology Bulletin* 137, Washington, D.C.

Burt, Jesse, and Robert Ferguson
1981   *Indians of the Southeast: Then and Now.* Nashville, 254.

The most detailed reports on Louisiana tanning were those of Robert S. Neitzel to Frank Speck, now in the collections of the American Philosophical Society in Philadelphia. They describe the techniques and tools of the famed Tunica-Biloxi tanner and craftsman Joseph Alcide Pierite.

Gregory, Hiram F.
1982   Indians and Wood. *Forests and People* (Spring):15–20.

Mrs. U. B. Evans of Ferriday, Louisiana, and the Late Caroline Dormon taught Gregory much about Louisiana plants and ecology. Further work in the swamps of Catahoula, LaSalle, and Rapides parishes under the keen guidance of the late Emerick Sanson and Gilbert Sanson, with Louis Wiley and William Hampton, has added insights into the wealth and complexity of the aboriginal and early European adaptive strategies.

These people related freely their knowledge of traditional and nontraditional farming and herding techniques, and spent hours discussing hunting and gathering. The worth of their contributions cannot be measured in conventional terms.

XII

TRIBAL LAW

Justice was a powerful factor in the lives of American Indians. The aborigines had no written legal codes, but long ago, they formulated definite ideas of right and wrong, and prescribed punishments suited to specific offenses. As in modern society, class distinctions prevailed to the extent that people of the upper classes were less frequently and less harshly punished than were those of inferior ranks found guilty of the same crimes. Among the more rigidly stratified societies such as the Natchez, persons of high standing who committed serious crimes often went unpunished, having the right to offer the lives of lower-ranking relatives in their stead.

Common to all tribes of the Southeast was an abhorrence of rape, incest, murder, and witchcraft. These were major crimes, most often punishable by death. Among the Choctaw, as among most tribes, the ancient *Lex Talionis*, the law of retaliation, prevailed: "An eye for an eye and a tooth for a tooth." So strong was the requirement for retribution that it sometimes set war parties on the march. A murderer might be sentenced to a whipping, but this was carried out with such vigor that the person punished rarely returned to good health. Although some aggrieved families agreed to accept compensation in the form of goods, death was usually considered the only proper punishment for a murderer.

Charges of murder and other capital crimes were brought by the family of the injured party and were heard by chiefs, medicine people, or both, who rendered judgment on the case. Tribal law (custom) was sacred; few believed that they could foil the system, and attempts to escape punishment were rare. Wherever the Choctaw lived, instances were recorded in which individuals condemned to death by kin groups and summoned by their chiefs reported voluntarily for their executions. In Louisiana, Rapides Parish plantation owners noted such behavior at the beginning of the nineteenth century. The person condemned to die surrendered rather than stain the honor of the family. Executions were carried out by members of the guilty person's family in the presence of the offended party. Oral histories recall the "blood for blood" law along Red River. It probably applied among the Biloxi and Pascagoula.

Witchcraft was a most serious offense, since it was believed to result in death or misfortune. Medicine men could diagnose witchcraft and were able to identify the witch. When a victim had been recognized, counter medicines were administered and the witch was confronted. If the clan, or family group, judged the charges valid and proven, the witch was executed. The execution was not a simple matter, since the magic involved might preclude the death of the witch. He or she might be put to death only to return to life or become a malevolent ghost. Sometimes the body of a witch was buried face down or dismembered and scattered in an effort to restrain the witch's powers. Both witches and screech owls (*kitini* in Choctaw), whose form they were thought to take, could be killed with menstrual blood.

Persons judged guilty of other serious crimes were severely punished. A thief, for example, was likely to be chastened by his extended family, since the act discredited the entire kin group. In most cases, the offender was beaten and the stolen items returned, and in more extreme instances the punishment might include expulsion from the tribal area. The death penalty might even be exacted for repeated theft. Sometimes the ears of a thief were cut off, even in the case of a first offense.

Adultery was a grave misdeed to all Indians, but the penalty exacted varied from tribe to tribe. Often women were chastised more severely than men guilty of the same transgression. Punishment might include beating, the cropping of ears, and the public branding of the woman as a prostitute. The Choctaw often allowed an unfaithful wife to submit to any man on demand, in a public place, and then she was left to become a mistress or a prostitute but never a wife. Sometimes she and her lover were driven away from the community. Among the class-conscious Natchez, an adulteress of higher rank than her husband might escape punishment entirely. Homosexuality went unpunished.

Offenses of a minor nature were punished less severely than major crimes. For example, persons assigned to building houses, both men and women, who were late for work or who otherwise failed to do their part were switched by the project supervisor. Indians, in general, were patient with their children, and punishments for failures to observe the rules were mild. Natchez parents were especially indulgent, and so was the old-man tutor assigned to the boys. Children were not beaten but threatened with the dire fate of banishment.

In sum, among the aborigines of Louisiana, criminal acts were not tolerated and were likely to incur heavy penalties. Beating, banishment, public humiliation, death, and economic restitution were sentences imposed by all the tribes. Particularly notable is the powerful influence on the behavior of Indian people exerted by their desire to protect the reputation of the family through strict adherence to traditional standards of conduct.

A major class of property among the Indians was tribal land, which was largely given over to hunting and which belonged to the tribe as a whole. No individual had a recognized claim to any area or to any species of game. Nominal tribal claims extended even to moderately distant hunting grounds, and chiefs threatened the trespassers who entered their claims. Control over hunting grounds was demonstrated when the Choctaw farmers ceded agricultural lands to the Chickasaw, and again when Caddo chiefs allowed tribesmen from east of the Mississippi River to hunt in Red River country. Jean Penicaut said that the Red Stick, a great cypress tree on the river bluff at present-day Baton Rouge, was the marker defining Houma and Bayougoula hunting territories, though the villages of the two tribes were sixty miles apart. If the Red Stick did serve that purpose, it was unique among the Indians as the marker of a definite boundary.

Maps showing the distribution of tribal properties neatly separate them with continuous lines, which are likely to be viewed today as inviolable boundaries. At times they may have been, but in most cases they were somewhat fictional lines of convenience, perhaps drawn through uninhabited, unused, and untraveled country.

Frequent excursions by the villagers well beyond their clearings were necessary and led the Indians to have little consideration for boundary markings as Europeans knew them. The collecting of seeds, nuts, berries, and fruits drew the gatherers far afield, but they remained largely within hailing distance of the village center. Fishing and trapping grounds used frequently and hunting areas contiguous to the margins of tribal farms were unquestionably tribal properties, and any violation by other tribes could lead to conflict.

Territorial claims and the vigor with which they were defended varied according to the use of the land. Of primary order were village or town lands cleared for agriculture, and any aggressive move against them prompted a fierce reaction. Today, the ancient territorial disputes most often are forgotten and replaced by tribal land claims filed against the federal government.

Like Europeans, Indians had definite practices with respect to property ownership and channels of inheritance. A distinction existed between real estate and chattel property on one hand, and incorporeal property, such as songs, dances, curing rites, and clan crests, on the other.

The ownership of agricultural land was rather clearly defined. Some fields were held by important chiefs and were cultivated by all the people of lesser rank, even males. Other fields, held by the town for its inhabitants, were assigned to families and worked by them, especially the women. To the extent that these lands were held by family groups, inheritance was reckoned through the female line, as with other kinds of property. In some cases land went from father to son. If the latter left the land idle for two years or if he died without issue, the land reverted to the village and was redistributed.

Dwellings went with the land on which they stood and also were inherited in the female line. However, in much of eastern central Louisiana, dwellings were destroyed, or at least dismantled and moved, upon the death of an occupant. Moving the substantial winter houses of the area was a considerable task. Even so, the practice was long maintained. As late as 1900, the Tunica still tore down frame homes and gave away the lumber.

Movable property was inherited through the female line. A man's chattels went to his sister's son, while his own son inherited from his father's sister's husband. This matrilineal mode of inheritance applied to tools, weapons, and ephemeral items such as clan symbols, privately owned songs, dances, and curing rites.

Another class of property, human slaves, existed in pre-Columbian time, but its place in Indian society remains uncertain. It appears that slavery did not actually exist as a formalized institution and that slaves were relatively few in number. After the appearance of the Europeans, more Indians were involved in slavery—sometimes as masters, but more often as slaves. Most Indian slaves in Louisiana were set free under Spanish rule in the 1790s. Only the Natchez were required to purchase their freedom from their owners—a penalty imposed as punishment for their 1729 massacre of Europeans at Fort Rosalie. French parties descending the Mississippi River late in the eighteenth century encountered individual slaves who performed menial tasks but normally were well treated. However, at the will of the owner, slaves might be given away, traded, or even put to death.

REFERENCES

The brevity of this discussion of the Indians' code of conduct reflects the lack of systematically derived information on the subject, and the information gap is a serious one. Ethnohistorical and ethnological sources are unequal in coverage and, in many cases, rather openly biased. European observers simply commented on those practices that mirrored concepts already familiar to them, such as the autonomy of chiefs, and on those that strongly contrasted. Indians, they felt, had customs, or "justice," and leadership, not polity.

Early documents, such as the *Papeles Procedentes de Cuba*, have been a major source of information relevant to this discussion, as have primarily archival and field-interview data gathered over the last fifty years. The material on witchcraft is taken entirely from fieldwork among five tribal communities. The numerous works of John R. Swanton have yielded much knowledge. His work on the Choctaw provides insights into the "tooth for a tooth" rule. Unpublished documents in the National Anthropological Archives at the Smithsonian Institution, the Library of Congress, and archives at Louisiana State University, Loyola University, Northwestern State University, and the University of Southwestern Louisiana attest to the strength and longevity of many of the customs described herein.

XIII

KINSHIP AND POLITICAL
ORGANIZATION

Kinship, at the time of initial contact between whites and Indians, was the most pervasive force touching Indian life in Louisiana. The kin group and its extension guided much of the Indians' behaviour, determining whom they married, whom they fought, and where they worked.

Prior to and after European contact, the tribes lived according to five different kinship systems. The first was the nuclear patrilineal family, composed of a man, his wife, and their children. The second, the egalitarian matriclan, was a clan system. A clan was an exogamous (people married outside it), unilateral kinship group made up of many families. The Koasati, Alabama, and Choctaw lived in clans. In the third system, ranked families—extended exogamous kin groups, perhaps clans—had more power and status than others. Chiefs emerged only from specific kin groups. The ranked clan system characterized the Caddo and Tunica. The fourth system was a segmentary lineage with social mobility by marriage. Such a society composed of hereditarily ranked exogamous social classes was the Natchez. Finally, there was a true endogamous caste system (people had to marry within their rank) in which there was no social movement, as among the Chitimacha. It has been suggested that at least some elements of these social structures relate to a single basic system, possibly the true caste, which had prevailed for a time but was evolving into more egalitarian structures.

The exact place of origin of the formal chiefdoms encountered throughout the Gulf Coastal Plain by the white men when they arrived in the sixteenth century is still a matter of speculation. An early beginning, perhaps about 1000 to 300 B.C., is suggested by the complex prehistoric earthworks displayed at the Poverty Point site in what is now West Carroll Parish. The construction of monumental earthworks in the form of large ceremonial and geometric mounds continued until the demise of the Natchez tribal centers about A.D. 1730.

Mound construction occurred in phases at some slight variance from one another. Temple mounds, essentially truncated structures that served as foundations for temples or the houses of chiefs, appeared about A.D. 800 to 1000. Some controversy surrounds these mounds, which are contemporaneous with the advent of maize, the bow and arrow, and more refined ceramics. They may have stemmed from Mexican influences or be the result of centuries of local development in the Southeast. Whatever the origins of temple mounds may have been, such controlled, massive constructions are suggestive of some centrifugal social forces in Indian communities. Perhaps the authority represented by the chiefdom could have provided the direction and discipline essential to such great efforts.

The nuclear family is probably the oldest of social structures, but in Indian communities in Louisiana it almost always has been secondary in importance to extended families in some form. Grandparents are still notable people, and older persons are respected for their knowledge and influence. Children often grow up in households that are multigenerational, a factor contributing directly to the continuity and conservation of ancient custom and language.

At the time of European contact, most Indian societies in Louisiana were matrilineal and matrilocal; that is, the children belonged to the mother's kin group and lived with other members of that kin group. The male responsible for the children's discipline and upbringing was the mother's brother, the uncle. Consequently, the biological father, in traditional families, was like an older brother. He was responsible for the rearing and behavior of his own sister's children. Koasati Indians recall an instance of this formal relationship, in which the "ugly uncle" was summoned when children misbehaved. It was this uncle who meted out the appropriate punishment. Usually, the children also had a "pretty uncle" who pampered and spoiled them, and tempered the image of the mother's other brother.

Aunts on the mother's side of the family stood in the same relationship to the children as did the mother. They were often called "mother," confusing early Europeans who used that term only in reference to the biological mother. Indian people often went beyond that, calling all the women in the social position of authority and responsibility "mother." Older Tunica, when interviewed in the 1930s, translated the English term *aunt* as *stepmother*, referring to one who had the mother's position in the family.

Many, if not all, of the tribes had some sort of totemic clan system, and in many cases these were exogamous matrilineal clans or family tribes, as some Koasati term them today. Such family groups were thought to have stemmed from mythical ancestors, usually animals. However, some clans were said to have descended from plants, wind, salt, or insects, like the daddy longlegs. These totems, as the northern Indians, the Algonkians, called them, offered special protection and aid. They were also the overt symbols of kinship and polity. The Choctaw revered the owl, the Biloxi the panther, the Koasati the garfish, the Tunica the rattlesnake, the Houma the crayfish, and the Natchez the sun. Unfortunately, the identities of many tribal totems have been forgotten. The protection of such guardian spirits and the potency of special individual symbols such as crystals and animal claws were thought to help ward off evil forces, including the powerful, dreaded witchcraft.

The Koasati still have true totemic matriclans. Their totems include Beaver, Wildcat, Lion or Panther, Bear, Daddy Longlegs, Turkey, and Alligator. At one time Wind, Wolf, and Salt were also included. Their Alabama relatives have those named for the Koasati today, plus a few others: Wolf, Wind, Salt, Bird, and Skunk.

The ethnologist John Swanton believed that the totemic clans were not true clans. Surely, however, they are so among the Koasati and Alabama. The rule of exogamy clearly applies. Donald Hunter recently demonstrated the strengths of modern exogamy among the Koasati. Searching through family genealogies and marriage records, he found only one instance of clan rule violation in nearly seventy years. Swanton questioned the assumption that the Choctaw had no totemic clans, noting the presence of matriclans. The Louisiana Choctaw near Jena recall *Tchula*, Fox (perhaps borrowed from the Chickasaw), and *Sinti*, Snake, as clan names. Clan names were also known among the Chitimacha—

Bear, Dog, Panther, Snake. The Natchez, among whom matrilineal descent was controlled by the role of exogamy, later borrowed the clan names of the Cherokee and Creek with whom they found refuge after the Natchez War in 1730. Apparently, matriclans were developing in tandem with matrilineal lineage systems and at an early period, but the lineages operated without true clan divisions.

Albert Gatschet compiled totemic names among the Biloxi, and there is some evidence in kin terms to suggest matrilineage. Most of the Louisiana Caddo were totemic, matrilineal, and exogamous. The Kadohadacho clearly had Beaver, Eagle, Raccoon, Otter, Wolf, and Panther, as well as Sun and Thunder, clans. It is unlikely that the "little" and the "great" divisions of the Louisiana tribes reflect anything other than the moieties, clan divisions, so common in the Southeast. The Choctaw were divided into groups sometimes called the "greater" and "lesser" divisions and the Six Towns, or Yowani. These correspond to major geographic divisions of the tribes.

Prior to European contact, and continuing into the early 1900s, elders from at least the Koasati and Tunica-Biloxi clans formed a sort of community council that advised tribal chiefs. Although men sat in the tribal councils, the women actually controlled much of tribal life and government. The matriclan clearly dominated political events. The Koasati tribe maintained this egalitarian structure well into the 1980s. The chieftainship was inherited from the father, so it eventually passed from his clan to that of his wife, to which the son belonged.

A slightly different system prevailed among the Tunica. It was apparently matrilineal, but the chieftainship passed to the maternal nephew, the son of the chief's sister. The Tunica chief Lattanache told the English at Manchac that his nephew would inherit the chieftainship. This is reminiscent of the Natchez war chiefs, who also received their rank through the matrilineage. This system served to keep the ranked position in one clan. With such a polity, referred to as a ranked clan system, one kin group becomes somewhat autocratic, holding authority for several generations. Caroline Dormon collected Tunica kinship terms that strongly suggest this system. It was still functioning among the Tunica until the 1780s, when they moved westward across the Mississippi. Shortly thereafter, they began electing their chiefs, perhaps in response to some Spanish governmental influence. From that time on, the

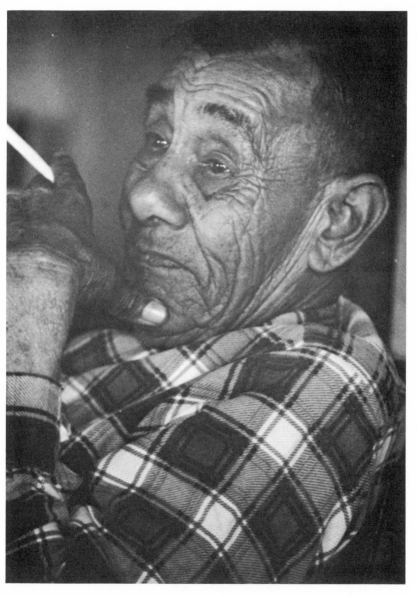

Fig. 28
JOSEPH PIERITE, LAST TRADITIONAL TUNICA-BILOXI CHIEF
Courtesy of Don Sepulvado

tribe legally recorded the vote. Even so, genealogical studies of chiefs have revealed that most of them were from one kin group, probably a single matrilineal family, the *Chiki*. Tunica family names show a measure of continuity (*Chiki* is equivalent to *belly*, *Casstete* to *tomahawk*, *Pierite* to *flint*, *Picote* to *tattooed*), though the apparent translation to French surnames occurred rather early. Such ranked families have not been adequately described or studied in the Southeast.

In most tribes, there often were two chiefs. The Tunica always had two, later recorded as a chief and a subchief. These were a peace chief who oversaw domestic affairs and a war chief who handled diplomacy and military matters. The Choctaw had a similar set of chiefs. Their *Mingo Puscus* (literally, Baby Chief) allocated hunting areas, farm fields, and other resources. Their *Mingo Huma* was the war chief. The *Xenesi* of the Caddo were in a sort of priest-chief rank that formed the ruling class, and under them was a *Tama*, or local chief, who organized work, meetings, and other affairs. The Caddo exhibited a unique trait: their elite, the *Xenesi* were patrilineal, while the rest of the tribe was matrilineal, though this may have been only another mechanism for transferring rank within a single class or clan. The Caddo system seems closer to Tunica than to the stratified societies of the Chitimacha and Natchez. Archaeologically, interaction between the Caddo and Tunica is well demonstrated.

These matrilineal systems, shared in varying degrees by the Biloxi and others, were markedly different from the lineage systems of the Chitimacha and Natchez. Those social forms, referred to by anthropologists as segmentary lineages, were probably older than both the ranked and egalitarian clan systems. Among the Natchez, a complicated social structure evolved in which two status classes were clearly defined—nobles and commoners. Within the nobility there were three ranks: Suns (the highest order), Nobles, and Honored people. The commoners, referred to as Stinkards, formed a single class. Nobles married into the commoner class, while the remaining commoners married among themselves. Children of these unions belonged to their mother's class, except the children of Suns and of Nobles, who were never Stinkards. The children of Suns and of Nobles belonged to the next rank below that of their fathers, Nobles and Honored people, respectively. Marriage did not

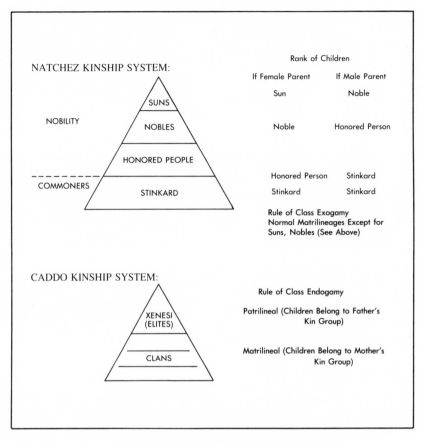

Fig. 29
NATCHEZ AND CADDO KINSHIP SYSTEMS
Courtesy of the authors and the Louisiana State University Cartographic Section

bring about a change in rank. A Stinkard remained a Stinkard, even if her children had a higher rank. However, a Stinkard could achieve Honored status by war exploits or by sacrificing a child at the death ceremony for a Sun. In such an instance, the wife was raised in status along with the husband. Like European knighthood, this advancement was for life only, and children of the couple took their parents' previous rank.

Some anthropologists have pointed to statistics indicating that if class or rank exogamy had continued among the Natchez, the tribe would have run out of eligible marriage partners within a century. Another anthropologist has reevaluated the figures and has found that it would have continued to work well. An equilibrium apparently was achieved, resulting from a low birthrate among the Noble and Honored women coupled with overreproduction among upper-class men and Stinkard women. This circumstance, combined with war losses among the Nobles and Honored men, balanced the population well. Jeffrey Brain, of Harvard University, has proposed a more nearly complete model based on both archaeological and ethnohistoric information.

Natchez political structure was closely wed to this kinship system. The chief, head of nine to eleven villages, was called the Great Sun and was the oldest son of the Sun Woman or White Woman, matriarch of the Suns. A war chief, the Great Sun's brother or maternal uncle, assisted him. His rank passed to his sister's son. Other Suns were lesser chiefs of the villages, and the Honored men were warriors. Stinkards controlled all subsistence activities. It is possible that the Natchez system was some variety of ranked class system and was misunderstood by French chroniclers who drew analogies with their own stratified society under the Sun King, Louis XIV. Such views, however, are only speculative.

Brain has suggested that the true caste system of the Chitimacha was preserved intact since it was isolated in the vast swamps of the Atchafalaya Basin, and that it was a direct descendant of the chiefdoms that arose in Plaquemine Period, A.D. 1200 to 1400. The caste system consisted of chiefs, nobles, and commoners. There was no social mobility. The Chitimacha chief could be as autocratic as he pleased, while in the clan systems the chiefs had little personal power. Their main function was to give the people of both their goods and their time.

Class endogamy, in which aristocrats married aristocrats and commoners were restricted to marriage with commoners, was maintained by the Chitimacha, while in the north other groups, under intense outside pressures, changed into the Natchez system. Faye Stouff, wife of the late Emile Stouff, the last traditional Chitimacha chief, recalls that she had to give his mother proof of her aristocratic European ancestry before she would sanction their marriage, the last vestige of an ancient social organization. Brain suggests that the class exogamy of the Natchez provided a mechanism for the assimilation of new people from other tribal groups, while at the same time matrilineage preserved the old Noble lineage. The Natchez integrated small tribes, most of them refugees from the Tunican north, into their Stinkard ranks, which would have disappeared if their class exogamy had persisted.

The Caddo political structure was somewhat like that of the Natchez, but it differed in several ways. There was a chief, the *Xenesi*, who dominated other ranks much like the Great Sun of the Natchez. Both abstained from manual labor, had sacrosanct religious duties, such as caring for the temple and sacred fire, and dominated lesser chiefs. The lesser chiefs were the *Caddi*, or principal village headmen, and the *Canaha*, sometimes called the captains or elders of the villages. The *Canaha*, possibly elected in each town and usually old men, were somewhat like council members. Other elite were the medicine men, or the *Conna*, and a man referred to as the *Tamma*. The latter coordinated work details, announced councils, and acted in the general capacity of overseer and town crier for the ranking chiefs. These hierarchical positions seem to have passed to lineal descendants. *Xenesi*, often blind men, were always replaced by male lineal descendants. The other, lesser ranks also passed to male heirs, perhaps in a bilineal or patrilineal way. A father-to-son sequence is documented for the *Caddi*. This complex of hierarchically ranked rules, like Caddo kinship, clearly shows its Mississippian roots or at least a close connection to them. Without question, it places the Louisiana Caddo in the southeastern United States culture area.

The several sociopolitical systems served to facilitate the allocation of people and resources, to provide protection and military organization, to control internal relationships, and to educate and control the youth. The extended family and, in some cases, the true exogamous clan, were reinforced by religious tenets and taboos regarding incest. These groups functioned as the agent for the enculturation of children, protection of members, and control of human sexual and economic needs.

Couples lived together in marriage as long as they were compatible, but that institution seems to have been quite flexible. Divorce was a simple matter, with no stigma attached. Afterward, each former partner moved closer to his kin group. Children presented no problems in such cases, since they usually belonged to the clan, class or lineage entities more powerful than the biological pair of male and female. The extended families simply assumed responsibility for mother and child. Since the maternal uncles usually held such a responsibility anyway, it was unlikely that children would be traumatized by the fragmentation of nuclear families. Fortunately, there were, at least in the matrilineal clans of the Koasati and the Choctaw, no illegitimate children. Each child had a clan; everyone knew the mother, grandmother, and aunts. Even more fortunately, such a system reinforced the child rearing and economic activities of the nuclear family.

When European and other-tribal pressures began to dislocate tribes, driving small, disparate groups into a number of culs-de-sac near the Yazoo River in Mississippi, in the Red River valley in central Louisiana, and elsewhere on the Gulf coast, social problems arose. It became necessary for tribes without clans and without families of responsibility to control the behavior of children and provide for their welfare. The progeny of a Choctaw mother and a Koasati father, for example, or a Tunica father and a Biloxi mother, might become isolated at some point from the maternal clan. The condition worsened if white women, who had no clan or extended family, had children by Indian men—a circumstance that seems rare but did occur. The Koasati sometimes adopted people; in one instance a Choctaw came to be considered a member of the Turkey (*Fito*) clan. The Alabama suggest that one of their clans came into being when they absorbed the Pascagoula.

There remain in Louisiana numbers of people who are of mixed racial or Indian descent and who therefore have no tribal identities. This was not likely to have happened in precontact times when tribal locations were more stable. It is probable that tribal fusion and the mixing of Indians with non-Indians that intensified in the nineteenth century produced new social problems all across the Southeast. Some communities became completely obscured in the process, lost to the ranks of other tribes or in white or black communities.

Little is known of the impact of slavery on Indians in Louisiana, but it must have forced changes in the social structure. Apacheans, held by French and Spanish families, were baptized Catholics, and they often married whites or free blacks. Patrilineage dominated.

The Natchez who sought refuge from slavery among the Cherokee and Creek changed to their egalitarian clan system.

Sometimes the offspring of Indians and non-Indians formed separate mestizo communities, which, over the years, developed their own identities outside of specific tribal groups. Nevertheless, Indian identities persisted, and traditional culture was frequently maintained relatively intact. This is the situation of the *métis* in Canada, though it is exaggerated. There, only the children of Indian mothers are considered Indians. Even so, mixed-bloods founded their own groups. At least three such old, well-documented communities with Indian identities exist in Louisiana. These are the Clifton Choctaw community, the various Houma groups, and the Spanish Choctaw-Apache community at Ebarb. Indian blood quantum is high in these groups, and the community organizations are strong, though established along slightly different lines than might prevail in a purely Indian group.

For most of these mixed groups in Louisiana, local communities tended to become endogamous. This policy was related to the fact that these people lived in marginal cutover and swamplands. The tendency to marry inside one's community has weakened as racism has become less important and as the social isolation once so marked has diminished. This has occurred since the 1950s and 1960s, due, in part, to the integration of schools and the loss of community school-church autonomy and its attendant isolation. Electricity and the resulting better communications have further reduced isolation, while surfaced roads provide access to services outside the communities.

Prior to the advent of modernizing influences, the basic sociopolitical organization of the mixed groups was the extended family. Families were sometimes tied together into named geographic bands, with perhaps thirty to forty families per region, as was the case at Ebarb and among the Houma. In each band, the family elders, generally males (a Spanish influence in Ebarb and French among the Houma), became leaders. The office of chief did not develop at Ebarb. At Clifton and among the Houma, chiefs were maintained, and the Muskogean clan system all but disappeared. Again, extended-family elders began gaining prestige and power. Cora Bremer has described a similar trend among isolated Choctaw in southeast Louisiana.

Churches, both Protestant and Catholic, were the focus of the communities. Churches seem to have replaced the temple centers throughout the Southeast and to have assumed secular as well as religious functions. Ministers, however, seem to have had only advisory capacities, if those. Most often they were non-Indians and outsiders. Decision making remained in the hands of the family elders, male and female.

The mixed-blood communities have retained some native languages, food habits, crafts, and even elements of religious and political organization. Although observably different from the more purely Indian groups, these communities also demonstrate that they differ equally from their non-Indian neighbors.

Named groups, somewhat like totemic clans, persist at Ebarb. Each can be identified with a geographic area and is often called by some animal name, such as Bear, Hawk, or *Tejon* (*badger* in Spanish, *raccoon* in the local dialect). There are taboos about the use of the group names. Only members of the group are allowed to use the label; a hawk may be called a hawk only by another member of the group with that name. Violence may result if a name is carelessly used. A Choctaw group at Ebarb has been named *Minti* after the verb they use in calling their children; *Ho Minti* is Choctaw for "You-all come." These named groups are still basically exogamous and usually live near their kin. They are apparently now mainly patrilocal. The persistence of Indian elements in these mixed communities, some two hundred years old and in almost daily contact with Europeans throughout that time, demonstrates the strength of the original Indian kinship systems.

In Louisiana, only the Koasati tribe has maintained the greater part of its native kinship system. Clan exogamy has remained intact in that group, but the general knowledge of clan membership is apparently weakening. In the early 1900s, every Koasati knew everyone's clan affiliation. Most of them still know their own, but clan memberships no longer appear to be community-wide knowledge. Residence after marriage has shifted to a mixture of matrilocality and patrilocality among the Koasati, too. In view of Koasati language, craft, clans, and religion retention, this is somewhat surprising. The change toward patrilocal residence probably reflects the influence of the Anglo-American legal system's effect on land titles. However, some of the first lands homesteaded by the Koasati tribe were filed on by women.

Among the Jena Choctaw, one of the more isolated groups, the Choctaw divisions disappeared. There the family elders were elected chief. These chiefs, like their Biloxi, Chitimacha, Koasati, and Tunica counterparts, struggled to preserve local tribal autonomy. They assumed, then, the functional roles of priests, ministers, and other titularies adjusted by white society. Marriages were traditionally made before the chiefs or, in more recent times, before the eldest man of the Choctaw, as was done by the Tunica. The Choctaw report the ritual to have been exactly the same as when spoken by a white minister. Prior to white influences, the couple merely offered gifts to each other or to the girl's family.

Although they did not intend to subvert civil authority, the chiefs increasingly came to be recognized as the symbols of Indian community identity. The Tunica chief Lattanache protested to the English that he had the right to take his people across the Mississippi River whenever he chose to do so. When, on one occasion, the Spanish authorities protested against the killing of twin infants who were thought to be evil, the Houma chief, according to the *Papeles Procedentes de Cuba*, replied that "the ways of the Spaniard are not the ways of the Houma."

After Europeans began to appoint medal chiefs, the status of the chiefs became separated from kinship to a much greater degree than ever before. The position was more secular, less social, and more of a public office. American Indian agents like John Sibley at Natchitoches crassly manipulated the position of chief among the Louisiana Choctaw. When the tribe chose a person whom Sibley disliked, he engineered a confrontation, told authorities that he had been attacked, and had the man arrested. Then he demanded that the Choctaw appoint another man more to his liking to be their chief.

Such instances of white circumvention of tribal policy imply sweeping changes in tribal life. Adaptation to white mores and land policy no doubt affected Indian sociopolitical structure early. Tribal governments have never ceded their sovereign status to the federal government and, while loyal to the state and nation, still feel that those agencies have only limited authority over Indian people, lands, and resources. This has been a point of legal contention for over two centuries, involving, at one time or another, several powers. The Louisiana tribes, with others in North America, hope to guarantee their rights not as wards of the government but as sovereign entities within the United States. State, national, and tribal leaders are struggling with the legal problems inherent in this concept, which is rooted in the longest occupation of North American soil. The concept of sovereignty is the modern manifestation of thousands of years of governmental organization developed by the Indians on this continent.

Today, extended families, often church or school centered, continue to be the rule in most Louisiana Indian communities. The old ways die slowly, and all Indian social life still shows much of its vital heritage from the past. The Koasati and Alabama have kept their traditions and are working diligently to maintain them vis-à-vis those of their neighbors.

REFERENCES

Few systematic studies have been made of kinship organizations in the lower Mississippi River valley and adjacent areas. Most of the information available pertains to the Natchez, whose elaborate scheme captured the attention of the Europeans. The French, stirred by the spectacle of a chief carried on a litter and linked to the sun, as was their own monarch, wrote detailed accounts of the Natchez that have been reprinted, quoted, debated, and reinterpreted for many years.

Brain, Jeffrey P.
1971   The Natchez "Paradox." *Ethnology* 10(2):215–22.

Fischer, J. L.
1964   Solutions for the Natchez Paradox. *Ethnology* 3(1):53–65.

Haas, Mary R.
1939   Natchez and Chitimacha Clans and Kinship Terminology. *American Anthropologist* 41:597–610.

Hart, C. W. M.
1943   A Reconsideration of the Natchez Social Structure. *American Anthropologist* 45:374–86.

MacLeod, W. C.
1924   Natchez Political Evolution. *American Anthropologist* 26:201–29.

Mason, Carol Irwin
1964   Natchez Class Structure. *Ethnohistory* 11:120–33.

Quimby, George I.
1946   Natchez Social Structure as an Instrument of Assimilation. *American Anthropologist* 48:134–37.

Tooker, Elizabeth
1963   Natchez Social Organization: Fact or Anthropological Folklore?
       Ethnology 10:358–72.

Van Tuyl, Charles D., and Willard Walker
1979   *The Natchez: Annotated Translations from Antoine Simon Le Page
       DuPratz' Histoire de la Louisiane.* Oklahoma Historical Society
       Anthropology Series 4, Oklahoma City. (The appendix on social
       structure is especially helpful.)

White, Douglas R. *et al.*
1971   Natchez Class and Rank Reconsidered. *Ethnology* 10:361–88.

Changes in the Koasati system have been documented recently in an unpublished study of kinship terms in a multigenerational household.

Pavy, David
1963   Notes on the Semantics of Koasati Kinship Usage. MS at Depart-
       ment of Anthropology, Tulane University, New Orleans.

Further information on Koasati kinship can be found in more intensive
studies.

Jacobson, Daniel
1954   Koasati Culture Change. Ph.D. dissertation, Louisiana State
       University.

Johnson, Bobby H.
1976   *The Coushatta People.* Indian Tribal Series, Phoenix.

Kinship was considered in H. B. Cushman's 1899 work, which has been reprinted, but its coverage is better on the Choctaw of Oklahoma than on
those of Louisiana. A small portion of the work is devoted to the Natchez.

Cushman, H. B. (Angie Deboe, ed.)
1962   *History of the Choctaw, Chickasaw and Natchez Indians.* New
       York.

Swanton summarized Choctaw kinship in several reports.

Swanton, John R.
1931   Source Material for the Social and Ceremonial Life of the Choc-
       taw Indians. *Bureau of American Ethnology Bulletin* 103, Wash-
       ington, D.C.
1932   Choctaw Moieties. *American Anthropologist* 34:357.
1932   The Rev. John Edwards' Account of the Choctaw Indians in the
       Middle of the Nineteenth Century. *Chronicles of Oklahoma*
       10(3): 392–425.

Fred Eggan, in the 1964 Lewis Henry Morgan Lectures at the University of
Rochester, addressed change and continuity in Choctaw kinship. He did

not include the Louisiana Choctaw communities, but in general, his observations on Oklahoma hold true for Louisiana as well.

Eggan, Fred
1966 The Choctaw and Their Neighbors in the Southeast: Acculturation Under Pressure. In *The American Indian*, Aldine, Chicago, 15–45.

A few items of information on kinship among the Bayou LaCombe Choctaw appear in Bushnell's study of that community.

Bushnell, David I., Jr.
1909 The Choctaw of Bayou LaCombe, St. Tammany Parish, Louisiana. *Bureau of American Ethnology Bulletin* 48, Washington, D.C.

Chitimacha kinship has been studied by Morris Swadesh and Gene Weltfish. Weltfish apparently did not publish her findings, and Swadesh narrowed his to a comparative study of tribal language.

Swadesh, Morris
1948 Sociologic Notes on Obsolescent Languages. *International Journal of American Linguistics* 14(4):226–35.

A book that contains stories, legends, and other cultural material from the Chitimacha has been privately published. It also includes contemporary kin terms and folk traditions.

Stouff, Faye, and W. Bradley Twitty
1971 *Sacred Chitimacha Indian Beliefs*. Pompano Beach, Fla.

Caddoan kinship has not been studied extensively, and the work done so far is limited to the time since the tribes were displaced, from 1835 to 1840.

Spier, Leslie
1924 Wichita and Caddo Kinship Terms. *American Anthropologist* 26: 258–63.

Swanton, John R.
1931 The Caddo Social Organization and Its Possible Historical Significance. *Journal of the Washington Academy of Sciences* 21(9): 203–206.

Parsons, Elsie Clews
1941 (rpr. 1969) Notes on the Caddo. *American Anthropological Association Memoir* 57.

Dorsey, G. A.
1904 *Traditions of the Caddo*. Carnegie Institution, Washington, D.C.

Many of the primary and secondary sources of material on the Caddo are summarized in a landmark study.

Swanton, John R.
1942 Source Material on the History and Ethnology of the Caddo Indians. *Bureau of American Ethnology Bulletin* 132, Washington, D.C.

An archaeological perspective, perhaps the only useful approach to the reconstruction of past sociopolitical systems, has been added to the literature on the Caddo.

Wychoff, Don G., and Timothy Baugh
1980 Early Historic Elites: A Model for the Material Culture of Governing Elites. *Mid-Continental Journal of Archaeology* 5(2):225–88.

The Atakapa people were so heavily impacted by European disease and settlement that few ethnographic materials on them were saved.

Swanton, John R.
1929 A Sketch of the Attakapan Language. *International Journal of American Linguistics* 5:121–149.

Source materials on Louisiana Indians are sometimes solitary and obscure.

Steckler, Marguerite C.
1932 The History of the Attacapa Indians for Elementary School Use. M.A. thesis, George Peabody College.

Only a few writers, among them William Sears, have essayed a broad synthesis of sociopolitical patterns in the Southeast.

Sears, William
1954 The Sociopolitical Organization of Pre-Columbian Cultures on the Gulf Coastal Plain. *American Anthropologist* 56:339–46.

XIV

THE CRISES OF LIFE

The crises of life are the several events that normally mark the major episodes in the life of the individual: birth, puberty, marriage, death. No matter how they may be obscured, these occasions are of concern in every society, and that of the American Indians was no exception. Among the aborigines, as in all human societies, long-established procedures marked the critical times of change and were learned as children advanced to adulthood.

Although complete information is not available for all the early Louisiana tribes, the procedures attending the event of childbirth seem to have been quite similar among them. It was customary for a menstruating woman to be confined to a small outbuilding, and to this same structure the pregnant woman went when about to give birth. There she remained unattended throughout her labor. Her husband was subject to certain taboos for the duration of this period, eating only at certain intervals and omitting specified foods.

Immediately after its birth, the child was placed in a cradle, and if that was the custom of the tribe, head flattening was begun. Today, the Koasati infant's head is shaved at four months, and Choctaw parents still paint their child's spinal area with grease and red ocher. The purpose, in both practices, is to make sure that the child will grow strong.

The Indian child was well cared for from the day of its birth. The mother might rub her baby regularly with bear oil to keep its muscles pliant and repel insects, and infants were suckled as long as they wished. Teething rings of alligator teeth or perforated nuts were tied to the infants' wrists, and necklaces of pain-relieving Jerusalem artichokes were hung about their necks to quiet them. Among the Koasati, newborn children were given tiny artifacts—

pots or baskets for girls, and bows and arrows for boys—intended to impress upon them the complementary roles of males and females.

The children learned to bathe daily and became capable swimmers at an early age. Constant physical exercise, including much swimming and running, was stressed, but work was not pressed upon them at first. Not until the age of ten or twelve did the boys begin to carry small burdens.

The traditional education of the boys was under the direction of an old man, and that of the girls was under an old woman. A mild but effective discipline was meted out to children who failed to bathe in the morning before eating and to boys who neglected to practice the use of weapons. The painful, embarrassing marks left by scratching the skin with garfish teeth were quite enough to bring the offender into line. One might be dunked in a chilly creek or spring, but this was usually a last resort.

It was established early in the minds of young Indians that males took precedence over females in virtually every activity. However, they also learned that a special role and significance were reserved for women. Women were revered as the bearers of life, and the fields belonged to them. The mystery of menstruation gave them great power over both men and game, making them dangerous and doubly respected.

Boys learned masculine skills and girls were taught the things that women did; thus they learned of the sexual division of labor. Men, they knew, were responsible for hunting, fishing, and felling trees and making things from them. The Natchez men cultivated the sacred fields of the tribe, and the Tunica men took care of their secular clearings. Men also waged war, built cabins, and performed similarly difficult physical tasks. Women pounded corn into flour, cooked and did other household chores, made pots, baskets, mats, and clothing, and were chiefly responsible for the growing of crops. They tended the fields and the children. The sexes at times joined together, having great power over the supernatural, for instance, and practicing medicine.

The attainment of sexual maturity seems to have occasioned no public ceremonial observance. Girls learned that they must occupy the isolated huts set aside for them during menstruation, for menstrual blood was considered a dangerous substance. Sexual mores varied extensively among the ancient tribes. Sometimes, as among the Natchez, unmarried women had great sexual freedom. In exchange for their favors, they demanded goods that constituted a kind of dowry for the day of their marriage. The Natchez thought that sexual freedom prior to marriage served to enhance a woman's status as she sought entry to the afterlife. Among the Caddo, sexual abstinence was desired in an unmarried female, even if it was hardly expected. Adolescent youths engaged in sexual activity as they wished, and marriage was usually delayed to the age of twenty-five or older. While considerable formality attended the wedding of a Caddo virgin, it was absent in the case of the sexually experienced female.

Indian young people of both sexes expected to receive help and guidance from a source outside of the family and tribe. Chitimacha boys were placed in solitary confinement in a house until they had experienced a revelation from a supernatural animal being, which then became their guardian spirit. The same procedure was followed with girls of that tribe. Young people of other tribes were isolated individually in the forest. A sign revealing the identity of the guardian spirit of each was encountered after much prayer and fasting. How widespread this practice might have been among Louisiana Indians is unknown. As part of the puberty rites, Chitimacha boys fasted and danced in the temple for six days, an ordeal sure to impress them with the serious nature of the occasion and with spiritual life in general.

The attainment of adulthood by a male entailed largely the assumption of the functions of a man in the economic, social, ceremonial, and martial life of the tribe. As he matured, his childhood name was replaced by one reflecting his warlike deeds. Among the Chitimacha, men's personal names often were taken from animals, though no totemism was implied. A man of the Atakapa, Chitimacha, or Choctaw dropped his own name as soon as his child was born and henceforth was known as the father of so-and-so. Frequently, men were addressed by honorifics that were war names. These often ended with -*huma*, meaning *red*, a power color, or with -*abe* or -*ubbe*, signifying "killer," the equivalent of "general" or "commander" in English. The Mobilian word *mingo*, or *chief*, was applied to powerful men. Females usually kept the same names throughout their lives. One name, not two, was sufficient.

The customs and usages associated with names were often taken very seriously and, in some cases, were quite complex. The Choctaw were averse to revealing their personal names and to mentioning the names of the dead. The system of terms used to designate relationships was extremely intricate and precise, with many degrees of distinction and, at the same time, many inclusions under the same term. For example, among the Choctaw the same term is used to refer to the grandmother and the father's sister. The latter referred to her brother's son as "grandchild." A man speaks of his sister's children as "nephew" and "niece," but their children are "grandchildren" to him. In a matrilineal kin system, these terms serve well to reflect the responsibilities and rank of the family.

Marriage among Louisiana Indians generally followed clan exogamy. If a clan existed, each member was required to marry a nonmember. A man called all of his female cousins "sister," and he could not marry them. A widower might marry one of his late wife's sisters or an unrelated woman. Marriages usually, but not always, were monogamous. Polygamy, usually polygyny, or marriage involving multiple wives, was allowed and probably persisted among the Choctaw until the 1920s. Polygamy was fairly common among the Natchez chiefs, the mother of the first child taking precedence over others. The married couple lived with the first wife's people, and incest taboos were strictly observed. Practices changed after European contact, so that it is not always possible to say what the aboriginal customs were for a specific tribe. The Koasati honor the clan rules of exogamy even today.

Events of the magnitude of marriage were surrounded by a great mantle of rules and attitudes. Marriages might be arranged but were never forced. Elopement was frowned upon, and the fleeing couple was pursued by a group somewhat like a posse. If the couple managed to avoid capture for one year, until the next green-corn ceremony, all was forgiven.

Among the Choctaw, marriage was preceded by an informal agreement between man and woman, evidently initiated by either of them. Then the man or a family representative approached a responsible guardian of the young woman. A gift was presented to the woman's mother, and a suggestion was made to her as to her part in providing for the wedding feast. A ceremonial race gave the young woman a chance to withdraw from the agreement, if she chose to do so. Otherwise, she let herself be caught, but only after a show of reluctance. Presents were given to her by the man's relatives and to him by her family. A few more preliminaries were followed by a wedding feast, a lecture by the chief, and an all-night dance.

Among the Indians, a faithless wife often paid a heavy price for her indiscretion. The typical Natchez wife, after having been encouraged in sexual freedom before marriage, was rarely unfaithful, was infrequently divorced, and could not be divorced after she had borne a child. Among some tribes a man avoided his mother-in-law, though this was never as stringent a rule in Louisiana as it was elsewhere in North America.

Female prostitutes were found in almost all groups. Wives were sometimes loaned to friends in a kind of hospitality prostitution. There existed a class of homosexuals, or berdaches, who performed the menial tasks of women. No stigma was attached to their position, and they were looked upon as "social women."

A death among the Indians was an occasion for genuine mourning and was marked by carefully prescribed ceremonial observances. As a rule, the more important the deceased, the more elaborate the rites, though the social distinctions of life were largely dissolved by death. The souls of the dead met varying fates depending, in part, on their earthly behavior. The Louisiana tribes exhibited considerable variation in the practices attendant upon death, the Natchez being foremost in retaining some semblance of the elaborate prehistoric mortuary complex.

During the eighteenth century, among the Choctaw, the house of a dead person and the provisions it contained were burned. The head of the deceased was painted red, and the corpse, covered with skins, was placed on a scaffold near where the house had stood. A fire burned underneath the scaffold on four successive days. Mourners hired for the occasion, their hair cut off, occupied benches around the scaffold and wailed three times a day.

After the flesh of the dead person was thoroughly decayed, a bone picker, or Turkey Buzzard Man, in the presence of the mourners, picked the bones clean. The bones then were put into a chest or hamper and placed in the mortuary house. Completion of this phase was followed by a feast, usually prepared by the bone pickers. When the mortuary house had been filled with chests, the house might be covered with earth or the chests might be piled on the ground and covered. Subsequent burials were sometimes added to a mound. As time went on, spring and fall mourning ceremonies honored the dead with displays of weeping, dancing, and feasting.

The early practices associated with death among the lower Mississippi tribes were somewhat the same. Mourning was displayed by cutting the hair, leaving the face unpainted, and avoiding public dances and meetings. The corpse was buried with utensils and food, and after burial the relatives went to the grave twice daily to mourn and leave food. The funerary practices of the Bayougoula, Chitimacha, and Houma were much like those of the Choctaw.

Most elaborate and costly of all rites were those that attended the death of a leading figure among the Natchez. Procedures familiar along the lower Mississippi were carried out and were accompanied by the execution of a number of persons who were to travel with the deceased to the spirit world. In this party there were his wives, some of his officers, and volunteers who sought honor for themselves and their children. Parents of sacrificed children were raised in rank for life. Pills of tobacco were swallowed, bringing unconsciousness, after which the victims were strangled with cords. Relatives performed the executions, after which they, too, advanced in rank. What the act truly symbolized is unknown. It certainly was connected with attitudes toward death and dying unlike those of most Indians. Le Page du Pratz described a mass burial of sacrificial victims in one grave, and that of a Sun and his two wives in another.

The mortuary practices of the Natchitoches Caddo on Red River seem to have resembled those of the lower Mississippi Valley groups more than the divergent rituals of the western Caddo. However, there were no scaffolds, and men killed in war were cremated. Burial traditions still prevail to some extent among the Oklahoma Caddo. The hands of the deceased are painted red, and the corpse is smoked with cedar smoke, as is the house of the deceased. Four times the coffin is carried around the grave, and then it is covered. Goods may be placed with the dead.

The Tunica traditionally buried their dead in family cemeteries, in relatively shallow graves. As late as the beginning of the nineteenth century, they placed carefully prepared goods in the grave and dressed the corpse in that person's most elaborate attire. A knife was always buried with a man so that he might overcome any attacker, usually an eagle, on his trip to the next world. Burial goods also included such personal items as eating utensils, saddlery, and sundries. When the last traditional chief, Joseph Pierite, Sr., died, each member of the family contributed special items to the coffin: blue beads, white beads, an eagle feather, and an open clasp knife. The chief wore the belt he had liked, carried a ceremonial pipe, and wore a beadwork tie with a shell gorget—his favorite dress. According to custom, a fire was lighted at the graveside to light the way for the soul at night. Today, the votive lamp, a Catholic custom, serves the same function.

The Koasati practices were similar, but also involved the placement of goods on top of graves. This practice seems to have become less frequent in the twentieth century. According to Alabama and Koasati belief, wicked people were destroyed by an eagle. A knife was buried with each evil person so that his soul might fight the eagle during its travel to the afterworld. In the Koasati practice, the weapon was placed in his right hand and the hands crossed over the chest. Favorite foods were placed with the corpse, most recently in the coffin itself.

Early Koasati burial practices were reconstructed by John Swanton in the 1920s, by Averill Taylor in the 1930s, and by Donald Hunter in the 1970s. The Koasati believed that the spirit of the deceased remained on earth four days, and so food was replenished each day, though the corpse was usually buried before the four days had expired. An individual who was not a member of the family prepared the body by washing and dressing the corpse. A man performed this duty for a man, and a woman for a woman. Usually, the man who prepared his friend's corpse also dug the grave. After these preparations, he removed his own clothing and bathed in an herb and water medicine. The tools and clothing were washed with water. For four days after the burial, the preparer took infusions of medicine and then, in seclusion, cleansed himself by vomiting while facing the sunrise. Throughout the four days and nights people stayed in their houses, since to touch or see the spirit might cause instant death.

The door of the house in which the deceased person had lived was left open at night, and a light was kept burning there. The personal items not buried with the deceased were laid out in one room, and food was placed there and replenished daily for four days. This gave the dead person's spirit access to goods and food it might desire.

For four evenings, at sunset, a male member of the family fired four shots above the grave, always aiming to the west, the direction souls took in their journey to the afterworld. On the first evening the spirit awoke, on the second it stood, on the third it gathered its possessions, and on the fourth it left for the afterworld.

The family of the deceased underwent ritual cleansing through the taking of medicine and vomiting. The house was scrubbed with herb medicine to keep ghosts away. The relatives also ate little dur-

Fig. 30
CHOCTAW-APACHE ROMAN CATHOLIC CEMETERY, ZWOLLE, LOUISIANA
Courtesy of Don Sepulvado

ing the four days the soul remained. The rules of mourning required that marriage not be made for a period of one to four years. The mourners also did not cut their hair for a period ranging from four months to a year.

Today, only the most conservative families still wash the house after a funeral, and the other customs have been replaced by standard Christian practices. Grave goods are not buried with the dead, except in rare instances, though some personal items could still be seen on Koasati graves in the 1960s. Now, this practice, too, seems to have ceased.

Choctaw burials in the Jena community still exhibit some old traditions. Older Choctaw still believe that each person has two souls, of which one resides at the grave while the other leaves. Consequently, some people offer delicacies at certain graves, remembering the favorites of the deceased. In the past, at both Jena and Indian Creek, in Rapides Parish, families gathered at the grave, where the women seated themselves in a group, covered themselves with large cloths, and wept for the deceased. The earliest record of such a practice among the Louisiana Choctaw involved a group on the lower Ouachita River, where the early explorers William Dunbar and George Hunter saw a woman crying for a departed child. The last cries among the Choctaw seem to have been held in the late 1930s. The nineteenth-century observer Cora Bremer discussed a cry followed by ritual feasting among the Choctaw on lower Pearl River. That practice, too, seems to have disappeared early in the twentieth century.

At Jena, the chief asked couples to wait a year before marrying, especially if an older chief had died—a custom somewhat similar to Koasati practices. Another similarity lay in the taboo against cutting hair—men refrained from shaving as well—that older Jena Choctaw still recall. The placement of grave offerings seems to have persisted until 1920 or 1930 at Jena, but now that practice has apparently been dropped in all the Choctaw communities.

Changes in funerary customs have continued under the strong influences of such factors as burial insurance, funeral homes, and legal requirements related to embalming the dead. Still, Indian burials continue to be among the most solemn, most important rites of passage in Indian life.

REFERENCES

The best sources on childbirth, and virtually the only secondary sources, are the works of John R. Swanton. He has provided most of the available material on the Chitimacha, Natchez, and others. Charles Hudson has developed some regional comparative information.

Hudson, Charles
1976   *The Southeastern Indians.* Nashville.

It is unfortunate, in some respects, that the earliest accounts all were left by men—soldiers, traders, and priests. Their writings yield little information about Indian women other than occasional observations on their sexuality and were given from the masculine point of view. Even so, they show that Indian women wielded considerable personal influence in the 1700s.

The topic of child care has been developed herein primarily from ethnographic fieldwork among contemporary Louisiana Indians. Part of this report is based on studies of four tribal groups: the Ebarb Choctaw-Apache, the Jena Band of Choctaw, the Koasati, and the Tunica-Biloxi. Research into mental health and social relations was funded by a grant from the National Institute for Mental Health and was conducted by Indian trainees from each tribe. Donald Hunter carried out a series of systematic observations and, with Bel Abbey, a Koasati, contributed much to the information presented here.

Indian slaves are much in evidence in Spanish colonial documents and old conveyance records at both Natchitoches and Opelousas. The reader is referred to the *Papeles Procedentes de Cuba*, dated 1790, from Havana, which are available at Loyola University in New Orleans and at the University of Southwestern Louisiana in Lafayette.

Swanton's work with the late Koasati chief Jackson Langley has left valuable records of Koasati ritual.

Swanton, John R.
1928   Social Organization and Social Uses of the Indians of the Creek
      Confederacy. *Bureau of American Ethnology 42nd Annual Report*, Washington, D.C.

Lyda Averill Taylor visited the Koasati at Bayou Blue in the 1930s. Her dissertation at Yale University contains much valuable ethnographic information on the tribe. Following in her footsteps, Daniel Jacobson noted the dynamics of social change among that same group. Jacobson has the original Lyda Taylor notes.

Jacobson, Daniel
1954   Koasati Culture Change. Ph.D. dissertation, Louisiana State
        University.

Swanton's 1937 field notes, on file at the National Anthropological Archives, Smithsonian Institution, Washington, D.C., contain much information on the rites of crisis for the Alabama and Koasati. Albert Gatschet's
earlier field notes offer data on the Chitimacha, Tunica, and Biloxi, and
also are in the National Anthropological Archives.

XV

RELIGION AND MEDICINE

The Louisiana Indians lived in a sacred world. They made no distinction between the sacred and profane, and saw none of the polarities inherent in the European world view. Their universe was a whole held together by spiritual forces that caused man to respect all things, living and nonliving.

Earth was part of a layered universe with a deep underworld and an upper world. The first humans had migrated upward through a hole, a hollow log, or a crayfish tunnel, onto earth. There the sun warmed them, and they stayed. From the chaotic, unpredictable underworld, they had ascended to a harmonic, balanced place. Everything fit somewhere; each part somehow related to the whole. The rule of existence for man was to perceive and respect this natural order. The harmony had to be maintained. Time was not a way to break apart a day but a never-ending circle of events. The repetition was an endless continuum of the seasons, days and nights, and life and death.

Animals, plants, and human beings were interchangeable parts of a single fabric. The woods were full of spirits, "little people" who could be mischievous or helpful. They often had the gift of shamanistic power. They took various forms but were known in the mythology of the majority of tribes. One had to take care not to offend them. In Indian myth, maize was once an Indian grandmother who gave her body to become food for her orphan children. Corn was analogous to a female; it had tassels like hair, and the kernels of new corn gave milk. It was the mother of life itself.

All Indians grew up feeling comfortable in the natural world. It was in the swamps, the forests, and the marshes, among the birds and animals, that man belonged. The rhythms of the land were shared by man. More than the efforts of missionaries or even the force of military control, the economy of the European finally altered the Indian religious pattern; the automobile making roads through the land, the chainsaw and the bulldozer eating away the forest, and the chemicals polluting the water and air, all played a part. The land, second only to the sun in sacredness, was torn, wasted, and broken. Even so, Indians have remained "in the woods," as isolated and as close to the natural landscape as possible. A modern Caddo leader, Melford Williams, once remarked, "I want to build a house in the trees where the birds and animals are, in the woods near the water. We belong there, with that."

Indians believed that animals and humans could converse freely and that certain powerful humans could change into animals and leave their bodies. Birds and animals could become humans, too. An old part-Choctaw man once remarked, when asked about the sanity of a person seen talking to a squirrel in the woods, "Your problem is simple. He speaks squirrel. *You* don't." The Indian system confused the Europeans who encountered it. Animals, plants, and even the dead were considered animate parts of life. Indians failed to understand why Europeans denied relationships with these entities.

In Louisiana, the native religions survived countless attempts by Christian missionaries to change them. Indian people were able to keep their basic view of things and to participate, to various degrees, in Christianity. Wise missionaries recognized this. Highly regarded, they had a great understanding and tolerance of traditional Indian religion. Others—perhaps less wise and certainly more zealous—punished, cajoled, and threatened Indian people. Indians politely withdrew or, more rarely, forced the missionaries to leave. In the 1700s a few were killed. Many times the liberal priests and ministers were understood less by their European peers than by their Indian flocks. In 1719 Bénard de la Harpe described the doughty missionary Father Davion, the beloved priest of the Tunica, in somewhat ambivalent terms.

> Since he [Davion] has been with the Tunicas, he has had to "surrender" to these peoples the greatest part of their idolatry, their household gods *Dieux penates* are a toad [crapaud] and a figure of a woman that they worship. They believe both represent the sun. This nation is composed, in all, of 460 people; they have two great chiefs of the assembled nations, speaking the same language. The first is called

Cahura-Joligo; he yields himself, with his family, everyday to the prayers and exhortations of M. Davion, who, although he is opposed to their feasts and plurality of wives, is strongly revered in this village.

Later, in the nineteenth century, another priest, Father Rouquette, lived with the Choctaw north of Lake Pontchartrain, near Bayou LaCombe. He wore his hair long, in Indian style, spoke Choctaw, and attended their annual ceremonial feasts. He was respectfully called Chahta Ima, "Choctaw-like," by his Indian friends.

Although the Chitimacha had killed the missionary St. Cosme in the eighteenth century, most of the priests and ministers went unmolested among the tribes. Their most common lament was simply that no one listened to them. Both the humble Spanish priests of northwest Louisiana and the politically affluent Jesuits, Dominicans, and Capuchins of the French colonies in lower Louisiana seemed equally frustrated in their efforts.

Documents from the colonial period show tribal tolerance even for excesses like the vitriolic outbursts of those missionaries who stormed temples and broke the sacred objects they found there. Even the French chroniclers seem amazed at such restraint. Had they but known that in the eyes of the Indians, such missionaries seemed mad. Surely, these sacriligious acts must have startled the Indians into their passive attitude. Even madness was a part of order, just as storms preceded great calms.

Owl hoots, the barking of foxes, and other signs such as cracks in house walls portended death. Individuals frequently announced the day and time of day when they would die. One Tunica medicine man cut a path across a field to the site where he wished to be buried; four days later he died, just as he had predicted. Indians, then, were not taken by surprise. The omens allowed for adequate preparation. Death was to be met at home, surrounded by family and friends. To live for a long time and to live life well was part of the natural cycle. Sudden or violent events—the death of children, of young people in their prime, of warriors caught off guard—were unnatural, surprising, and usually attributed to witchcraft. A child was given a pet to grow up with; if witchcraft was directed at the child, the pet intercepted it and died.

The dead were respected and were dealt with carefully. If disturbed, they became ghosts—spirits without conscience or obligations. Ghosts were dangerous and greatly feared. Some living per-

Fig. 31
ST. PETER'S CONGREGATIONAL CHURCH, THE OLDEST INDIAN CHURCH IN
LOUISIANA, KOASATI SETTLEMENT, BAYOU BLUE
Courtesy of Don Sepulvado

Fig. 32
NINETEENTH-CENTURY ROMAN CATHOLIC MISSION TO CHOCTAW ON BAYOU SCIE,
SABINE PARISH
Courtesy of H. F. Gregory, Don Sepulvado, and Jim Toby

sons could talk with the dead and even ask them for favors, such as providing company or opening gates. Such conversations, however, were perilous and were available only to the most powerful persons.

Despite the Indian's belief that all events were part of a harmonic whole, death was traumatic, and the gaps left in family and community brought deep, genuine mourning. Although the dead were merely moving from one world to another, the path between the two might be an odyssey filled with dangers, temptations to go astray, monsters that might attack, or slippery logs that must be used to cross the streams. Consequently, the dead were prepared for such eventualities. Food and water, favorite weapons, and sacred objects were interred with the dead to help with the journey into the next life.

Some tribes, among them the Tunica, made special fires to light the paths of the deceased. Others prayed at the graves and fired guns to frighten away demons and open the road. The Alabama, Choctaw, and Koasati believed that each person had two souls, *Shillup* and *Shilombish*. One stayed at the grave with the remains for four days and nights, while the other traveled prior to the journey to the afterworld. The soul that remained at the grave might become a ghost, wandering malevolently. Cemeteries were holy places, and gifts of food were often placed there long after a person's death. The Koasati still refer to burial places as *Ilhani Snaho*, "rich man's land." Stillborn infants were buried in hollow trees with the umbilical cords of children who had lived.

The destination of the dead was conceptualized in various ways. It was a place like the home of the Indians on earth, but conditions in the upper world were better. The Choctaw described the afterworld as a place of green grass, water, and trees. The Koasati saw a land of song and dance to the west, across a rainbow. The Tunica knew of a land, like their own on earth, at the upper end of the Milky Way.

Conversion to Christianity is sometimes described by old Indian people as "being taught to pray." Prayer existed in Indian culture to express thanks and tell of need. What the European brought was prayer for salvation. Most tribal religions lacked the concepts of eternal punishment and sin. There was no hell from which to be saved. The Choctaw feared being lost in a desert of thorns, but virtually all of the others expected another life in a place much like the earth at the end of their dangerous journey. Death, then, was not confused with punishment. It was merely a part of the intricate web of natural phenomena.

To the Indian, evil simply existed, like all other things. It was a natural occurrence with which people had to contend, like cold and hunger. Although understood, evil remained locked in the context of power, a gift from the spirit world that surrounded man. Power could be used for great good or turned against one's peers and community; hence it was a danger. Antisocial behavior was evil. Punishment was immediate, not delayed to the other life, and was handled in a number of ways.

Human sacrifice, infanticide, and suicide must all be considered, at least partially, in the light of the Indians' attitudes about death. Louisiana Indians observed these practices, and some of the tribes participated in all of them.

Sacrifice, noted archaeologically and ethnographically, served to release spirits to accompany the dead. Objects including weapons, pottery vessels, horses, dogs, and human beings were killed, literally or figuratively, to release the essence of their beings to accompany individuals into the next world. The Natchez chief Stung Serpent contemplated suicide so that he might enter the next world with his brother. Wives, children, and slaves were customarily strangled and interred with the deceased as retainers and friends in the other world. Close friends and family might volunteer to accompany the dead. This practice seems to have reached exaggerated peaks among the Natchez and Taensa. The roots of the once widespread custom are definable far back before the historic record began, as evidenced by multiple burials in mounds. However, it seems to have persisted into European contact times only among the Natchez and related tribes. Frightened Europeans, shocked and revolted by the behavior of the Indians, failed to understand the theological reasoning behind such actions. Only Le Page du Pratz, who lived with the Natchez, suggested that they considered sacrifice a noble deed reflecting honor and glory on surviving relatives.

Infanticide seems to have increased after white contact. Le Page du Pratz noted that women used plants to abort unwanted pregnancies, and later the Spanish authorities protested against the

killing of newborn twins. The birth of twins was considered an ob-
vious break in the natural scheme by most tribes. Charles Hudson
has noted that many other phenomena were similarly regarded by
Indians of the Southeast and that such drastic measures were justified as attempts to restore the natural order, the harmony of the
world.

Later, infanticide was practiced by Indian women held in slavery
by the French, most likely to prevent the children from becoming
slaves. As late as the nineteenth century, a Tunica woman attempted
suicide rather than be considered socially on the same level as a
slave. Such practices were not sanctioned forms of Indian behavior
but probably were responses to European impacts on traditional
Indian conduct. Infanticide by women slaves is not on the same
order as the killing of twins or the sacrifices described above. The
numerous accounts of human sacrifice and infanticide in the colonial period may also reflect the unprecedented stresses of new diseases and attempts to maintain the Indian world view under continuous pressure from non-Indians.

One of the oldest religious entities was a sun and temple cult. Like
the corn, beans, and squash cultivated by the Indians, this religious cult had its roots in the Southwest and Mexico. The Acolapissa,
Caddo, Houma, Natchez, Taensa, and Tunica all maintained sacred
buildings, some of which were raised on truncated pyramidal earth
mounds reminiscent of temples in Mesoamerica. Practices of the
Atakapa and Chitimacha differed somewhat. They built sacred
dance houses and charnel houses, but no temples. In most of the
tribes, the skeletons of the upper classes; sacred objects connected
with the sun, especially figurines of humans, frogs, and rattlesnakes; and quartz crystals, were kept in the temples.

A sacred fire was ritually kindled in the temple every year and
kept burning by temple guardians for the ensuing twelve months.
Each family fire was relit from this new fire. The temple guardians
protected the building from intruders. It was an extremely holy
place. Le Page du Pratz has left a detailed description of temples as
he saw them in 1725.

All the peoples of Louisiana have temples, which are more or less well
cared for according to the ability of the nation, and all, as I have said,
put their dead in the earth, or in tombs within the temples or very

near them, or in the neighborhood. Many of these nations have only very simple temples, which one would often take for private cabins. However, when one comes to know he distinguishes them by means of two wooden posts at the door made like boundary posts with human heads, which hold the swinging door with a fragment of wood planted in the earth at each end, so that the children may not be able to open the door and go into the temple to play. In this way the door can be raised only above these posts, which are at least 3 feet high, and it requires a strong man to lift it. These are the little nations which have these temples that one would confound with cabins. The latter have in truth posts and similar doors, but the posts are smooth, and these doors open sideways, because there is no fragment of wood at the end. A woman or child is able to open these doors from the outside or inside, and at night one closes them and fastens them inside to keep the dogs from coming into the cabins. The cabins of the Natchez Suns have, in truth, posts like those of the temples, but their temple was very easy to recognize in accordance with the description I have given of it. Besides, near these little temples some distinctive marks are always to be seen, which are either small elevations of earth or some little dishes which announce that in this place there are bodies interred, or one perceives some raised tombs, if the nation has this custom.

These temples are clearly associated with the cult of the sun and the dead, sometimes termed the Southern Cult or the Buzzard Cult by anthropologists. From a city complex that developed near what is now East St. Louis, Missouri, it spread across the major river drainages of the South from about A.D. 1000 to 1400. Remnants of the Buzzard Cult were still functioning in Louisiana when the first Europeans arrived. The residual elements included temples and mounds, stratified social organizations headed by priest-chiefs, sacred fires, and special concerns with the sun, moon, wind, and cardinal directions. Life and death, the sun and moon, and rain and crops were all implicated in the temple cult.

Each day the Natchez chief climbed the temple mound and called out his father, the sun. This ritual reaffirmed his connection to the source of life, the most powerful of all the forces in the universe. The sun rose at the exact time of his call—a precise piece of astronomical knowledge. According to Archie Sam, the cross-in-palm symbol indicated the point where the power of the sun entered the worshiper's body. The crosses represented the sun and were displayed when the palms were raised toward the morning sun.

Worship of the most sacred element of the universe, the sun, seems to have been universal. The Tunica considered it a female deity. The Chitimacha had a female sky god, Kutnahin, who probably was a personification of the sun. The moon, the "night sun," was equally sacred to most of the tribes. The Alabama considered it best to wash one's body by moonlight. Myths about the sun and related human deities persist among the tribes. Dances are performed around a fire because it represents the sun. Among the Choctaw and Koasati, the discovery of red toads living under one's house is a lucky sign, as are dreams of fire.

The temples were integral not only to worship of the sun but also to the annual celebrations at the ripening of the new crops. In 1736 Father le Petit noted that fathers of families carried their first harvests of corn and other vegetables to the temples. The priests then distributed the harvest in the villages.

Mound building had begun to lose its significance in Indian life at the time of the first white settlement in Louisiana. Both the Chitimacha and the Natchez interred their dead in mounds well into historic times. The de Soto narratives point out that both temples and chiefs' houses were raised on mounds, but by two centuries later, only the Natchez, probably the most conservative of the southeastern Indians, seem to have retained the once universal tradition. Temples, however, did survive longer, and most tribes built some such sacred edifice. Among the Alabama and Koasati, the *Ischoba*, "Big House," is still central to community patterns. Today, the word *Ischoba* is applied to Christian churches, which fulfill the sacred function.

Some tribes erected brush arbor structures at the first-fruits ceremonial. Medicine men, the ritual specialists, called the people together at the harvest of the new corn, which usually occurred in July or August, depending on the phases of the moon. The people were summoned to a ceremony called *posketa* or *bosketa*, at which many of them drank the Black Drink. The English called the ceremony the Busk. The drink, termed *asi* by the Muskogean speakers and *La Cassine* by the French, was a tea often brewed from a variety of holly (*Ilex vomitoria*). Taken in large quantities, it caused those who drank it to vomit, ritually cleansing their bodies and minds before they ate the new corn. No one could enjoy the new crop until this ceremony had been conducted. Eventually, the annual ceremonials seem to have become detached from the early temple-mound complex. The Biloxi and Tunica preserved almost the entire new-corn ceremony, but not the temple mound, as late as 1941.

Each family harvested its own crop. The men and older boys went to a sacred water hole with the chief, usually a medicine man, in whom were combined the roles of priest and chief as observed by early Europeans. There the men and boys faced the rising sun, dove naked into the water, and bathed. The chief called them from the water and marked the forehead of each with a cross, the ancient symbol of the cardinal directions. Then each was given a kernel of corn to eat. After this ritual, they returned home, where the women had been arranging an elaborate feast in which corn was prepared in every way they knew.

Another element in the Tunica practice, called by the French the *Fête du Blé*, Corn Feast, was the ritual feeding of the dead. Small boys chosen from each family were given packets of corn folded in shuck containers to place on the graves in family burial areas. This had to be done before dawn, and the dead fed before others broke the corn fast.

Except for the ancient ritual drink and vomiting, the elements described above clearly show Southern Cult roots. The sun, the cardinal directions, corn, and water all were integrated, or reintegrated, in the ceremonial. The connection between the living and the dead was reaffirmed, and the corn admitted to sacred standing.

The ritual *posketa* ceremony centered on the taking of *asi* or *ahissi*, the emetic drink. The rites were held at the square ground, an area often set apart from the community itself. Four logs pointing to the cardinal directions were laid on flat ground in the center of the dance plaza in preparation for the sacred fire. The Natchez and Cherokee departed from this custom by building the fire on a small mound raised in the plaza. According to a number of tribes, the most powerful fires were kindled from logs taken from trees that had been struck by lightning.

Then, for four days and nights at the new-corn ritual, the people of the tribe gathered. All day the medicine men in the arbors taught the men and boys, and orated. The lectures dealt with leading a virtuous life and behaving properly toward other people and nature. All night and day the people fasted; at night they danced around a fire. Koasati males drank great quantities of ritual tea, usually brewed from the roots of *toola* (bay) or *skafoto hatka* (horsemint), while women washed in it. Then all went to the edge of the sacred area, vomited, and returned. In another cleansing ritual, men and boys were scratched with a sharp implement to shed blood for the people. The scratching might be done with the teeth remaining in a garfish jaw, a sharp piece of bone, or trade needles set in a bent turkey quill by the medicine man. A dried raccoon paw was used among the Choctaw for this purpose. Scratches were inflicted on forearms, chest, calves, and the length of the spine, and the bloody marks were swabbed by the medicine man who had done the work.

Married people reaffirmed their vows, each Indian made peace with his enemies, and the harmony of the world was restored. The resolution of conflicts at every level within the community was an aspect of the green-corn feasts that Europeans generally failed to understand. Indian etiquette was complicated; one had to be careful not to give offense. Making amends was difficult, and some Indian languages had no word for "sorry." The Busk ceremony allowed people to atone; there was ritual forgiveness, wherein each reaffirmed his ties to all the others. It is most likely that other ancient forms contained similar components that were not apparent to outsiders.

Witchcraft was universally dreaded, and it persisted long after tribal religion began shifting to Christianity. The colonial Europeans feared witches as much as the Indians did. Malevolent acts disrupted the natural order and led to unpredictable events disharmonic with normal life. Almost always, such abnormal events were discussed with the medicine people or doctors and then attributed to witchcraft.

A witch apparently had certain unnatural powers, but he or she could be overcome if the medicine person who was asked to deal with the witch was strong enough. A particularly strong Tunica witch sometimes reportedly took off her skin and traveled invisibly through the night, but when a medicine man caught her, he filled her skin with salt. The burning sensation she felt when she put it back on before dawn supposedly cured her.

The Louisiana Indian saw witchcraft and medicine as being closely related. What was great power for good could easily be turned into great power for evil. If a patient died while being treated by the medicine person, the cause of death might be considered witchcraft. In such cases, the medicine person was killed, a radical sort of compensation for malpractice.

Medicine people had various ways of diagnosing witchcraft and dealing with it. Cures were complicated and secret. In 1719 Bénard de la Harpe described a case.

> The chief of this nation had a son of 15 years, who had been baptised and instructed in the mysteries of our Saints by M. Davion. Less than a month after my departure from the Tunicas, he fell ill and died in the hands of his pastor and father, Deville, Jesuit. . . . The recovery of this young man was given over to a Tioux medicine man; after the death of this young man it is repeated that he had said had the father given him a present, he would have saved the boy's life. The Tonica chief, having received these words, ordered the immediate execution of this medicine man. Before this execution, he, the medicine man, says to Cahura-Joligo, in the presence of M. Davion, that he sees he clearly cannot avoid death, but in order to prove he is a great sorcerer; after his death the beasts and birds will respect his body without the services of the dead being performed upon him. After the Tioux was executed he was thrown on the road and truly, like he had predicted, the birds and wild beasts, though in great numbers, did not touch the body.

La Harpe attributed the incident to the use of herbs, rubbed on the body, which were repugnant to the scavengers. The role change from curer to sorcerer, nevertheless, is well demonstrated by this incident.

The term *medicine* in Indian usage connotes both power and preparations used in the treatment of disease. The medicine people who combined magic with their knowledge of plants and anatomy were the most powerful and, possibly, the most dangerous of medicine people. Each had his own territory, and like the Tioux described by La Harpe as serving the Tunica, could cross tribal and linguistic boundaries. The territories were respected, for it was believed that their violation led to vicious, magical conflicts among the medicine people.

The medicine, or power, was obtained from a visionary being, through long apprenticeship to an older practitioner, or as a gift from an animal or other spirit, such as one of the "little people" of the forest. Not everyone who sought the medicine found it, even if he heeded items essential to the search—specific herbs, thorns, water—and underwent complete isolation. Exactly what transpired during the period of isolation was never revealed. Certainly there was prayer and fasting.

The Choctaw danced around a dead tree until they saw a vision. The tree was expected to burst into life when the medicine was acquired. Some tribal medicine men knew special songs and recitations for curing, which, along with herbal medicines, are still used by Louisiana Indians.

Some forms of religious belief existed apart from the medicine involved in curing, though there was no sharp dichotomy. The medicine people existed alongside the cult leaders. It is not quite clear when, if ever, the functions of priests and medicine people fused. As early as 1718, the anonymous author of the *Luxembourg Narrative* described the medicine people in this fashion:

> They have among them doctors, who, like the ancient Egyptians, do not separate medicine from magic. In order to attain to these sublime functions a savage shuts himself into his cabin alone for nine days without eating, with water only; everyone is forbidden to disturb him. There holding in his hand a kind of gourd filled with shells, with which he makes a continual noise, he invokes the Spirit, prays Him to speak to him and to receive him as a doctor and magician, and that with cries, howls, contortions, and terrible shakings of the body, until he gets himself out of breath and foams in a frightful manner. This training being completed at the end of nine days, he comes out of his cabin triumphant and boasts of having received from Him the gift of healing maladies, driving away storms, and changing the weather. From that time they are recognized as doctors and are very much respected; people have recourse to them in sickness and to obtain favorable weather; but it is always necessary to carry presents. It sometimes happens that having received them, if the sick person is not cured or the weather does not change, the doctor is killed as an imposter; a fact which causes the most skillful among them only to receive presents when they see an appearance of cure or of change in the weather.

The medicine people became the complicated crux of Louisiana Indian religion. Religion was the combination of philosophical concepts of how to live in the world—how to maintain the role of humans in the natural order—and the ritual and herbal magic used to maintain harmony.

Religious specialists, or priests, existed in many tribes. Among the Natchez and their neighbors in the lower Mississippi Valley, these men were Suns, descended from the sun and more like gods than men. However, in this tribe the keepers of sacred temple fires were not the Suns but old men chosen for their piety and faith. The Caddo priestly caste, the *Xenesi*, had great supernatural powers but were not necessarily medicine men. Among the more egalitarian tribes, the medicine men were sometimes religious leaders.

Some tribes, like the Choctaw, made a clear distinction between herbal and ritual medicines. The herbalists, usually older men and women, offered plant remedies and occupied a position somewhat like that of the modern pharmacist. Herbal medicine, as practiced by the Indians, was far from simple. In the 1930s, one Houma medicine man revealed to Frank Speck seventy-nine plant cures, only three of which involved plants of European origin. The French-speaking Houma called such a physician a *traiteur* or *traiteuse*. Of thirty-nine plant cures learned by Lyda Taylor from the Koasati, only four were possibly of European origin. Speck pointed out that European plants were utilized in Indian ways; dosages, for example, were computed in fours, not threes.

The application of plants in medical practice was complicated. Plant stems, blooms, bark, leaves, and roots all had their specific efficacies, and their employment varied from cure to cure. Animals, too, played a part in herbal medication. The Choctaw believed that knowledge of the mayapple medicine, used in the treatment of stomach upsets, came from the crow. The bear taught other cures, and even the dog had some medical knowledge to impart. The herbalists were careful observers of nature and especially of animals, their teachers.

Various factors were part of the Indian doctor's lore. Claude Medford has noted that the time of day was an important consideration in the gathering of medicinal plants, as were some seasonal changes. The various colors associated with the cardinal directions as well as with life and death were relevant to medicine. Red was especially powerful and almost universally viewed as a life color. Other sacred colors were black, yellow, and white. To the Koasati and Tunica, blue was sacred, signifying death to the former and winter to the latter.

Parts of plants, such as blooms, stems, and roots, were sorted by color as well as place of origin. Bags of different colors, often red flannel or a black or white fabric, were filled with medicine and carried on the sick person as amulets. The power associated with clays and natural pigments was probably derived from their association with certain sacred colors. In Louisiana and elsewhere, the Indians' emphasis on plants as agents of healing set them apart from European practitioners of medicine. Indeed, the aboriginal herbal pharmacopoeia lengthened the life of many an early American pioneer.

Among the Indians, medicines were usually administered orally, some being made into teas. Others were applied as poultices or sudorifics. The Houma and Choctaw measured medicines by "swallows" and "half-swallows." Traditionalists still find hypodermic medicine distasteful, for witches "shot" objects, including lizards and insects, into their victims.

Hypnosis, psychological suggestion, and cupping, or bleeding, were employed, along with herbal medicines. These treatments were carefully selected and skillfully administered with restraint. The feeling of balance, for example, precluded the exhaustive bleeding practiced by Europeans. Among the Indians, this treatment appears to have been cleaner and more efficiently done than by the Europeans. Choctaw curers used cups of cow or buffalo horn and lancets of flint or glass in a procedure Le Page du Pratz described as superior to the European method. Contemporary traditionalists almost always identify small lancets found at prehistoric sites as those used in bleeding, opening boils, and extracting thorns. Some of the Europeans were quick to learn that willow tea, the equivalent of aspirin, was more helpful than leeches and knives.

Smoke was also a remedy of some importance. Warm smoke blown into the ear, for example, was a widely employed cure for earache. Broken bones were skillfully set, though surgical procedures were almost unknown. Other than in the removal of bad teeth, such techniques violated the natural order.

Some aboriginal specialization developed, such as midwifery, and some curers were widely respected for their treatment of burns, fractures, and lung ailments. Some doctors were capable of handling ghostly manifestations and ghost fear. In Indian Health Service hospitals among the Mississippi Choctaw, the practices of these efficient, careful doctors, as the medicine people are still known among the Indian communities, have been integrated with modern medicine.

These medicine people were among the first practitioners of holistic medicine. They realized not only the inadequacy of a dichotomy between the mind and body but the lack of clear distinctions between the natural and supernatural as well. They used what many now consider to be advanced medical techniques. Patients, for example, were usually treated at home and were not isolated from their social unit, the family. Whenever possible, the doctor lived with the family. Sweat baths, massage with a warm object such as a stone, the use of herbal incense, herbal inhalations, and the recitation of sounds that induced a sense of exaltation had all the benefits of contemporary relaxation therapy. People displaying symptoms of depression or melancholy were gathered into group sessions with family and friends. The medicine people used these support sessions to reintegrate the patient. Such meetings are clearly the forerunners of community mental health activities.

As late as the 1930s, a Koasati medicine man rejected surgery on his injured feet. He resorted to herbal medicine, and the resultant slight limp with which he walked was infinitely better to him than would have been the amputation of a foot. To be buried in two places, he explained, was unnatural. The manipulation of one part of the body, with no idea of how it fit into the larger system, was alien to the medical tradition of many American Indians, including those of Louisiana.

Le Page du Pratz, a pharmacist, was quick to note the efficacy of herbal medicines. His observations were supported by others. In the eighteenth century, French observers were amazed at the Indian doctors' abilities in curing wounds. They thought, however, that Indians had little knowledge of internal medicine. Such observers knew little of Indian herbals such as sweet-gum sap, willow-bark tea, and the various emetic plants used to treat internal problems. Le Page du Pratz not only understood the treatment of wounds to be superior but noted that the Indians' internal medicine was also excellent.

I shall not undertake to particularize all the virtues of this sweetgum or Liquid-Ambar, not having learned all of them from the natives of the country, who would be no less surprised to find that we used it only as a varnish, than they were to see our surgeons bleed their patients. This balm, according to them, is an excellent fabrifuge; they take ten or a dozen drops of it in gruel fasting, and before their meals; and if they should take a little more, they have no reason to apprehend any danger. The physicians among the natives purge their patients before they give it. It cures wounds in two days without any consequences; it is equally sovereign for all kinds of ulcers, after having applied to them for some days a plaster of bruised ground-ivy. It cures consumptions, opens obstructions, afterwards affords relief in the colic and all internal diseases; it comforts the heart.

Many of the other herbal medicines noted by Le Page du Pratz eventually were taken into modern pharmaceutical usage.

Notable, too, was that the Indian doctors were not paid. They accepted gifts, but only if they felt certain that the patient would get well. Not surprisingly, the largest gifts were given after recovery. Especially welcome rewards were tobacco and colored cloth folded in special ways. The punishment for failure might be exile, permanent ridicule, or even death.

The appearance of previously unknown diseases, particularly those brought in by Europeans, confronted the native practitioners with new problems. The fear of witchcraft increased, and the shaman became more cautious in the application of his healing arts. As early as the 1700s, the execution of medicine men may have reflected their growing inability to cope with the new diseases sweeping the tribes. Other new pressures, among them alcoholism, tribal migration and warfare, and Indian slavery, seem to have provoked more frequent accusations of witchcraft. In many cases, the medicine people suffered unjustly when their skills failed.

The medicine people, in spite of all difficulties, survived. The new strains drew the people and the practitioners closer together, and those socioeconomic stresses unique to Indian communities seemed best handled by the traditional medicine. Ancient skills had to be applied to serious new problems, worse than arrow or even gunshot wounds. The tribes were crowded onto smaller land holdings. The elders and the children, the repositories and the hope of tribal traditions, were dying. Increased involvement in the European trade brought more competitive attitudes, violating the oldest of all Indian virtues, hospitality and the sharing of resources. These problems intensified malevolent feelings, factions developed everywhere, and the medicine people had to combat witchcraft more diligently, emphasize the need for sharing, and constantly remind the people of the need to be cooperative with, and supportive of, each other.

The white men, who had transmitted their ills to the Indians, often denied them the remedies that were available. Indian leaders like Tinehouen, a Caddo chief, sought new medicine against smallpox for their people; it was never delivered. The medicine people did what they could. As the government of the United States began to treat Indians as wards, Indian doctors were driven underground, fearful of prosecution for practicing medicine without licenses.

As late as the 1930s, anthropologists could observe the old religion and collect the medicines. By the 1950s, the traditional medicine had become something understood by Indians only, and it was for the most part no longer shared with those who did not understand the depth and intensity of its spiritual components. When given to outsiders, the gift was always predicated on the admonition, "not for publication." The sacred prayers and recitations needed to make the medicines effective were once known to many people but had become carefully guarded knowledge by 1900.

By the 1920s, the medicine people had become increasingly pan-tribal and had extended their activities. Some, like Emma Jackson of Indian Creek and Mark Robinson, a Koasati, traveled from one tribal community to another. The late Arzalie Langley, a Choctaw from the Koasati tribal area, visited almost every Indian community in Louisiana except the Houma and the Chitimacha.

Protestant mission work among the Indians began in earnest after 1890. The first ministers were Indian medicine men, who were admirably suited to the work and were sought out for the task. Most of them knew the Mobilian Jargon and so could communicate across tribal boundaries. The medicine men were sober, honest, and giving of themselves. In many ways, they surpassed the white Christians.

Their rewards, at least in this life, tended to be meager. Once conversions had been made, churches had been built, and con-

gregations established, these early Indian leaders were often replaced by whites. One early Koasati minister, Mark Robinson, who
walked fifteen miles to preach in 1922, was eventually displaced
from his hard-won position, though it took two whites to do his job.
Perhaps the early Indian ministers were too tolerant of the Indian
medicine to relinquish that tradition; whatever the reason might
have been, the Indian preachers were quickly dismissed. Non-
Indian preachers drove the rituals and integrative traditions far
underground. Christianity was compatible with the ministry but
not with the old Indian ways.

As Indian youths began to attend schools, new assimilative pressures were felt. Not only did the native languages come under attack, but western religion was strongly advocated. Young Indian
people began to acquire the notion that white values, for better or
for worse, would be dominant in the world, and they began to
learn the distinctions of European science and mathematics. The
old ways were left for the old people. Yet the religion and medicine
survived. In Indian communities, where income levels were low
and children were plentiful, it fell to the lot of the older people, the
grandparents, to baby-sit and to raise the children. So the earliest
learning experiences were resoundingly Indian in orientation.

In colonial times, there was a tendency to exchange cultural values and behavior. Elements of European culture crept into Indian
ways and vice versa. After 1900, there was a strong tendency to
compartmentalize the two cultures. Recently, when a young Louisiana Indian asked his grandfather about the old ways, the reply
was terse. The youth was asked if he preferred the Christian religion. When he answered that he did favor the nontraditional faith,
the old man simply replied, "The medicine is for Indian people."
Young Indians increasingly seem to feel that they must make a
choice between the old and the new ways.

Ethnologists and others, in a well-intentioned rush to preserve
the Indian culture, are equally well admonished by Chief Joseph A.
Pierite, a Tunica-Biloxi traditionalist: "We have a promise from the
Sun. As long as the Sun will shine we will have the medicine. As
long as there is the medicine there will be Indian people. If we
have, as you anthropologists say, been here 10,000 years, then we
have kept the medicine. We do not need it written down!" The
medicine will survive in one form or another. The Sun's promise

will be kept. In marshes, pine hills, and smoky streets, most Louisiana Indians continue to seek harmony, to maintain the natural balance of life. The medicine goes with them, wherever they go.

REFERENCES

While Indian religions long have quickened the imaginations of non-Indian observers and writers, anthropological literature reveals surprisingly little information on the subject. John R. Swanton discussed the Indian religions of the Southeast in most of his standard works cited herein and has provided other significant sources.

Swanton, John R.
1928 Sun Worship in the Southeast. *American Anthropologist* 30: 206–13.
1929 Myths and Tales of the Southeastern Indians. *Bureau of American Ethnology Bulletin* 88, Washington, D.C.

A good summary of Swanton's works coupled with a broader southeastern Indian perspective appears in two relatively recent syntheses.

Hudson, Charles
1976 *The Southeastern Indians.* Nashville.
1979 *Black Drink, a Native American Tea.* Athens, Ga.

A work tracing the connections between the archaeological evidences of religion and magic and ethnographic descriptions of those beliefs has become a classic.

Howard, James H.
1968 The Southeastern Ceremonial Complex and Its Interpretation. *Missouri Archaeological Survey Memoir* 6, Columbia.

Antonio Waring's formulation of evidence of a widespread ceremonial complex is also seminal.

Waring, Antonio J., and Preston Holder
1945 A Prehistoric Ceremonial Complex in the Southeastern United States. *American Anthropologist* 47:1–34.

Waring, Antonio J. (Stephen Williams, ed.)
1968 The Southern Cult and Moskogean Ceremonial. In the Waring Papers, the Collected Works of Antonio J. Waring, Jr., *Papers of the Peabody Museum of Archaeology and Ethnology, Harvard University*, Cambridge, 30–61.

Another important perspective has been developed.

Witthoft, John

1949   Green Corn Ceremonialism in the Eastern Woodlands. *Occasional Paper from the Museum of Anthropology* 13, University of Michigan, Ann Arbor.

Many primary sources on the religion of the Louisiana Indians and their neighbors have never been translated from the original French or Spanish. Especially important are the *Papeles Procedentes de Cuba* and the letters from the commanders at the various Spanish colonial posts of Louisiana: Lafourche (now Donaldsonville), Rapides (now Alexandria), Punta Cortada (Pointe Coupee near modern New Roads), Ouachita (now Monroe) and Natchitoches.

John R. Swanton, in 1911, used the abundant French colonial material in the *Bibliothèque Nationale* in Paris. However, he most often seems to have used translations by the nineteenth-century Louisiana historian Pierre Margry. Margry's work has unfortunate deletions, some errors in translation, and some unnecessary though interesting additions to the original sources. He has gathered a whole series of accounts in his work.

Margry, Pierre, ed.

1880–1883   *Découvertes et Etablissements des Français dans l'Ouest et dans le Sud de l'Amérique septentrionale (1614–1754)*. Paris, 6 vols.

Perhaps the best observers of the religious practices of the tribes, especially in the eighteenth century, were the Jesuit priests traveling up and down the Mississippi. A look at their material is valuable.

Thwaites, Reuben, ed.

1896–1901   *Jesuit Relations and Allied Documents: Travels and Explorations of Jesuit Missionaries in New France, 1610–1791*. Cleveland.

Another good eighteenth-century source on Louisiana Indian religion is Jean-Baptiste Bénard, Sieur de la Harpe. Most often his name is misspelled, and he is called Benard de la Harpe. He went to Louisiana from France to found a post on Red River, and left a journal covering the period 1718 to 1720. The only manuscript copy of his journal is located at the *Bibliothèque Nationale* in Paris, as are his journals of two later trips in Louisiana and a memoir. A rather bad translation of La Harpe, by Pierre Margry, contains alterations, deletions, and additions. This version, dated 1876 to 1886, has been translated again by Ralph A. Smith.

Smith, Ralph A.

1958–1959   Account of the Journey of Bénard de La Harpe; Discovery
Made by Him of Several Nations Situated in the West. *Southwestern Historical Quarterly* 62, Nos. 1–4.

Much information from the journal of Bénard de la Harpe on the Lower
Mississippi Valley and its tribes can be found in Swanton's work.

Swanton, John R.

1911   Indian Tribes of the Lower Mississippi Valley and Adjacent Coast
of the Gulf of Mexico. *Bureau of American Ethnology Bulletin*
43:318–26, Washington, D.C.

An important discussion of European and Indian attitudes toward witchcraft appears in Jean-Bernard Bossu's narratives.

Dickinson, Samuel Dorris, ed. and trans.

1982   *New Travels in North America by Jean-Bernard Bossu, 1770–1771.*
Natchitoches.

An interesting reference to the execution of witches by the Caddo in the
nineteenth century is available.

Williams, Stephen

1964   The Aboriginal Location of the Kadohadacho and Related Tribes.
In *Explorations in Cultural Anthropology* (Ward H. Goodenough,
ed.), Princeton, 545–70.

One of the best primary accounts of shamanism remains the so-called *Luxembourg Narrative*, housed in Paris. The author remains unknown, and the
document apparently written in French seems to have been published at
Luxembourg. The passage most pertinent to shamanistic activity is quoted
in Swanton's 1911 work. Swanton believed the document was written before 1718. The full title is:

1752(?)   *Mémoire sur la Louisiane en le Mississipi.* Luxembourg.

Other early accounts appear in the Spanish descriptions of the Caddoan
groups in the western area of the state. Herbert Eugene Bolton has summarized some of these in his extensive work on Texas. Further information
is in the Library of Congress.

1805–1835   Letterbooks of the Caddo Agency. Ms on microfilm at Library of Congress, Washington, D.C.

References to witchcraft among the Choctaw appear in a number of places.

Cushman, H. B. (Angie Deboe, ed.)

1962   *History of the Choctaw, Chickasaw and Natchez Indians.* New
York.

Bushnell, David I., Jr.
1909   The Choctaw of Bayou Lacombe, St. Tammany Parish, Louisiana. *Bureau of American Ethnology Bulletin* 48, Washington, D.C.

Some material herein came from the field notes of Hiram Gregory and the late Caroline Dormon. These references are based on work among the Koasati, Choctaw, and Chitimacha in the 1930s and 1970s. Gregory has synthesized an overview of Louisiana Indian traditional culture—religion, magic, folktales, and so on.

Gregory, Hiram F.
        A Promise from the Sun: The Louisiana Indians. In *A Guide to Louisiana Folklife* (Nicholas Spitzer ed.), Department of Culture, Recreation, and Tourism, Baton Rouge.

Chief Pierite's statement near the end of this chapter can be found in Gregory's 1973 field notes. Donald Hunter, with several Koasati, among them Bel Abbey, Nora Abbey, and Louisa Wilson, has produced good accounts of tribal custom.

Hunter, Donald
1975   The Cicada in Southeastern Archaeology and in Coushatta Tradition. *Louisiana Archaeology* 2:219–26.

The continuity of Tunica burial customs has been documented.

Brain, Jeffrey
1976   From the Words of the Living: The Indian Speaks. In *Clues to America's Past*. National Geographic Society, Washington, D.C.

Tunica practices and attitudes toward the dead have been described, along with an account of a late nineteenth-century burial.

Gregory, Hiram F.
1978   A Historic Tunica Burial at the Coulee des Grues Site in Avoyelles Parish, Louisiana. In *Texas Archaeology* (Kurt D. House, ed.), Dallas, 146–64.

Le Page du Pratz described Indian temples.
1758   *Histoire de la Louisiane*. Paris, 3 vols.

The Tunica corn feast, as described by Sesosterie Yuchigant, has been documented in a series of linguistic texts.

Haas, Mary
1950   Tunica Texts. *University of California Publications in Linguistics* 6(2):1–174.

The late Louise Allen, Clyde Jackson, Mary Jones, Mr. and Mrs. Anderson Lewis, Jesse Lewis, and Dorothy Nugent, all of the Jena Choctaw, along with Clementine Broussard and the late Florence Jackson, have contributed much to our understanding of Choctaw and Tunica-Biloxi traditions. Oney Brown, a nontribal Indian, has also given of her knowledge. The late Emerick Sanson, a part-Choctaw, materially advanced our knowledge of relationships between animals and humans.

A recent work on folklore and myth among the Houma, by Bruce Duthu, a young Houma, is an impressive beginning for Indians teaching non-Indians about their tribes.

Duthu, Bruce
1979   Folklore of the Louisiana Houma Indians. *Louisiana Folklife* 4(1): 1–32.

Faye Stouff, widow of the late Emile Stouff, a Chitimacha chief, shared some of her insights into the tribe and the medicine it used. Her publication on the tribe contains much important material.

Stouff, Faye, and W. Bradley Twitty
1971   *Sacred Chitimacha Indian Beliefs*. Pompano Beach, Fla.

Lester Sepulvado's report on curing and witchcraft along the Sabine River remains the only documentation of Hispanic and Indian syncretism in that area.

Sepulvado, Don Lester
1980   Folk Curing in a Spanish Community. *Louisiana Folklife* 3.

Many unpublished field notes are available; the notes on the Alabama, Koasati, and Tunica contain numerous references to the tribal myths and traditional religion. These are in the National Anthropological Archives. Albert Gatschet's notes are also in the National Anthropological Archives and, like Swanton's, contain many bits of information virtually impossible to find elsewhere today.

Spanish documents covering nearly forty years of Spanish administration in Louisiana are filled with detailed information on topics such as infanticide. The *Papeles Procedentes de Cuba* are now available at the Library of Congress, the Loyola University library in New Orleans, and the Archives of the University of Southwestern Louisiana, Lafayette. The Bexar Archives in San Antonio, Texas, contain references to the Caddoan tribes, including some on their religion.

The Library of Congress holds English documents covering 1765 to 1790 and dealing with the tribes on the east ascending bank of the Mississippi River. More important than these sources may be the traditionalists who have shared their cherished beliefs with us: Bel Abbey and the late Mark Robinson of the Koasati; and the late Joseph Alcide Pierite, Sr., and his brother, the late Herman Pierite, of the Tunica-Biloxi.

In his work, Frank G. Speck set admirable standards—respected by Indians and anthropologists—which extended to the study of herbal medicine. His work among the Houma was seminal to the study of ethnobotany.

Speck, Frank G.
1941 A List of Plant Curatives Obtained from Houma Indians in Louisiana. *Primitive Man* 14(4):49–73.

The regional authority on southeastern Indian plant usage, Lyda Averill Taylor, completed her dissertation at Yale University on the Koasati. Her work, which has been published, is filled with references to herbal medicines from Louisiana.

Taylor, Lyda Averill
1940 *Plants Used as Curatives by Certain Southeastern Tribes.* Cambridge, Mass.

XVI

PLAY

Formal and informal play constituted a significant element of the Indians' social life. By playing at being adults, children learned tribal skills. Boys practiced wrestling, running, throwing, and lifting weights, played at the ball and chunkey games, and sought skill with the bow and blowgun. Girls learned and practiced the domestic arts. These activities were undertaken in fun but were preliminary to the games of adults, which were viewed as seriously as our modern athletic contests.

Variations of the ball and chunkey games were found among all the Louisiana tribes. The ball game is related to the lacrosse of the northeastern American Indians, now an intercollegiate sport. The Indians of the Southeast used two rackets made of hickory, each with one looped end in which there was a deer-hide webbing. Only men were allowed to play with the rackets. Women might be permitted to join the game but could use only their hands. The ball was of deerskin stuffed with deer or squirrel hair, or it might be plaited of rawhide with a flea inside to "make it jump."

Playing fields were of various lengths and seem to have become shorter in recent times. The ends of a field once were marked with single goalposts topped by fish or bird effigies, which later gave way to paired posts with crossbars. In Louisiana, the single-post game was retained for contests in which both men and women participated. A score was made by striking the goalpost with a thrown ball or by touching the post with a ball held in a racket.

Teams ranged in size from a few players to the entire adult male population of a town. Pregame activities included body painting, scratching, and anointing to make the player elusive, and dancing and singing to prepare him spiritually. In the course of play, the ball could be carried up or down the field in the racket or thrown to a teammate. Each team had a ball witch to help it control the ball, and women switched the men to keep them running. The game was exceedingly rough, with only head butting barred, and injuries were common. Even deaths occurred in the violent action. The game ended when an agreed-upon number of points, usually ten, had been scored by one team or the other, and was followed by the distribution of the vast amount of goods wagered on the out-

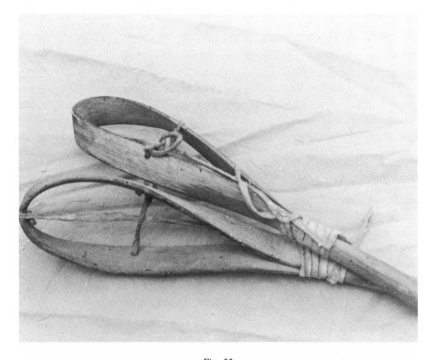

Fig. 33
TUNICA BALL STICKS
Photograph by H. F. Gregory, Courtesy of the Dormon Collection, Special Collections, Eugene P. Watson Library, Northwestern State University, Natchitoches

come. Although this was primarily a man's game, women might play when the men were finished.

According to reports, the Natchez played a version of the ball game in which hands were substituted for sticks or rackets. Players tried to keep the fist-sized ball, stuffed with Spanish moss, from touching the ground during play. The game ended with the scoring of a single goal. Ceremonies were held before and after a game, and hundreds of people participated. The chief of the losing side presented gifts to the winners. This game was played until after 1900 in the isolated Clifton settlement in Rapides Parish, where it may have been learned from the Apalachee or from itinerant Natchez. The popular Creole game *racquette* was borrowed directly from the Indian game, even retaining the custom of each team having its own songs. *Racquette* remained popular in French Louisiana throughout the nineteenth century, and, in the 1950s, attempts were made to revive it at Mamou. In other parts of Louisiana, interest in the game as a spectator sport ceased to exist after the Indians stopped playing it about 1900.

Highly popular, at least in early colonial times, was the chunkey game. This variation on the widespread hoop-and-pole game was largely a spectator sport, since only two players usually took active parts. Each contest was an occasion for heavy betting among the watchers. The equipment and rules of the chunkey game varied among the tribes. Common to all was the chunkey stone, a polished stone disk some six inches wide and two inches thick, with concave sides. It was owned by tribes or clans. Goal-posts were of slender hickory poles ranging in length from eight to fifteen feet and bearing crossbars or other markings.

Almost every early Indian town in Louisiana had a chunk yard, a smooth, well-worn space about one hundred feet long and ten to twelve feet wide. One player rolled the stone, and as it moved, one or both players threw sticks, their object being to hit the stone, strike the opponent's stick, or to come to rest nearer the stone after it had stopped rolling. The playing sticks were about five feet long and an inch wide, and rings were cut around them several inches apart. These helped measure the distances involved in scoring the game.

Other games, usually less athletic in nature, afforded further opportunities for gambling. One seems to have been a variant of the western hand game, a guessing game in which two sides, generally of four men each, tried to outguess each other as to the location of an object. There was chanting by the contestants on the side whose leader was trying to guess where a designated object had been hidden. Among the Choctaw, the object was concealed under moccasins, socks, or gloves. The Caddo hid a bead, and no gambling was associated with their game. Both sides sang lustily during a contest, the object being to enlist supernatural help or to cow or confuse the opposition.

A favorite gambling game among Indian women was played with three or four short sections of cane, split lengthwise. These "dice" were thrown into the air, and the result was scored by the position in which they landed—so many pieces with concave sides up, and the like. Choctaw women played a game resembling jackstones but apparently were reluctant to be seen playing it.

For the chunkey game the Caddo seem to have substituted the hoop-and-pole game familiar farther west. Wrestling, foot racing, and archery competition were much pursued, perhaps more so in Louisiana than to the east. The Caddo also played a game resembling ticktacktoe and another somewhat like a modern game in which the object is to jump one piece over adjacent pieces until only one is left.

The Indian games and sports were often important only because they justified many other activities. Almost any contest was likely to be an occasion for all sorts of fun, particularly gambling. The Indian was an inveterate gambler and seemed ready to bet on the outcome of any competition—an attitude that added excitement to even the dullest events. This tendency led missionaries to discourage all sorts of recreation, especially stickball.

Feasting, when it had no ceremonial significance, must be considered recreational. Occasions for feasting sometimes arose fortuitously, the result of a good catch of fish or an exceptional bag of game. Sometimes warm weather or another circumstance made it impossible to preserve the fish or game for future use. The Indians were accustomed to eating heartily when food was plentiful and to reducing consumption when supplies ran low. This was no more than a rational adaptation to circumstances over which they had little or no control.

At both formal and informal affairs, feasting was commonly accompanied by dancing and singing. The dancers sometimes performed as a group, dancing in a circle, while others danced individually or in pairs. A tune usually went with each dance, rendered vocally or on pipes accompanied by rattles and drums. On informal occasions, there seems to have been much spontaneous composition of songs and variations on the dances. Quite different were the eagle dances of the Choctaw, in which the participants wore masks. European observers found these dances impressive. They were more ceremonial than recreational, though they surely were enjoyed by the dancers.

Each of the Louisiana tribes had its own musical tradition, which, like other American Indian music, was wedded to dance. Other music and dance forms were more widespread or pantribal in distribution. Long before the powwow circuit had spread eastward from the Great Plains, Louisiana Indians and their neighbors, even non-Indians, were sharing dances and songs. The pantribal music generally was secular, and songs were almost invariably in Choctaw or the Mobilian Jargon. They were performed for fun or served as a focus for courtship, trade, or, on occasion, politics.

Stickball games, by their nature rousing affairs, were enlivened still further with team songs somewhat like the fight songs of colleges and universities. Running songs were performed en route to ball play to reinforce team spirit. Among their modern counterparts is the singsong cadence so often heard at military training centers. Since each stickball player had a personal song, it would seem that the typical stickball game was more of a musical than an athletic event. While singing his song, the player also performed his own dance steps, usually at or near the goalpost. More like prayers than a dance, the steps were intended to insure the athlete's success and well-being during the forthcoming game.

Many songs were call-response songs, most accompanied by drums. The Choctaw simply struck hardwood sticks together to keep time. Call-response songs were often sung by men and women. Leaders could be of either sex but most often were males. As in earlier times, the songs are beautifully performed today, but only a few old singers remain. The Koasati tribe has a dance team for its young people, but it is difficult to find a singer to work with them.

A number of dances were cataloged among the Bayou LaCombe Choctaw early in the twentieth century. These included a tick dance, chicken dance, and horse dance. They had spread to other tribes, especially the Tunica and Biloxi, and had been added to the sacred dances of those tribes. "Stealing partners," a highly popular Choctaw secular dance, is still performed regularly in southeastern Oklahoma. Girls chase boys from the crowd around the dance

Fig. 34
TICK DANCE, BAYOU LACOMBE CHOCTAW, *ca.* 1914
National Anthropological Archives, Smithsonian Institution

ground. Boys and men hold back, pretending shyness, but are pulled into a dance line. The singer and drummer start a song, and the dancers, holding hands, begin moving around the dance area. At intervals, someone dashes from the crowd, pulls a dancer free, and leads him to the end of the line. By the time the dance is finished, all the participants have danced holding the others' hands.

Snake dances, or double-head dances, were popular among several tribes and, in spite of their secular nature, once may have had religious significance. The Tunica enjoyed a snake dance in which a line of dancers, holding hands, spiraled into a tight group. Then they spun quickly out from the coil so that a long line was almost instantly formed, and spiraled back into the cluster. The line of dancers coiled and straightened with such speed that those at the end of the line were likely to be snapped off. People not acquainted with the dance found themselves hurtling through the spectators or into the bushes. The coils of the snake dances were drawn from the spirals that were the symbols of the sacred winds, the center of the world, and the origins of life. Fire and technology were linked to the spiral, as were the concepts of duality and continuity, the beginnings and ends of things being powerfully interconnected.

Many dances were imitations of animal behavior. In the Tunica raccoon dance, for example, individual dancers mimicked that familiar creature's shuffling and shoulder-humping movements. Other dances mirrored the horse, chicken, horned owl, rabbit, turtle, and even the humble but aggressive wood tick. Some dances had magical properties. The Koasati garfish dance supposedly called that fish to the dancer. Claude Medford, who lived many years with the Alabama and Koasati, swears to the efficacy of this dance.

Dancing was secularized from the more complicated celebration of the new corn. The animal dances, performed as part of the Green Corn ceremonial to thank the animals for their help to man, became for secular fun during the rest of the year. The Alabama and Koasati girls performed a dance in which they winnowed corn in fanner baskets without losing a grain or missing a step—carrying work into play. Even dancing for fun often had ritual connections. Some dances were purely recreational; the classic round dance and "changing partners" dance of the Choctaw and other Muskogean tribes are the best examples.

The Tunica, in the first part of the twentieth century or earlier, performed a long series of songs and dances much like an orchestrated ballet at certain times of the year. The *Elohara*, or midnight dance, of the Tunica was dedicated to the full moon and was sung, in part, as a tribute to the moon "dressed in silver." It was the high point of their dance cycle.

Some tribes danced only at night, and some avoided dancing until the snakes had hibernated so as not to attract them. As a rule, men and women danced separately in sacred dances and together during recreational dances. Isolated boy-and-girl couples were not permitted, for a dance was a community affair.

After the Europeans went to Louisiana, they often attended Indian dances, some of which incorporated European elements. Changing partners and dancing in mixed couples in a sort of Indian schottische is an Alabama dance called the Alabama two-step.

The last regular Louisiana Choctaw dances were held at Bayou LaCombe at the turn of the twentieth century. An attempt at revival has begun; in 1974 the Jena Choctaw held a barbecue and dance attended by singers and dancers from Oklahoma and Mississippi. The songs and dances were traditional. The Caddo now located near Gracemont, Fort Cobb, and Binger, Oklahoma, have maintained their dance ground at Binger. They hold their traditional dances there each year, during August. Their turkey dance, bell dance, and other dances were once sung and performed in northwestern Louisiana. The traditional costumes of these Caddo echo those from the days before the cession of their Louisiana homeland.

Costumes vary considerably from tribe to tribe. Usually, dancers simply wear their best, and often most colorful, clothes. The Tunica, however, as late as the 1930s, dressed in special costumes for their dances. The tailored costumes of men were fringed, and small bells were sewn along the fringes to provide additional music to accompany the dance. Sacred colors, especially red and white, appeared in dance costumes.

Today, costume is still an important element of the dance among Louisiana Indians. Women frequently wear long, brightly colored dresses, with additional color provided by long streamers or ribbons attached to the hair, to headbands, or, sometimes, to the shoulders. The ribbons originated in the Old World, where they had long been worn to indicate revolutionary sympathies, patriotic causes, and other relationships. The French probably introduced the custom to the Indian trade in the New World after the French Revolution. Now they are worn simply to add color and change to the movements of the dancers.

As a rule, the traditional dances are performed outdoors, by the light of fires. The Caddo refuse to dance inside any sort of building, though they sometimes sing and drum indoors. The Chitimacha were the only tribe to erect large buildings, at some distance from their villages, where they gathered for rituals and dances. These dance houses were sacred structures, like temples. All other groups resorted to special grounds where dances and songs were performed. The Caddo still maintain small camps, or brush-arbor structures, which they call "houses," about their ground in Oklahoma, where a visit may last several days.

Indian musical instruments were simple. Drums made of skin-covered logs were used by the Choctaw at Bayou LaCombe. The Tunica-Biloxi made drums of skin-covered cypress knees, the pneumatophores by which the sacred trees "breathe." Indian drums were played with one stick. Playing them with the hands is an African style not adopted by the Indians.

Rattles were made of gourds filled with gravel or garfish scales and attached to a handle. Another popular instrument for syncopation was a rattle made of deer hooves strung so as to strike the handle. The Choctaw singers sometimes used two sticks to keep time, striking them together to provide the rhythm for dancers and singers.

Indian musicians readily adopted European materials and some of their musical instruments. The simple Indian rhythms were augmented with bells and rattles of metal, and the fiddle became a popular item among Indian musicians. Deo Langley, who is Choctaw and Koasati, and the late Choctaw Amos Blue Eye helped make the fiddle a part of traditional Indian music. Turtle shells were worked, covered with rawhide, and made into crude fiddles and guitars by descendants of the Apache in northwest Louisiana.

A few flageolets, or flutes, were made of cane, as were great numbers of whistles. Some musicians had copper-covered panpipes as early as A.D. 700 or 800. Scratchers of alligator hide produced a

Fig. 35
CYPRESS-KNEE DRUM
Courtesy of the Museum of Geoscience, Louisiana State University

somewhat droning, scratching sound that may be heard today in the Indian version of Scottish fiddle music.

In spite of the simplicity of their instruments, Indians managed to produce beautiful, fascinating music. From the solemn movements of the isolated Chitimacha dancing in their dance house to the mass confusion of the Choctaw "stealing partners" at social dances, the Indians displayed their skills in this art form. The tonal principles of Indian music often inhibited the participation of whites in Indian social life, especially in the sacred and secular dancing. So, to be Indian came to mean to be a dancer, to attend the sacred Busk or Yaupon Tea ceremonies, and to maintain tribal connections.

Missionaries in the nineteenth century strove to eradicate, at least in northwestern and central Louisiana, the dancing, music, and ball play that were so much a part of Indian life. Betting and drinking, commonplace at these gatherings, were anathema to Protestant fundamentalists. Converts to the white man's faith were urged not to dance. Sometimes they did refrain, but often the Indians retreated with their old music and religion into the deep swamps. There they could sing, dance, pray, and have a good time together, as a tribally sovereign group.

As early as the 1890s, medicine shows and theatrical events had introduced the feathered, tepee-dwelling Indian stereotype into the East. Plains cultural elements gradually turned into symbols of Indian identity, even among the Indians. The powwow reached Louisiana sixty or seventy years later, by the middle to late 1960s. Using a communal drum, several drummers, and chant songs that had no words helped integrate the Indian society. Plains songs were popular. The Indian Angels, an urban, pantribal group, began organizing powwows in Baton Rouge, Louisiana. Today, the annual Baton Rouge powwow, usually held in July or August, attracts Indians from all parts of the Southeast. Cherokee, Creek, Pueblo, Sioux, and others attend this gathering, which is replete with gift and music exchanges between the groups. In a north Baton Rouge teamsters' hall, one can hear drumbeats and see the dancers. Old people sit and watch while younger people dance together. Around the edges of the crowd, whites buy traditional and nontraditional crafts. There is almost a carnival atmosphere. In a corner, a Sioux, far from the plains he knew as a young man, unwraps a cedar flute from a deerskin and plays the gentle, sweet notes of courtship. Older people, watching and listening, nod and smile.

The powwows cut through petty tribal differences and ethnocentrism, and give urban Indians a feeling of gain rather than loss. At least in the cities, Indians can dance and sing their songs. At the powwows, they listen eagerly and break down linguistic barriers.

Outside the powwow circuit, there are few opportunities to see and hear Indian dances and music. The Tunica-Biloxi sing their songs for their children, and sometimes older Alabama and Koasati return to the forest to sing and dance, far from alien eyes and ears. The Tunica-Biloxi Harry Broussard, who toured the nation playing jazz saxophone, often recalls breaking into a Tunica song in the midst of a performance and how much the audience liked it. Koasati fiddlers long have surpassed the fiddling of their Cajun neighbors and are undoubted masters of that instrument.

Indian songs and dances have been performed to meet individual needs for thousands of years. The white planters used the Indian arts and artists to entertain their guests; Indians danced for help and harmony. Even though the settings in which they are performed are sometimes foreign, the ancient Indian traditions of music and the dance remain. They are strong but are increasingly influenced by more popular Plains Indian powwow music and dance. The forms native to the Louisiana tribes are becoming increasingly rare.

REFERENCES

Louisiana Indian music and modes of recreation have attracted the attention of visitors—both anthropologists and laymen—since before the Civil War. The slave Solomon Northup left descriptions of 1850 Indian dances at Indian Creek in Rapides Parish.

Northup, Solomon (Sue Eakin and Joseph Logsden, eds.)
1968   *Twelve Years a Slave.* Baton Rouge.

Another account is of Indian dances near Lecompte and Marksville, and of ball games attended frequently by non-Indians near Natchitoches.

Saucier, Corinne
1943   *The History of Avoyelles Parish, Louisiana.* Baton Rouge.

Steward Culin discussed Indian games, including stickball, and described a Louisiana *racquette* game in some detail.

Culin, Steward
1907   Games of the North American Indians. *Twenty-fourth Annual Report of the Bureau of American Ethnology.* Washington, D.C.

In various reports John Swanton presented data on the stickball game and on various other recreational topics. Swanton is the primary authority on traditional Indian games.

Swanton, John R.
1911   Indian Tribes of the Lower Mississippi Valley and Adjacent Coast of the Gulf of Mexico. *Bureau of American Ethnology Bulletin* 43:318–26, Washington, D.C.
1931   Source Material for the Social and Ceremonial Life of the Choctaw Indians. *Bureau of American Ethnology Bulletin* 103, Washington, D.C.

Another writer left firsthand accounts of both the ball game and chunkey.

Cushman, H. B. (Angie Deboe, ed.)
1962   *History of the Choctaw, Chickasaw and Natchez Indians.* New York.

Few systematic data on dance and music have been synthesized, though Bushnell, Swanton, Cushman, and, more recently, Charles Hudson, have written briefly on them.

Hudson, Charles
1976   *The Southeastern Indians.* Nashville.

Canyon Records has released two recordings of typical Muskogean ceremonial music with excellent commentary by Claude Medford, Jr.

Canyon Records
1969   *Songs of the Muskogee Creek.* Taos, New Mexico.

Two recordings of traditional Caddo songs and dances have been released by Indian House Records.

Hasinai Cultural Center
1976   *Songs of the Caddo.* Taos, New Mexico.

Another researcher left Tunica songs in her texts and recordings.

Haas, Mary R.
1950   Tunica Texts. *University of California Publications in Linguistics,* 6(2):1–174.

The unpublished papers of the late Caroline Dormon contain some songs she recorded from Milly Brandy, a Choctaw, near Alexandria, Louisiana—the only record of Louisiana Choctaw music. Her notes are on file in the archives of the Eugene P. Watson Library, Northwestern State University, Natchitoches. Tapes of Tunica-Biloxi songs exist in the field collections of Mary R. Haas, Claude Medford, Jr., Hiram F. Gregory, Ernest C. Downs, and Emanuel Drechsel. Unfortunately, these recordings are not generally available to the public.

Natchez music taped by Mary R. Haas may be heard at the ethnohistory archive of the University of Indiana. Archie Sam, a Natchez-Creek revivalist, reconstituted part of that music at the Natchez square ground in eastern Oklahoma.

Howard, James H.
1970 Bringing Back the Fire: The Revival of a Natchez-Cherokee Ceremonial Ground. *Oklahoma Anthropological Society Newsletter* 18(4):11–17.

James Howard was nearing completion of a detailed study of Choctaw music at the time of his death in 1984. It is expected that it will be finished soon and published posthumously. The contrasts between urban and more traditional activities were well described in Dennis Booker's thesis.

Booker, Dennis A.
1973 Indian Identity in Louisiana: Two Contrasting Approches to Ethnic Identity. M.A. thesis, Department of Geography and Anthropology, Louisiana State University.

A single Houma song fragment has been recorded by Jan Curry, but little else remains of that tradition or language. The fragment is preserved in the field collections of Hiram F. Gregory and Claude Medford, Jr.

Bowman, Greg, and Janel Roper-Curry
1982 *The Houma People of Louisiana: A Story of Indian Survival.* Mennonite Central Committee, Akron, Ohio.

The veteran student of all Indian music, Frances Densmore, left an excellent monograph on Choctaw music.

Densmore, Frances
1943 Choctaw Music. *Anthropological Paper* 28, *Bureau of American Ethnology Bulletin* 136, Washington, D.C.

Densmore also managed to collect snatches of the Chitimacha musical tradition.

Densmore, Frances
1934 A Study of Indian Music in the Gulf States. *American Anthropologist* 36(3):386–88.
1934 Studying Indian Music in the Gulf States. *Explorations and Fieldwork of the Smithsonian Institution in 1933*, Washington, D.C., pp. 57–59.
1943 A Search for Songs Among the Chitimacha Indians in Louisiana. *Bureau of American Ethnology Bulletin* 133:1–15, Washington, D.C.

Ralph Renzler of the Smithsonian Folk Festival collected Koasati folk songs by Arzalie Langley and Dee Langley in the 1960s. Tapes of the songs are in the collections of the Center for Creole and Acadian Studies at the University of Southwestern Louisiana but are generally available only to researchers. Folklorist Alan Lomax in 1983 began recording Koasati fiddle tunes and traditional songs. He hypothesizes that much Acadian folk culture, including some of the music, was borrowed from the Indians—a distinct possibility, if one is to judge from language and food in Louisiana.

Lomax, Alan
1984 Personal communication to H. F. Gregory.

XVII

TRIBAL WARFARE

The waging of war was an integral part of life for Louisiana's Indians, and armed conflict was rather easily provoked. A strong chief, feeling his position menaced by a neighboring tribe, might launch a campaign. Real offenses such as an intrusion on tribal lands or the killings of a tribesman without an acceptable offer of compensation could lead to war. Fancied offenses stemming from the desire to secure captives could also lead to war.

It has been suggested that the Indians of the Southeast made war in hopes of acquiring more or better farmland. This was probably not so in Louisiana, since many square miles of excellent bottomland were never cleared and occupied. Perhaps the objective was the conquest of agricultural land already under cultivation or the winning of a position of strategic or trade value.

Although the reason for going to war might be capricious, the conduct of hostilities was a serious business. Winning military glory was virtually the only path by which a young man could advance to accepted adulthood. If war was decided upon, those youths without honors sought places in the war party, hoping to kill an enemy and take his scalp, or capture hostile warriors or civilians. Failure to achieve military distinction doomed a male to a menial position for life. Cowardice and desertion in battle were major crimes; one who had left his post was forever scorned by his people.

Among the Muskogean speakers, men assumed honorific titles after they had distinguished themselves in battle. Many such names appear in the literature on the Louisiana Indians. The suffixes *-tubbe*, *-mico*, and *-huma*, or *-houma*, were more in the nature of insignia of military rank than simple name endings. Many Indians, as late as the early twentieth century, carried these war names as well as French or English Christian names.

Indian wars were frequent, breaking out and ending almost abruptly. Combat was preceded and followed by ritual and ceremony, much of which was religious. The season for military operations among the Indians lasted from late spring to early fall. Perhaps the warriors could leave their families unattended for longer periods at that time of year, and life in the open was less rigorous. Armies around the world followed the same scheme, campaigning during the warm months when roads were passable and going into winter quarters with the onset of the cold season.

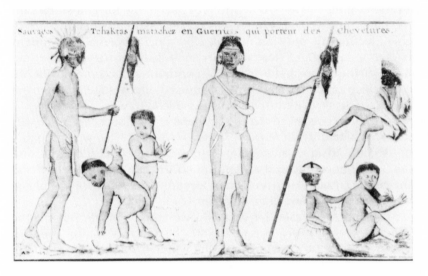

Fig. 36
EIGHTEENTH-CENTURY CHOCTAW WARRIORS AND CHILDREN
sketch by A. De Batz
National Anthropological Archives, Smithsonian Institution

The preliminaries to hostilities varied from tribe to tribe but were a matter of some concern to all, because the outcome of a campaign might be determined by what was done or not done before it began. In one instance, the Choctaw met in council and declared war on another group. Members of the expeditionary force assembled several days prior to departure to prepare themselves for the ordeal of battle. They painted their bodies, rubbed themselves with herbs possessing magical powers, fasted, performed the war dance, and sought auguries of victory from the conjurer, who was the medicine man. Each warrior, stripped to breechcloth and moccasins, carried rations of dried meal and was well armed with bow and arrows, knife, tomahawk, war club, and, in ancient times, a shield.

In the approach, the party of approximately twenty men sought to surprise the enemy. Near their objective, they moved at night, traveling quietly two or three paces apart in single file, imitating animal sounds and movements, and employing other ruses to avoid detection. On the march, the leader carried the sacred ark of war medicine belonging to the town. A bad dream or questionable incident, even the unnatural song of a bird, might force the party to turn back without ever meeting the enemy.

If possible, secrecy was maintained until the actual assault. Engaging in individual combat meant discarding the bow in favor of a weapon better suited to fighting at close quarters, perhaps knife or war club. Cane knives were used to remove scalps and even heads. The success of the attacking party was measured by the number of the enemy killed, scalps taken, and prisoners of all ages captured. The leader was most triumphant if he achieved his objective without loss to his own force.

As the returning victorious warriors neared their home village, they signaled their coming with loud whoops. Spoils of the expedition were distributed to the relatives of slain warriors. Adult male prisoners were tortured to death and scalped. Women and children were taken in by local families and soon were indistinguishable from others of the group. Captured women could attain full acceptance by marrying local men. After a purification ceremony, the winners strutted about, displaying a count of enemies slain, and records of their feats of war were tattooed on their bodies. Scalps stretched on cane frames to dry and skulls on poles were exhibited, and women danced around them. A calumet peace ceremony brought an end to hostilities, and a truce was declared, usually lasting until another incident provoked a new raid.

Martial procedures among the Natchez differed somewhat from those of the Choctaw. Preparations for a war effort involving the entire nation were carried out on a large scale. A council house was designated by the presence of a war calumet, a sacred reed or wooden tube to which a pipe bowl was usually attached. The council sought to determine if the offense against the nation could be resolved by sending a party carrying the peace calumet to the offender. If the overture was made and failed, preparations for hostilities began in earnest.

The war calumet, moved from the council house, was displayed on a pole before the house of the war chief. There was dancing and feasting, oratory, the drinking of the black potion *Ilex vomitoria* or the emetic redberry, and the proclaiming of individual warlike exploits. Those involved were not only the young volunteer warriors of the war party but also the older men who reddened the war clubs and incised the wooden objects to be left in the enemy's country. While the bow was the principal general-purpose weapon for all the tribes, the club was the symbolic war weapon among the Natchez. Perhaps this reflects old ways or the fact that the club, unlike the bow, was rarely used for any purpose other than fighting.

The war dance terminated the preparations for war. Three days later the attacking force set out, marching in single file in one or more columns, depending on the size of the force. They moved cautiously, preceded by scouts, avoiding fires at night and carrying with them a fetish or war medicine. The assault was delivered at daybreak.

While the Indians could and did fight fierce battles with Europeans according to conventional European methods and were often superior to unmounted whites, their engagements with other Indians took the form of raids launched against unsuspecting villagers whenever possible. An important objective was to leave visible evidence of their intrusion in the form of carved or painted sticks. The scalps of both friend and enemy, if the former was slain far from home, together with the prisoners, were brought back to the hometown.

Captives were made to sing and dance for several days. The hair of female prisoners was cut to indicate their status. Males taken by the Natchez were stunned and scalped, spread-eagled on a rectangular upright frame of poles, and then tortured and burned to death. A prisoner's life was spared if a local woman chose to marry him. The victors who had taken scalps had to avoid their wives and were placed on a special diet for six months. Finally, the calumet ceremony ended the conflict.

The Natchez, unlike the Choctaw, allowed individuals to organize private war parties and lead them against the enemy if they wished. A man seeking to recruit his own force erected two posts ornamented with feathers and painted red. Those who wished to join the war party gathered at the posts to dance, recite the accounts of their military deeds, and drink of the Black Drink to induce ceremonial vomiting. This rigorous cleansing freed the men of the ghosts and witchcraft that might have been encountered in previous wars.

The culturally marginal Atakapa followed practices in warfare quite different from those of the river tribes. According to Cabeza de Vaca, he observed conflicts erupt over women in the villages. The rivals struck and beat each other until worn out. In combat against outsiders, the men resorted to lethal bows and arrows. When expecting attack, villagers built fires in their houses but slept outside in order to confuse attackers. The Atakapa fought in a crouch, darting here and there to evade arrows. When the supply of arrows was exhausted, the combatants of both sides returned home without pursuit.

Some conflicts might have been termed formal warfare, but others took the form of massacres. Such was the case when the refugee Tunica, who had been sheltered by the Houma, followed the urging of the French and fell upon their hosts, killing some and driving others from their own town. In another instance, the Bayougoula, who earlier had nearly exterminated the Mugulasha living among them, granted asylum to the Taensa, only to be set upon by the newcomers and slain or expelled.

By modern standards in many countries, some practices associated with armed conflict among the Indians in colonial times seem extremely cruel. Mutilation of the dead and the prolonged torture and killing of prisoners are customs many consider repugnant, but a glance at recent events shows that this attitude is far from universal. Surely, the Indians' cruelties are dimmed by comparison with the savageries that have been perpetrated on a vastly grander scale in modern times. Also, such practices are no worse than the sufferings inflicted by adherents of the major religions of the world at that time in the name of their faith.

The military heritage of pre-European times remained firm throughout succeeding generations of Indians. The Choctaw and Tunica of Louisiana served as mercenaries with the French during the Natchez wars. Later, the Choctaw, along with some called "Seminole," more likely Pacana, fought under Andrew Jackson at the Battle of New Orleans. The Alabama and Koasati raised a Confederate unit to fight during the Civil War.

Recent events have shown that the warrior tradition among Louisiana Indians is as strong as ever. The Indians have transferred their martial allegiance from their tribe to their country. Long before they were considered citizens of the United States in 1914, many Louisiana Indians served in the United States Army as volunteers. Like that of other American Indians, their service in two world wars was exceptional. They also served in the Korean conflict and the Vietnam War. Although the Tunica, among other Louisiana Indians, objected to the military draft during World War II, claiming that only the tribe held sovereignty over its manpower and refusing to let Tunica youths be inducted into segregated units, virtually all the young men of that tribe went to war as volunteers. The Indians of Louisiana are unified by the pride they share in their record of military service.

REFERENCES

Almost every reference to the Southeast in the extensive literature left by early European arrivals in Indian America speaks of warfare. The de Soto narratives seem to open the window to a view of warlike southeastern tribes.

De la Vega, Garcilaso (Jeanette Varner, John Varner, eds.)
1980   *The Florida of the Inca.* Austin.

Bourne, Edward G., ed.
1904   *Narratives of the Career of Hernando de Soto.* New York.

A detailed treatment of the de Soto narratives as they relate to warfare is available in an unpublished source.

Duke, John
1980   De Soto's Travels on the Ouachita River in Arkansas and Louisiana. Ph.D. dissertation, Texas A and M University.

After his long association with the United States de Soto Commission, John R. Swanton paid special attention to the explorer's descriptions of the Louisiana Indians. Swanton's pertinent publications after 1930, cited elsewhere in these notes, reflect the influence of his fellow commissioner

Caroline Dormon. The major summary of their viewpoints was published in 1939.

Swanton, John R.
1939 Final Report of the United States de Soto Commission. *House Documents*, 76th Cong., 1st Sess., 71, Washington, D.C.

The Natchez wars have drawn the attention of historians and ethnohistorians to warfare as a significant aspect of intertribal relationships. These encounters, like those of de Soto, made possible a traditional historical focus on wars—with models of winners and losers.

Various sources, most notably Swanton's 1931 work, recounted Choctaw martial practices and accomplishments in detail. Cabeza de Vaca's observations of conflicts among the Atakapa can be found in:

Cabeza de Vaca, Alvar Nuñez (edited by A. F. Bendelier)
1904 *The Journey of Alvar Nuñez Cabeza de Vaca*. New York.

The activities of the Louisiana tribes after the mid-eighteenth century are best read in the untranslated *Legajos* of the *Papeles Procedentes de Cuba*, now available in several American libraries. The Alabama, Biloxi, Houma, Tunica, and others are described as participants in numerous raids and counterraids.

The little-known reports of the English agents on the east bank of the Mississippi River, especially John Thomas, after England had assumed control of that territory in the period after 1764, contain excellent accounts of Indian warfare. These are the reports to John Stuart, Superintendent of Indian Affairs, Southern District, 1764 to 1780, in the Library of Congress and the British archives in London.

Early French accounts by Le Page du Pratz and Penicaut contain much pertinent material, some of which has been summarized by Swanton.

Swanton, John R.
1911 Indian Tribes of the Lower Mississippi Valley and Adjacent Coast of the Gulf of Mexico. *Bureau of American Ethnology Bulletin* 43:318–26, Washington, D.C.

Another often-used source comprises the three volumes of the Mississippi State Archives.

Rowland, Dunbar, and Albert Sanders
1927 *The Mississippi Provincial Archives, 1701–1729*. Mississippi State Archives, Jackson.

A better, more carefully edited version is now available.

Rowland, Dunbar, and A. C. Sanders (Patricia Galloway, ed.)
1984 *Mississippi Provincial Archives: French Dominion*. Baton Rouge.

A history of French Louisiana long available only in the French versions has been translated and published.

Giraud, Marcel
1974 *A History of French Louisiana, Volume 1: The Reign of Louis XIV, 1698–1715.* Baton Rouge.

This work, based largely on the extensive holdings of the French archives— the Archives of the Colonies, the Archives of the Navy, the Archives of the Ministry of Foreign Affairs, and the departmental archives of La Rochelle and Nantes—remains the best historical source on early Louisiana.

The six volumes by Pierre Margry are a valuable source of descriptive material on Indians and warfare.

Margry, Pierre, ed.
1880–1883 *Découvertes et Etablissements des Français dans l'Ouest et dans le Sud de l'Amérique septentrionale (1614–1754).* Paris, 6 vols.

An English account by James Adair, first published in 1775, is the best source on the Chickasaw and Choctaw military attributes.

Adair, James
1775 *The History of the American Indians.* London. (1980 rpr., New York.

Lewis H. Larson has addressed the precontact role of southeastern Indian warfare.

Larson, Lewis H.
1972 Functional Consideration of Warfare in the Southeast During the Mississippi Period. *American Antiquity* 37:383–92.

Jon L. Gibson also wrote on warfare, using many examples from the lower Mississippi region.

Gibson, Jon L.
1974 Aboriginal Warfare in the Protohistoric Southeast: An Alternate Perspective. *American Antiquity* 39:130–33.

XVIII

LOUISIANA'S INDIANS TODAY

There is no accurate figure available for the number of Indians in Louisiana today, and estimates range from 3,000 to 20,000. The 1950 count was 490. In 1960 it was 3,587, and in 1970 it was 5,294. Growth continued, and the population reached 16,000 by 1980. It would seem that these figures do not represent actual numbers of Indians. The substantial difference in numbers between 1950 and 1980 reflects a new approach to Indian demography in which Indians, for the first time, were employed as census takers and self-identifications were accepted. Government programs offered new incentives for identification, and racial considerations were of little concern.

The uncertainty in numbers stems from the question "Who is an Indian?" If the individuals are allowed to decide, some with little Indian blood may be counted as Indian while others with much Indian blood may be omitted. If the count includes those affiliated with a recognized Indian group possessing a land base, even though some may live in a city, the total number indicated by the 1980 census is 12,600. This figure includes several hundred persons living apart from Indian groups and claiming to be Cherokee, Puebloan, Chipewa, Commanche, Sioux, or of some other exotic tribe. Not included in the figure are hundreds, perhaps thousands, who are from other populations and have partial Indian ancestry. As Clyde Jackson, chairman of the Jena Choctaw, has remarked, only Indians have to "prove" their identities.

Indians living in definable communities, in tribal groups, or in affiliation with such groups can, in broad terms, be divided into three classes: the federally recognized tribes, of which there are three; the state-recognized tribes, of which there are five; and the mixed-blood and full-blood kin groups scattered about the state.

An unknown number of people of Indian descent known as Red Bones live in southwestern Louisiana, some of whom reside in isolated, endogamous communities.

Federal recognition of an Indian tribal group is based on the demonstration that the group has existed with its own political integrity over a long period of time, preferably "forever," and retains a political or social structure that can be seen as an extension of traditional policy. The Chitimacha in St. Mary's Parish were recognized as such a group by the United States Congress in 1925. The Allen Parish Koasati were similarly recognized in 1971, and in 1981 the Bureau of Indian Affairs recognized the Tunica-Biloxi of Avoyelles Parish. During the 1970s, the Tunica-Biloxi were one of only two tribes recognized in the Southeast by the United States Department of the Interior. More than thirty tribes had petitioned.

While retaining traditional chiefs, the federally recognized tribes restructured themselves according to the Indian Reorganization Act of 1934. Today, each community elects a tribal chairman or chairwoman, who works in concert with an elected council. The chairman is not a chief, since that ancient title still refers to a respected hereditary position. Many tribal chairmen are descended from chiefs or medicine people, but they hasten to remind outsiders that they gained office by election, not inheritance.

Factionalism has long been inherent in Indian political affairs, involving such rivalries as kin versus non-kin and traditionalist versus modernist. In traditional Indian communities, factionalism contributed to a balance of power. Even the powerful Suns of the Natchez, because of factions, were not entirely independent of their subjects. Today, ancient intertribal and intratribal differences surface in tribal politics. Although appearing divisive to outsiders, they contribute a system of checks and balances essential to tribal structure.

The seemingly chaotic nature of Indian organization has mystified outsiders, but is, in fact, egalitarian. Each person is entitled to his opinion, and most councils, like the chiefs before them, cannot act until nearly full agreement is achieved in a negotiated action. In many respects, the Indian system is the most democratic of American governments.

The Tunica-Biloxi, among other tribes, had to work hard to achieve federal relationships, even though it had retained part of its communal land base, some religious practices and crafts, a traditional chiefdom (it had not "reorganized" and had kept a chief and a subchief well into the 1970s), and even cemeteries and traditional autonomy. The Bureau of Indian Affairs simply neglected its obligation to the tribe.

Fig. 37
CADDO TRIBAL EXPERTS DISCUSSING CADDO CULTURE, 1983
Courtesy of Don Sepulvado

The Apache, Choctaw, and Houma are attempting to follow the Tunica-Biloxi lead. Perhaps they, too, soon will be "Federal Indians." Still, tribalism remains strong. Each tribal group reflects periodically on more, instead of less, traditional government, and each remembers, or has maintained, a traditional chief.

The Louisiana Choctaw kept their alliances with the more powerful Mississippi chiefs as long as they could. By the American pe-

Fig. 38
ERNEST SICKEY, KOASATI, FIRST INDIAN TO SERVE AS COMMISSIONER OF INDIAN
AFFAIRS, WITH CONGRESSMAN JERRY HUCKABY
Courtesy of the Williamson Museum, Northwestern State University, Natchitoches

Fig. 39
CARROL TYLER, COMMUNITY LEADER, CLIFTON CHOCTAW
Courtesy of Don Sepulvado

riod—the time after Spanish domination—Indian agents in Louisiana were pressing the Choctaw to elect chiefs with whom they could work. Eventually, elections were held, and each Choctaw community had its own leadership. This resulted in the communities remaining essentially unaware of each other until the 1930s, when some movement was made toward pantribal organization. Ely Barbry, then chief of the Tunica, sought to organize the Biloxi, Choctaw, Koasati, and Tunica so that he could represent them in Washington. His efforts, though admirable, failed, and the tribes have since gone their separate ways. The Koasati leader Ernest Sickey has been active on behalf of all the tribes since the early 1970s and has brought their plight national attention.

State and federal recognition are substantial prizes. They guarantee land rights and provide educational and health services to the tribes. Further, they confirm the sovereignty of the communities by giving to Indian people the rights legally allowed nations, states, and municipalities.

State legislative recognition was extended in the 1960s in order to develop programs for Indian concentrations. Except for the Red Bone groups, virtually all Louisiana Indian communities now have such recognition: The Jena Band of Choctaw, the Houma, the Clifton Choctaw, the East Baton Rouge, or Louisiana, Band of Choctaw, and the Choctaw-Apache of Ebarb. A state Office of Indian Affairs, headed by a full-time commissioner, was established in 1972 to work on program development and the collection of demographic and other basic data on the Indians in Louisiana. Four of the five commissioners who have served have been Louisiana Indians. Koasati, Houma, Jena Choctaw, and nontribal Indians have held the post.

With the exception of the Chitimacha, all of the recognized groups represent migratory tribes that entered Louisiana in the last half of the eighteenth century. The Ebarb community (actually occupying a larger geographic area in that vicinity) includes families of Lipan Apache whose ancestors were imported as slaves by the French and Spanish on the eighteenth-century frontier between Louisiana and Texas. John Sibley relocated a number of Choctaw families west of Los Adaes in the nineteenth century. These people mixed with Hispano-Indian groups already there, further spreading the Choctaw westward.

Courtesy of the Louisiana State University Cartographic Section

THE CHOCTAW

The Choctaw of Louisiana are the most widely dispersed group, the East Baton Rouge Parish community representing principally mixed-blood Choctaw descendants now living in an urban setting. The other relict Choctaw groups represent eighteenth-century bands that moved into the present state under Spanish dominion. The only exceptions are the families scattered in the Mandeville area, which constitute a southerly extension of the larger body of Mississippi Choctaw. The largest contemporary Choctaw populations are descended from eighteenth-century Choctaw settlements in Rapides Parish and on the Ouachita River. These groups now compose the Jena Band of Choctaw and another, unrelated group, the Clifton community. In 1903 some of the Louisiana Choctaw joined members of their tribe living in Oklahoma.

Although most Louisiana Choctaw have been conservative, only the Jena Band has retained the language and traditional Choctaw crafts. Their old religion continued intact until the 1940s. They make good use of a tribal center funded by a grant from the Department of Housing and Urban Development and a tribal recreation facility. The Clifton community operates a recreation area for its youth and, depending on the availability of grant funds, a tribal center or office. Both groups feature tribal organizations with elected officials.

Today, many Indians work in industrial areas, on offshore oil rigs, on crew boats, as farmers, and as loggers. A few are college graduates, and though they share in Louisiana's lamentably high dropout rate, more and more are finishing high school. Still, incomes remain low, and the tribes suffer from years of exclusion from schools or, as in Terrebonne and Lafourche parishes, from a poorly developed tripartite school system.

The Ebarb community, for whom a state-supported public school was provided earlier than for other Indian and mixed-blood communities, probably has the most college-educated members. That community has experienced the greatest cultural change and, in the 1980s, works at restoring both its Indian and Spanish heritages. The annual Tamale Fiesta in Zwolle, Louisiana, has added local interest and fostered better community relations.

THE TUNICA-BILOXI

The Tunica-Biloxi are a small tribe. Fewer than a hundred live in the Avoyelles area, and as many more live and work in other places, maintaining some kind of connection with the parent group. On moving to the Avoyelles Prairie in 1779, the Tunica were granted land by the Spanish authorities. Such a grant should have been a square league, or nine to ten square miles. The 160 acres of land remaining occupied has never been taxed; it has also never been recognized as a reservation and has been placed in federal trust for the tribe. The Tunica-Biloxi are now receiving government benefits like those accorded the Chitimacha and the Koasati as organized tribes owning such a trust land base.

The Tunica-Biloxi seem to have retained many of their arts and crafts, though their native languages are virtually extinct. Their educational and economic attainments are low, perhaps lower than those of the Jena Choctaw, Clifton Choctaw, Chitimacha, Ebarb Choctaw-Apache, Houma, and Koasati. Approximately 60 percent have had a measure of formal education, but it is often of a low level. Attempts to establish the validity of the Tunica-Biloxi claim to the land they occupy and to use it as a basis for recognition have borne fruit. The tribe was granted federal recognition in 1981, making it elegible for much-needed aid to health and education. At the time of federal recognition, housing was poor and high unemployment existed. With the help of the United States Department of the Interior, Bureau of Indian Affairs, the tribe has funded a new housing development, a job placement service has begun operations, and an active crafts program is under way. A tribal planning program has begun, and the tribe is working toward the development of a small shopping center to provide income and employment.

THE KOASATI

The Koasati, in several respects, are the most purely Indian of all the Louisiana tribes. They are almost entirely full bloods. Their native tongue is spoken by all as their first language. They preserve and respect the rules of their matrilineal clans, and a traditional chief works with the tribal council and chairman.

Even so, cultural changes have occurred. Forty years ago the Koasati made a substantial array of functional plaited-cane baskets and wooden crafts. Today, pinestraw basketry, some beadwork, and occasional wooden items have replaced the utilitarian technology. The latter artifacts are made for a developing crafts industry that incorporates efforts to revive and maintain the old crafts, but the items that have proved most successful are those with some outside market potential.

The productive maize-based agriculture that once so distinguished the Koasati among the southeastern tribes was only faintly recalled forty years ago and now is practically forgotten. Tribal men and women work for wages in hospitals, on farms, and in the oil fields; others haul timber. Significant numbers have found employment in their own tribal services programs.

Fig. 40
KOASATI TRIBAL CENTER, ALLEN PARISH, 1984
Courtesy of Don Sepulvado

The federal school aid the Koasati have received since the 1930s continues, though it was interrupted for a time. They have completed a tribal organization based on elected representatives who serve on a council, and two hundred acres of land have been acquired to be held in trust by the federal government as a reservation. A new tribal headquarters building located on reservation land includes offices, recreational facilities, a meeting hall, and a medical dispensary. The last is essential for the treatment of diabetes, which afflicts about 40 percent of the tribe. The tribal organization required for the administration of the federal program has maintained a good tribal census, which presently totals approximately three hundred.

The settlement pattern is dispersed and is characterized by individual households situated in small clearings in a pine forest. Houses have been reconditioned or replaced, and road maintenance is good. Numerous water wells have been drilled to solve the ancient problem of a sanitary drinking supply, and steps have been taken to reintroduce agriculture, horticulture, and animal husbandry. A new venture is the production of Christmas trees. Favorable responses have met a proposal to establish an assembly plant to employ about eighty people. The former Elton railroad depot has been moved near a highway and converted into a museum and craft shop, selling baskets and other artifacts. Old crafts, including cane basketry, are being revived, and the elders have been enlisted to teach the dances, songs, tales, and crafts of long ago to the young people of the tribe.

The impact of the federal programs can be better appreciated by reference to prior economic and social conditions among the Koasati. In the 1970s, 90 percent of the people had annual incomes of less than three thousand dollars. Fifty percent of the wage earners were unemployed. Only about half the heads of families were literate, and housing and sanitary facilities were highly inadequate. Much improvement has been made in these and other conditions of life. Today, most wage earners have some employment possibilities. Educational levels, too, are higher. Many young people complete high school, and several have begun their college careers.

The Koasati now operate adult education classes, summer work programs, and reading assistance programs for elementary-school children. With the help of a linguist, Eugene Burnham of the Wycliffe Bible translators, they have begun publication of the first readers in their language, the most viable Indian tongue still heard in Louisiana.

THE CHITIMACHA

In some ways, the Chitimacha are unique among the Indian tribes of Louisiana. They are the only people who now live where they did in 1700, at Charenton on Grand Lake. From the first decade of the twentieth century until 1973, the Chitimacha were Louisiana's only reservation Indians and the only group to receive full federal benefits. They are the best situated financially and the best educated.

Before federal aid began to reach them, the Chitimacha were threatened with extinction as a tribe. Their language was almost forgotten, and the people were scattered and culturally disoriented. Supported now by federal recognition, a protected reservation of 262 acres, and a revived tribal identity, the Chitimacha comprise a healthy community of about 250 people. Another 400 or so live off the reservation but return to attend tribal meetings.

The Chitimacha reservation encompasses a school and a community or council house. In 1984 the tribe and the National Park Service signed a cooperative agreement for museum development. The tribe also operates a community grocery, and a fishery and meat-processing cooperative. It boasts a new school, kindergarten through eighth grade, under the administration of the Bureau of Indian Affairs.

Employment opportunities on or near the reservation are few. Many are employed in the petroleum industry, some in positions of responsibility. The future of jobs related to declining oil production are in jeopardy, but job training and placement are active tribal concerns.

It is unfortunate that much of the ancient Chitimacha way of life has been forgotten. The language is dead, the tribal lore is lost, and many arts and crafts are moribund. Only the beautiful cane basketry survives, but even its future is by no means assured. Chitimacha efforts to achieve and maintain unity and purpose are interesting to observe. Recent attempts to settle tribal land claims have met with little success, but developments on the reservation have continued.

THE HOUMA

The Houma tribe, by far the largest surviving Indian group in Louisiana, numbers approximately three thousand persons scattered from the banks of the Atchafalaya River to St. Bernard Parish, and boasts a healthy birthrate. "Sabine," an appellation with derogatory implications, is applied by some whites to the Indians.

The dispersal of the Houma over several parishes has precluded the development of a unifying organization. In the eighteenth century these people joined in small groups on the bayous that fan out southward to the Gulf coast and in the neighboring swamps and marshes, accessible only by dugout canoe. Since the advent of improved roads, powerboats, and automobiles, the Houma have tended to cluster at the ends of roads down the bayous. By 1940, for example, there were about seven hundred Indians living within walking distance of Dulac, which was at the end of the road on Bayou Grand Caillou.

Opinions on the nature of the Houma have differed. As early as 1907, Swanton declared that the Houma were so Gallicized in language and other cultural practices that they could barely claim Indian status. However, in 1943, Frank Speck declared the Houma physical type to be distinctly Indian and noted the retention of large portions of material culture and plant knowledge. Although the Houma have lost much that is traditionally Indian, a great deal of their lore of hunting, fishing, and trapping tends to be aboriginal.

At times the Houma have been impoverished. Their extractive pursuits, yielding fish, furs, and shrimp, have supported them moderately well, and jobs have been available in the oil fields since the 1930s. Now the oil industry is declining, and development of the marshes threatens the fragile fabric of that environment. Acres of marshland, fragmented by oil-field canal dredging, are lost to the Gulf of Mexico each year. The shrimp and oyster industries are severely curtailed by pollution, and the Houma find both their old and new life-styles endangered. Even their famous Lafitte skiffs may disappear.

Education was long a problem, since Houma children were not admitted to white schools and refused to attend black schools. A belated resolution of this difficulty came in the 1940s with the opening of special Indian schools that served until all schools were integrated in 1964. Still, it was not until the 1970s that the Houma began to produce college graduates, and the tribe still suffers from a low level of literacy.

The Houma's quest for federal recognition as Indians has been a troubled one. They presently have a unified organization, the United Houma Tribe, which meets the preliminary requirement for recognition, but the merging of so many scattered communities is difficult. The United Houma Tribe offers some hope, however, and the petition for federal recognition is in motion.

Through lethal selection, American Indians have, to a considerable extent, developed about the same degree of immunity to diseases as have whites. The result has been an increase in numbers, and at present there are approximately as many Indians in the United

States as there were in 1492. The present number of Indian people in Louisiana seems to be as large as, or larger than, in the past.

Time has not favored the ancient Indian ways. Within a single lifetime, languages have been lost, lore forgotten, and the skills of arts and crafts have been discarded. Survival has required the descendants of the aborigines to equip themselves suitably for life with their more numerous, more powerful contemporaries. Computer technology offers more jobs and better pay than traditional basketry.

Most important, at this time, is the realization by the Indian people that the ancestral ways were good, that they were as rich and meaningful as those of the outsiders, and that they are worth remembering. Periodic episodes of fantasy may seem to focus on bits and pieces of remembered material culture, but the tangible traits are vehicles that carry into the future the lore and learning that served so long and so well. Those descended, even only in part, from America's aboriginal inhabitants can take pride in the accomplishments and qualities of their ancestors. Without their contributions, modern life in Louisiana would be different indeed.

REFERENCES

It is unfortunate that information on the Indian tribes of Louisiana is not more generally available. Publications on the subject have appeared only irregularly, and some recent studies have quickly gone out of print. The findings of some investigations are available only through contact with the sponsoring tribal or governmental agencies, and others of value have not been published at all. Much information on the period since 1900 is to be found with the ethnohistorical data in the writings of Swanton and others.

Two more recent works that deal with the period 1900 to 1930 are available in manuscript form.

Gregory, Hiram F.
1981   On the Road to Recognition: The Louisiana Indians Since 1900. MS at Jean Lafitte National Park, New Orleans.

Drechsel, Emanuel, and T. Haunani Makuakane
1982   An Ethnohistory of the 19th Century Louisiana Indians. MS at Jean Lafitte National Park, New Orleans.

The tribes have published concise, up-to-date histories. The Indian Tribal Series contains two of the best of these.

Hoover, Herbert
1975 *The Chitimacha People.* Phoenix.

Johnson, Bobby H.
1976 *The Coushatta People.* Phoenix.

Recent efforts to secure federal aid and cooperation have led to a new series of reports on community history and life.

Gregory, Hiram F.
1977 Jena Band of Louisiana Choctaw. *American Indian Journal* 3: 2–16.

Downs, Ernest C.
1979 The Struggle of the Louisiana Tunica Indians for Recognition. In *Southeastern Indians Since the Removal Era* (Walter L. Williams, ed.) Athens, Ga. 72–8.

Juneau, Donald
1980 The Judicial Extinguishment of the Tunica Indian Tribe. *Southern University Law Review* 7:43–99.

Gregory and his associates have produced a recent synthesis of the Indians in Natchitoches Parish, Louisiana.

Gregory, Hiram F., James McCorkle, and Hugh K. Curry
1979 The Historic Indians of Natchitoches Parish and Significance. *Natchitoches Parish Cultural and Historical Resources*, Natchitoches Parish Planning Commission, Natchitoches.

The above work is an echo of an earlier paper on the Indians of Grant Parish, Louisiana.

Ethridge, Adele
1940 The Indians of Grant Parish. *Louisiana Historical Quarterly* 23: 1107–31.

Recent efforts of the tribes to settle land claims have generated a useful series of documents.

McGinty, G. W.
1963 Valuating the Caddo Land Cession of 1835. *Louisiana Studies* 2:59–73.

Jacobson, Dan
1960 The Origin of the Koasati Community of Louisiana. *Ethnohistory* 7:97–120.

1974   Alabama-Coushatta Indians. In *Creek Indians, Alabama-Coushatta* (David Agee Horr, ed.), New York, 1–255.

Horr, David Agee
1974   *Caddoan Indians IV.* New York.

These studies either present the accumulated pleadings heard by the American Indian Claims Commission or, as done by Webb and Gregory, synthesize tribal documentation.

Webb, Clarence, and Hiram F. Gregory
1985   *The Louisiana Caddo.* 2nd ed. Archaeological Study 2, Department of Culture, Recreation, and Tourism, Baton Rouge.

Another source of tribal information is the series of documents presented by the Inter-Tribal Council of Louisiana. These are economically functional in nature but often contain syntheses of tribal demography, economics, and cultural situations that are virtually unobtainable elsewhere.

Gulf South Research Institute
1973   *American Indians of Louisiana: An Assessment of Needs.* Gulf South Research, Baton Rouge.

Spicker, Jean R., Halk R. Steiner, and Rupert Walden
1977   *A Survey of Rural Louisiana Indian Communities.* Inter-Tribal Council of Louisiana, Baton Rouge.

Chapman, Bill, and Ted Schilling
1979   *A Bilingual Survey of the Inter-Tribal Council of Louisiana Tribal Members.* State Department of Education, Baton Rouge.

Skeeter, Andrew *et al.*
1978   *Summary Analysis of Clifton Choctaw Community.* Oklahoma City.

Faine, John R.
1986   *The Tunica-Biloxi Indians: An Assessment of the Status of a Louisiana Indian Tribe.* Institute for Indian Development, Baton Rouge.
1985   *The Clifton Choctaw Community: An Assessment of a Louisiana Indian Tribe.* Institute for Indian Development, Baton Rouge.
1985   *The Jena Band of Choctaws: An Assessment of a Louisiana Indian Tribe.* Institute for Indian Development, Baton Rouge.

Faine, John R., and Hiram F. Gregory
1986   *The Apache-Choctaw of Ebarb: An Assessment of a Louisiana Indian Tribe.* Institute for Indian Development, Baton Rouge.

A number of popular promotional papers are available from the Inter-

Tribal Council of Louisiana and its companion agency, the Institute for Indian Development.

The coastal Houma have also been studied of late. The works of Janel Roper-Curry, Greg Bowman, and other Mennonite volunteers have done much to elucidate the contemporary Houma and their sociopolitical situation.

Bowman, Greg, and Janel Roper-Curry
1982   *The Forgotten Tribe: The Houma People of Louisiana.* Mennonite Central Committee, Akron, Pa.

A study by Ann Fischer of Tulane University has bridged the generation gap between the activism of the 1930s and the integration of the 1960s.

Fischer, Ann
1968   History and Current Status of the Houma Indians. In *The American Indian Today* (Nancy Lurie, ed.), Baltimore, 212–35.

Edison Roy and Max Stanton have attempted syntheses of the Houma. The earlier work is flawed by an overriding concern with race and the schools, but both are useful sources.

Roy, Edison
1959   The Indians of Dulac: A Descriptive Study of a Racial Hybrid Community in Terrebonne Parish, Louisiana. M.A. thesis, Louisiana State University.

Stanton, Max
1979   Southern Louisiana Survivors: The Houma Indians. In *Southeastern Indians Since the Removal Era* (Walter L. Williams, ed.), Athens, Georgia, 90–120.

Since the 1960s all the tribes have become economic and sociopolitical entities. Their success with management and program development is mirrored in the numbers and kinds of publications that have resulted from their self-determination. Indians in Louisiana have at last begun to be a voice for their own cultures.

INDEX

Abbey, Bel, 8

Acolapissa: in 1700, pp. 50–51, 52; meaning of name, 50; absorbed by Houma, 63, 90; pantribal alliances, 65, 125; enmities, 72; movements and relocations, 78, 83; ceremonial art, 166; fishing, 203; temples, 257

Adai: Spanish expedition and, 6; in 1700, p. 47; interference from Europeans, 63; movements and relocations, 75, 91; attacked by Choctaw, 85; trade, 211

Adair, John, 209

Adolescence, 242. *See also* Children

Adultery, 219, 244

Agriculture, 142, 188–94

Ais, 76

Alabama: movements and relocations, 10, 84, 85, 89–90; pantribal community, 125; languages, 126; spinning device, 145; clothing, 179; kinship system, 223, 225, 236; absorption of Pascagoula, 232; death and burial, 246, 255; religion, 259; dancing and music, 282, 283, 287; Civil War and, 296

Alcoholism, 211, 213, 267

Algonkians, 124, 225

Allen, George, 8, 199

Allen, Louise, 8

American Indians: Louisiana population, 1, 22, 299; contemporary lifestyle, 1, 213, 215, 299–311; European influences, 2, 5, 62–66; accounts of, 2–7; experts from different tribes, 7–10; relations between tribes in 1700, pp. 51–53, 55–56; culture in 1700, pp. 56–57; diseases, 62, 92, 211, 213, 267, 268; movements and relocations, 71–80; warfare, 72, 74, 291–96; relations with blacks, 92, 93–94; relations with whites, 97–98; concept of sovereignty, 235–36; sexual division of labor, 241; personal names, 242–43; marriage, 243–44; death and burial, 245–48, 253, 255–56, 259; assimilative pressures, 269; games, 276–79; dancing and singing, 279–87; identity of, 299–300; federal recognition of, 300–301, 303; state recognition of, 303. *See also* names of tribes

American Revolution, 64, 75

Aminoya, 48

Amos Blue Eyes, 284

Animals. *See* Fishing; Hunting

Apache: language of, 65; spinning device, 145; slaves, 211, 232; federal recognition of, 301

Apalachee: settlement in hill country, 19; movements and relocations, 77, 83, 84, 85; land grants, 88; home at end of nineteenth century, 90; languages, 126; games, 278

Archaic Period, 29–31, 186

Archaeology, 28–34

Army, 296

Arrow points, 163

Arts and crafts: wooden objects, 137–46; cane objects, 146–53; baskets, 154–57; handiwork, 157–62; stone objects, 162–64; ceremonial art, 164–68; pottery, 164–68; revitalization of, 167–68

Atakapa: Cabeza de Vaca's description of, 3; hunting, 19, 197; in 1700, pp. 44, 46–47, 53; in twentieth century, 46; incorporation of other tribes, 75, 78;

19; prairie country, 19–20; coastal marshes, 20–21, 22; floodplains, 21–22; lakes, 22; environmental ruin, 22–23; in prehistoric periods, 28–34; recognition of Indian tribes, 303

Louisiana Indians. *See* American Indians

Louisiana Purchase, 88

Lozieres, Baudry de, 7

Lumbee, 92

Luxembourg Narrative, 6, 263

Margry, Pierre, 7

Marksville Period, 32

Marquette, Jacques, 6

Marriage, 243–44

Martínez, Wesley, 9

Matrilineal and matrilocal societies, 221, 224–26, 232

Medford, Claude, Jr., 9, 75, 147, 149, 156, 264, 282

Medicine, 262–68

Medicine people, 259, 262, 263, 265–68

Membre, Zenobius, 6

Men: clothing, 172–73, 175; hairdressing, 179; body ornamentation, 180–82; head deformation, 182; responsibilities of, 188, 241; names, 242–43

Menstruation, 240, 241

Métis, 63, 89, 93, 124, 233

Mézières, Athanase de, 211

Missionaries, 6–7, 63–64, 252–53, 268–69, 286

Mississippian Period, 33, 166

Mississippian-Plaquemines Period, 163

Mobile, 83, 84

Mobilian Jargon, 65, 97, 124–25, 129, 210, 213, 268, 280

Montigny, Dumont de, 6

Mortar and pestle, 139, 142, 144

Mortuary practices. *See* Death and burial

Moscoso, Luis de, 4

Mound building, 259

Mounds Plantation, 33, 149

Mourning. *See* Death and burial

Mugulasha: in 1700, pp. 50, 51, 52; meaning of name, 51; amalgamation with other tribes, 74; movements and relocations, 78, 83; absorbed by other tribes, 90; warfare, 295

Murder, 218–19

Music, 279–87

Musical instruments, 284

Muskogean tribes: in 1700, pp. 49, 50, 53; languages, 122, 123, 126; basketry, 156; uses of shells, 162; warfare, 291

Nacogdoches, 76

Nadarko Caddo, 76

Nahuatl, 65, 94, 124, 126, 130

Napochi, 51

Narvaez, Panfilo de, 3

Nasoni, 91

Natchez: relationship with Taensa, 3; de Soto expedition and, 4; French accounts of, 6–7; in 1700, pp. 47–51, 53, 55, 56; slavery of, 62, 65, 94, 222, 233; warfare, 64, 84, 293–95; enmities, 72; position after French and Indian War, 84; tribal settlements, 108, 109; buildings, 110, 114, 115, 257, 258; languages, 122, 123, 126, 129; weapons, 143; featherwork, 157; flint knapping, 163; games, 164, 277–78; pottery, 165; ceremonial art, 166; clothing, 173, 175; hairdressing, 179; body ornamentation, 180, 181, 182; agriculture, 189–91; fishing, 203; food preparation, 204, 205; trade, 208, 209, 210; tribal law, 218, 219, 220; kinship system, 223, 224, 226, 228–30; totems, 225, 226; political system, 230, 231; male responsibilities, 241; sexual mores, 242; marriage, 243, 244; death and burial, 245, 259; suicide and, 256; religion, 260, 264; factionalism within, 300

Natchez War, 226, 296

Natchitoches: French accounts of, 6; in 1700, pp. 47, 48; interference from Europeans, 63; enmities, 72; movements and relocations, 75, 76; in nineteenth century, 91; languages, 124, 126; ceremonial art, 166; hunting, 199; trade, 208, 211; death and burial, 245

National Park Service, 309

Native Americans. *See* American Indians

Neitzel, Robert S., 147, 149

Newkumet, Vynola, 9

Northup, Solomon, 175

Nugent, Dorothy, 8